HOW TO PRAY

After You've

Kicked the Dog

Terry Teykl

Prayer Point Press

HOW TO
PRAY
After You've
Kicked
the
Dog

How to Pray After You've Kicked the Dog

© 1999 Terry Teykl
Published by Prayer Point Press
Co-authored and edited by Lynn Ponder

First Edition, March 1999
Second Printing, August 1999
Third Printing, October 2000
Fourth Printing, May 2002
Fifth Printing, February 2005

Unless otherwise indicated, all Scripture quotations are from the Holy Bible, New International Version © 1973, 1978 by the International Bible Society. Used by permission.

ISBN: 1-57892-014-0
Printed in the United States of America

To order, contact:
Prayer Point Press
2100 N. Carrolton Drive
Muncie, IN 47304
(888) 656-6067

www.prayerpointpress.com

This book is dedicated to my five precious grandchildren—Robbie, Austen, Emily, Annalise and Tyler, and those yet known only in the heart of God.

Table of Contents

**"For as he thinketh in his heart,
so is he" (Proverbs 23:7, KJV).**

$\mathcal{P}$rologue

$\mathcal{J}$ remember quite well the night I arrived in Quito, Ecuador. My plane was very late, and as a result, my ride had obviously given up and gone home. I spoke no Spanish, and could find no one in the airport that spoke a word of English. Because of the late hour, everything was closed. I checked the phone book—Spanish; all the signs—Spanish. I was tired and frustrated, rendered helpless by my inability to speak or understand the language of this country. At that moment I felt lonely.

As I sat down on a bench to try and devise a plan of action, I had a strange thought: "This is the way a lot of people probably feel in church. They need help but they simply do not understand the language."

I imagine that to many, the church world can be confusing and intimidating. Some might even become fearful over deciding which is the right approach to finding God. We "church folk" speak a different language and have a different set of unwritten rules and expectations. We may not always be aware of the need to interpret what we do for those who are new to the faith.

I wanted to write a book that could help people talk to God and feel good about the experience. I wanted somehow to communicate the fact that prayer was His idea and that He will make it work. I think anybody can pray and feel at home with God if they truly understand what is in His heart toward us. He is our Father and He is eager to hear from us.

I saw a bumper sticker once that caught my eye. It read, "Call home—PRAY." Prayer is just that—calling home. You can do it with confidence and know you will be heard.

Introduction

Things Are Not Always As They Seem

It was a blistering summer day, and she was ready to get home. She pushed her crooked grocery cart across the parking lot, opened the back door of her car, and began shoveling the bags in. The heat rising out of the car made it almost difficult to breathe, and as she closed the door on the last bag of groceries, she wiped the sweat off of her face. Exhausted, she slipped behind the wheel, turned the key in the ignition and cranked up the air conditioner. But as she reached for the gear shift, she heard a loud "POP," and she felt something strike the back of her head.

"Oh, God!" she thought, "I've been shot!"

She slumped over the steering wheel, unable to move or even cry for help. Feeling numb and confused, she reached up and placed her hand on the back of her head. She could feel the moist warmth of the wound, and it made her stomach queasy. Tears began to roll down her cheeks.

Several people gathered around the woman's car as they noticed her distress, but no one seemed to know quite what to do. "Why don't they help me?" she thought. "Can't they see I'm bleeding?"

Just then the store manager reached the scene. Seeing no visible signs of violence or injury, he gently opened the woman's car door and said, "Are you alright, ma'am? Can I help you?"

"Please," cried the woman, "Call an ambulance. I've been shot in the back of the head!"

Confused, the store manager glanced around the car and then took a closer look at the back of her head, which she was still holding with one hand. Then, with a half-smile, the manager said, "Ma'am, I think you are going to be just fine." He reached in the back seat and pulled out of the top of one of the grocery bags an exploded biscuit can.

Things are not always as they seem. The things we hear, see and feel can sometimes lead us to believe something that is not actually true. In many ways we have a natural propensity to assume the worst, only to find out later that the situation is really not as bad as we thought. A child assumes he will be punished for breaking a glass; a husband assumes his wife will be angry because he was transferred to a new location; a construction worker assumes he will get blamed for delays due to bad weather; a business woman assumes she will get fired for losing a big account. All of us, at some point, have fallen prey to this kind of negative thinking.

Years ago, when I was pastoring in a small town, my wife and I saved enough money to take our kids on a family vacation. We packed the car and headed out, only to be stopped on the edge of town by a policeman. As he approached the car, I could feel my neck getting hot with frustration, remembering that in my haste to get out of town, I had put off the task of renewing my inspection sticker and license tag. I rolled my window down and said, "I'm sorry about my inspection sticker, Officer. I'll take care of it first thing when we get back."

Glancing at my windshield, he said, "I didn't stop you because of your inspection sticker, but you're right, it expired two months ago."

"Oh, well, about my license tag—I'll take care of that, also. I promise," I told him.

"That's fine, but that is not why I pulled you over either," he said, shaking his head.

Sinking lower and lower into the seat, I said, "Look, I know I was going a little too fast. But we are headed out of town on a vacation and we have a long way to drive. I'll slow down."

The officer kind of laughed. "Actually, I didn't even have my radar on, but you were moving pretty fast."

Exasperated, I finally asked, "Then why did you stop me?"

"One of your suitcases fell off the top of the car back there, and I thought you might want to pick it up!"

I cannot tell you how foolish I felt, or how long it was before my children stopped reminding me of that incident. Because of my negative outlook, I talked my way into $250.00 in tickets that day. I knew I had messed up, and my guilt did such a number on me that I could not receive help from someone who only had my best interest in mind. My intense awareness of my own shortcomings had corrupted my thinking. The whole conversation that took place between the officer and me would have been completely different had I simply understood his motive when he pulled me over.

The way we perceive situations is critical. In fact, the way we interpret the people and events around us makes us who we are. You have no doubt known people who have the innate ability to believe the best about everyone and everything, and as a result, they go through life fearing nothing and trusting everyone. On the contrary, we have all run across those who manage to focus on the dark side of every circumstance, and they suffer through life enslaved by their pessimism. A psychologist would probably tell you that a well-adjusted person functions somewhere in between.

When we fall prey to a misconception, we are in danger because misconceptions determine our attitudes or feelings, which in turn motivate our actions. In other words, we act on what we feel about what we believe to be true. If we believe we are in danger, we act with fear or aggression. If we believe someone is our friend, we respond to that person with trust and openness.

> *We* want God to fit in our box because He is easier for us to understand that way.

If we believe in our ability to accomplish a certain task, we act with confidence. If our perception of the truth is off in some area, then our actions are likely to be inappropriate in that area as well.

When it comes to spiritual matters, truth can be difficult for us to identify because we simply do not have the capacity to think like God. Spiritual truth sometimes seems to contradict earthly laws or norms, making it easy for us to buy into misconceptions that may line up more closely to our systems of thinking. We want God to fit in our box because He is much easier for us to understand that way. Fortunately, God does not oblige.

Having pastored for twenty-eight years and spoken to thousands of people in conferences and seminars, I have concluded that most people, to some degree, suffer from some kind of perception problem when it comes to prayer. Because prayer is such a miraculous gift, we have a hard time wrapping our minds around God's heart in the matter. We second guess Him. We look for the "catch." We focus on all the reasons why prayer makes no earthly sense, and in general, we make it harder than it was meant to be.

Why is this? Why do so many people who believe in God have so little faith in prayer? Why are we so skeptical about talking to God? Why is it that even our churches are filled with people who, in the depths of their spirit, wonder if God really hears them when they pray? I believe the answer is related to our problems with perception—with identifying and acting on the truth. We have allowed ourselves to swallow some myths about the nature of God and prayer. In most cases, the myths have their origin in truths that are either incomplete, misunderstood, or have been taken out of context.

However, it is not actually the myths that keep us from enjoying a rich prayer life, but rather the feelings and attitudes that develop in us as a result of our misguided thinking. These misconceptions all produce in us a toxin, fear, which in turn produces a behavior—we sit slumped over the steering wheel holding the back of our heads. We feel like we have "kicked the dog," or maybe even killed the critter, so we rule ourselves out, thinking that surely God will not hear our prayers. And even if, by chance, He happened to hear, He certainly would not respond.

If we approach God at all, it is with our tails tucked and our fingers crossed. Or we pray with a "lottery attitude"—maybe we will win, but probably not. The odds are not in our favor. We reason that prayer only works for really "holy" people. We feel unworthy, unqualified and undeserving. "Prayer? Maybe for some, but not for me." Our feelings of guilt and inadequacy leave us spiritually paralyzed, robbing us of the most precious privilege we have as Christians—communicating with God. Ultimately, we do not pray, or we pray tiny little prayers with great hesitation, because we are afraid.

I have identified three fears which hamper our prayer lives, and the myths on which they feed. The purpose of this book is to replace the myths with truths, and the fear with confidence and joy.

The Fear of Rejection

We are afraid that God hears our prayers based on a debit and credit system. Going to church, tithing, volunteering time to charities, performing good deeds and other notably righteous acts are all credits to our account. However, every time we let a bad word slip, sleep in on Sunday morning, yell at our spouse or children or cut someone off in traffic, we have created a debit. And of course "big" sins, such as divorce, abortion or abuse, so tarnish our spiritual credit history that we can never really recover. As we examine our track record and assess our worthiness to be heard based on performance, we all come up short, and we imagine that in God's economy, we will certainly be turned away and labeled, "Reject."

Myth #1: God will not answer my prayers if there is sin in my life.

Myth #2: Prayer is like an international phone call—distance is extreme, the connection is shaky, the rate is high and the number is hard to remember.

The Fear of Failure

Many of us, whether we have been going to church all our lives or have never set foot inside one, are afraid to pray because we are afraid that it will not work. Our perception is that we do not know *how* to pray and therefore do not stand a very good chance of being successful. Our thinking gets bogged down in questions like, "How often do I have to pray for it to work? How long do I have to pray? Are there special words I have to use? Is there a formula to follow? Do I have to kneel or be at an altar? Does it help if I cry or go without food?" And the most intimidating question of all, "What if I pray and nothing happens?" Nobody likes to fail at anything, but failing at prayer is especially frightening because it shakes our faith. We want some assurance that if we ask God for something, He is going to respond.

Myth #3: Some prayers are better than others.
Myth #4: Prayer is crisis-motivated.
Myth #5: The main goal of prayer is to get God's attention.

The Fear of Embarrassment

In any area of life, one of the most dangerous habits we can fall into is that of comparing ourselves to others. When we compare our own prayer life to someone else's, we are most likely headed for trouble. In our desire to feel accepted, we may try to be something that we were never created to be, which only leaves us frustrated.

Myth #6: In order for my prayer life to be legitimate, it should look like someone else's.

Myth #7: Prayer is a gift—some people have it, and some people don't.

Someone once said to me, "Fear is the darkroom where the enemy drags us to develop our negatives." We get so focused on our own shortcomings that we fail to see the true nature and purpose of this thing called prayer. These myths have squelched any confidence we might otherwise have had in approaching the throne. Preachers preach them, Christians internalize them, and non-Christians live in them. Because we do not understand God's heart in the matter, we are unable to receive. Young or old, rich or poor, churched or unchurched—much of what we see, feel, hear and read leads us to believe the worst about ourselves and our ability get through to God. The input we receive makes us wonder, "Why would God want to listen to me?"

A young woman was driving across town late one night when she found herself running low on gas in a neighborhood known for violent crime. Too afraid to stop, she kept driving, hoping to reach a familiar gas station several blocks away. To her horror, however, she felt the car begin to sputter as the engine choked out for lack of fuel.

It was too dark to see much around her, and she sat motionless for a few moments, trying to calm herself enough to think clearly about what to do. Suddenly, she looked up and saw the silhouette of a man who began to bang on her car window. Terrified, she screamed even though she knew that she probably could not be heard. The man disappeared momentarily, only to return with a metal pipe, which he began hurling at the woman's back window again and again until it shattered, throwing bits of glass everywhere. He climbed into the car and reached for the woman.

Hysterical, she fought and screamed, but she was exhausted and he was too strong. He managed to kick open her car door and then put most of his weight against her body, causing both of them to fall out of the car and onto the pavement. The man pulled her to the side of the road and collapsed with her in the grass, winded from the struggle. Within seconds, sparks lit up the sky and the sound of screeching metal pierced the night air as a freight train barreled into the side of the woman's car which had come to rest on the train track.

> *I* want you to see prayer for what it really is—for what God intends it to be.

Things are not always as they seem, and for many people, this is never truer than in the area of prayer. Our misconceptions create irrational fears in our lives, and keep us from realizing the truth about relating to God.

This book is not about formulas or recipes for prayer. It is about recognizing the truth and letting the truth set you free. It is about changing your perception of the big picture and seeing clearly the reality of God's intent for you. It is about the true nature of God and how He desires, even yearns, to relate to you. Although fear and feelings of inadequacy may dominate your prayer life, just as for the woman who was "shot" by a biscuit and the woman who was dragged from her car, things are not as they seem. I want you to see prayer for what it really is—for what God intends it to be. You need not be afraid because perfect love—God's love—has done away with all fear.

If you can replace myth with truth, then you can dismantle fear and approach God with confidence, knowing that He will hear and answer. It does not matter who you are, where you are, what you do, how much money you have, what color your skin is, what is in your past, whether or not you go to church or how many hymns you know! God wants to hear from you and speak to you. He is your Father, and He loves you whether your life is all together or in a million pieces.

> Spirit of the Living God, be the gardener of my soul. For so long I have been waiting, silent and still—experiencing a winter of the soul. But, now, in the strong Name of Jesus Christ, I dare to ask:
>
> Clear away the dead growth of the past;
> Break up the hard clods of custom and routine.
> Stir in the rich compost of vision and challenge;
> Bury deep in my soul the implanted Word.
> Cultivate and water my heart,
> Until new life buds and grows and flowers. Amen
>
> (Foster 3).

Part 1

Overcoming the Fear of Rejection

Chapter 1

Shame on You!

Most of what I know about shame I learned as a little boy. I was the youngest child, born some ten years after my two older sisters, but I was really raised more like an only child, since they both left home as teenagers. We were very poor. My dad worked in the oil fields, making barely enough money to keep a roof over our heads and second-hand clothes on our backs. We ate a lot of beans and casseroles, and thanks to our strong German heritage, a lot of sausage, sauerkraut and potatoes.

My father worked hard, drank heavily and was seldom home. He spent a good deal of time in bars and run-down pool halls. He did not actually pay much attention to me, which probably saved me from a good deal of much needed discipline. I remember coming home one afternoon proudly carrying my first little league uniform. As I walked in the house, my dad looked up at me from his chair and said, "Oh, you're playing baseball?"

I did some interesting things to earn extra money back then. For example, I sold cow manure to sweet gray-haired ladies to

put in their gardens and ran a paper route. When I was four-
teen, I saw my father raiding the cigar box where I kept money
I had collected for newspapers. To me, that felt like the worst
kind of injustice.

One Christmas I decided to sell mistletoe, which grew in
abundance in that southern part of Texas. All I had to do was
gather enough from the trees and carry it door to door. In the
yard of the Presbyterian church that we attended, right in front
of the stained glass window depicting Jesus, stood a tall tree
that was covered with the Yuletide vine. I picked up some rocks
and sticks and began to harvest. Unfortunately, I did not have
very good aim, and one of the rocks I hurled flew right through
the tree and hit the stained glass window just hard enough to
take a small chunk out of Jesus' left cheek. I will never forget
the shame of sitting in church the next Sunday looking up at
that window wondering what kind of punishment God might
inflict on me for "defacing" His Son.

Like many who grow up in poverty, the shame I felt about
my life and my family ate away at my self-image. I always had
my mother drop me off three blocks away from the school I
attended because I did not want anyone to see the piece of wood
that my dad had taped to the side window of our car, which we
could not afford to repair. I remember not wanting any of my
friends ever to see my house because I was so embarrassed about
our rat-infested attic and the galvanized tin sheets that covered
several walls and part of the roof. I remember kids laughing at
my shoes and at how skinny I was. In fact, I failed seventh grade
physical education because I was too embarrassed to undress in
the locker room! On many occasions, I walked with my mother
to a nearby park to fill buckets with water when, for some reason, there was not any flowing through the pipes.

Shame is more than a feeling; it is a state of being—one that
I understood long before I had the vocabulary to explain it. It is
a mindset that says, "I am not acceptable." Shame attaches who
I am to what I do, have or look like. It evaluates my worth as a

person based on external factors. The result is that every time I fail to measure up—for each standard I cannot seem to reach—I become less and less important as a person.

The interesting thing about shame is that it is no respecter of persons. It is not just a disease that afflicts the poor, the down-and-out or the young. Looking back on my childhood, I realize now that, contrary to what I might have thought at the time, I was not the only person who felt ashamed about who I was. My sisters felt ashamed; that is why they left home almost as soon as they could drive a car. My parents felt ashamed, which is why my father drank, and

> *Shame is more than a feeling; it is a state of being . . .*

my mother tolerated it. Even the rich kids who lived on the other side of the tracks probably all felt their own kind of shame because even though they had more than I did, they did not have as much as some other family down the street. Shame has no existence outside of comparison—thus the adage, "Ignorance is bliss."

No one is immune to shame. It is like a cancer that we have, as a society, allowed—even invited—to live among us and have access to us. No amount of money, status or physical beauty can shield us from its effects. In fact, shame is so familiar to us that often we fail to recognize the symptoms. But if you look closely, you can see that it is woven into the very fiber of our society. "I am too fat." "I do not spend enough time with my children." "I can't seem to make ends meet, no matter how hard I try." "If people knew the truth about me, they wouldn't like me." "There must be something wrong with me."

Needled with Pain

Not long ago in an airport, I picked up an unusual magazine called *Texas Tattoos*. Page after page was filled with incredibly detailed and colorful designs that had been permanently needled onto various parts of peoples' bodies. Now I have seen plenty of tattoos before, some sentimental or military symbols traditionally on the upper arm of a man with really big muscles. But these tattoos astounded me, both because of the territory they covered and the intricacy of some of the designs. Standing there in the airport newsstand, I faced that awkward dilemma of feeling slightly embarrassed about gawking at the pictures yet not being able to put the magazine down. I was fascinated.

I guess one thing that struck me about the body art was the permanence of it. My understanding is that well-applied tattoos are difficult to remove even with the skill of a plastic surgeon. To bear such an imprint temporarily would be interesting enough for me, but what if the tattoo styles changed? What if I woke up one morning and decided I was tired of jungle wildlife and wanted something different? What if I had to have surgery that involved my tattoo, and the surgeon sewed my picture up crooked?

Shame is a little bit like a tattoo that gets inked into your heart and mind. Once it is there, it is not easy to remove. You may try to hide it or cover it up, but it leaves an indelible stain. It is always there, underneath, an ever-present reminder of lack.

Sadly, we begin to encounter the shame message at a very early age, and I would say that we face it every day in some form until we die. Sometimes it is direct: "Shame on you!" And sometimes it is more subtle: "I'm sorry, you are a great employee, but your promotion has been denied again due to your lack of education." Often it is self-inflicted: "I should exercise more." "I ought to stop smoking." Regardless, it gets etched into our very being, and if it is not dealt with, it will dominate our thinking.

Although I am not a trained counselor, my wife is, and she has shelves of books that have been written on the causes and effects of shame. I have read very few of them. I have, however, been a pastor long enough to have seen first-hand many of the stories that are no doubt told in those books. One by one, they paraded through my office, prisoners of shame over past failures, unable to deal with the feelings of inadequacy.

One such man was a well-respected and successful attorney who attended my church. He was happily married and had a beautiful family. Then one day he cashed all of that in, leaving his wife to run away with one of the legal assistants who worked in his office. Although he stopped coming to church regularly, for years after his divorce he called me almost weekly to tell me how miserable he was and what a mistake he had made. He would have done anything to rewind the clock. He never could shake the guilt and shame he felt over the

---

Shame is a little bit like a tattoo that gets inked into your heart and mind.

---

fact that he had devastated his family in order to satisfy his own momentary desires. He felt used-up and condemned.

Another example was Lisa, a young single woman in our church who had answered two ads in the "personals" column and was date raped by both of the men whom she met. Not only did she struggle with the normal feelings that rape victims experience, but she also struggled with a great deal of shame over having made the same mistake twice. It was bad enough that she had been taken advantage of, but knowing that it was by her own choice that she had gone on the dates made the ordeals even harder to cope with. She felt useless and foolish.

I could tell story after story of people who live in shame over something in their past. I could tell you about Joe, the young Korean student who became a Christian in our church while studying at Texas A&M, and was rejected by his entire Buddhist family. Or I could tell you about the town drunk in one of the small communities where I pastored who felt so much shame over having killed a man in World War II that he stayed intoxicated all the time just to avoid the pain. Perhaps you can relate to these people because you, too, have some skeleton in your closet that emerges anytime you start to feel too good about yourself.

Sources of Shame

Past mistakes are common sources of shame, but there are many people who feel ashamed simply because of who they are or who they aren't—ashamed of how short they fall in trying to live up to the expectations they shoulder. As I have contemplated shame in relation to prayer, I have become very sensitive to the many ways in which the culture we live in contributes to the message of shame every day.

1. Family Hand-me-downs.   Often, shame is passed along in families as a hand-me-down. Unless shame is dealt with, it becomes like a virus that infects everyone who lives in the household. Shame is contagious. It is transmitted through statements like, "You should…," "You ought to…," "I can't believe you…," "Why can't you ever…," "What's wrong with you?" "You need to be more like…." These types of statements are devastating when they come from a person we respect and whose approval we naturally seek, regardless of whether it is a parent, boss, coach, or friend.

2. The Comparison Trap.   The media—everything we view on film or in print, including television, movies, magazines, newspapers and billboards—and especially the advertising world, is another toxic mixture of shame messages. The glamorous pseudo-reality of Hollywood defines such unrealistic standards of physical attractiveness that neither men nor women can possibly live up to them. While millions of teenage girls and even grown women starve themselves in an effort to fit into Barbie's clothes, men pump their bodies full of steroids and other drugs in the hopes that they, too, can be shaped like Arnold

Schwarzenegger. Billboards, TV commercials and magazine advertisements inform us that we either need to remove hair or grow some more; enlarge one part our body or reduce another; get a deep, dark tan or get rid of our wrinkles. We are enamored with a standard of beauty and youth that few can attain.

3. Dying to Succeed. Another source of shame lies in the yardsticks society uses define success: wealth, position and power. If we are enamored with beauty and youth, then we worship success. We celebrate winners and cast losers aside. We judge people based on the house they live in, the car they drive, the clothes they wear, the work they do and the number of people they oversee. We are, to an extreme, a society that places great emphasis on achievement, education, independence and wealth. The message is clear: the higher you climb and the more you have, the more important you are.

The Fruit of Shame

When shame goes unattended, it bears fruit such as resentment, anger, insecurity, loneliness and fear. It will eventually lead to aggression and violence. I believe that shame in some form is at the root of virtually every criminal act that is committed. We resent those people or circumstances that have caused us to feel inferior—parents, poverty, an ex-spouse, a past financial failure. And we may feel angry toward those who we feel cannot relate to our shame—the "perfect" family, the rich, the happily married, the financially successful. Shame almost always produces insecurities in us because it erodes our sense of confidence. And because we constantly fear being laughed at, ridiculed, "found out" and ultimately rejected, we may choose to isolate ourselves from other people in order to avoid the risks.

Too Ashamed to Pray?

So what does shame have to do with prayer? Everything! Our attitude toward prayer depends on how we perceive God and how we believe He perceives us. It depends, in other words, on our spiritual identity. How often and in what manner we approach God is determined by what we believe to be true about His nature and His willingness to hear and answer.

We are as vulnerable to feeling ashamed before God as we are in any other area of our lives—probably even more so. He is holy and supreme, all-knowing and all-powerful. He had no beginning and He has no end. In the light of His glory, we seem to amount to very little. We know that the Bible says God is love, but for some reason, going to church may feel more like a good thrashing than a tender embrace. All too often, the spiritual messages we hear sound strikingly familiar: "Where were you last Sunday?" "Why aren't you in a Bible study?" "You really should tithe more." "How much time did you spend in prayer last week?" "And by the way, you can only serve on this committee if you: have never been divorced, have never had an abortion, don't smoke or drink, are not a single parent, have a lot of scripture underlined in your Bible, and can recite the Lord's Prayer, the books of the Old Testament and John 3:16 from memory!"

Philip Yancey tells a story in his book, *What's So Amazing About Grace?*, which he heard from a friend who works with the down and out in Chicago:

> A prostitute came to me in wretched straits, homeless, sick, unable to buy food for her two-year-old daughter. Through sobs and tears, she told me she had been renting out her daughter—two years old!—to men interested in kinky sex. She made more renting out her daughter for an hour than she could earn on her own in a night. She had to do it, she said, to support her own drug habit. I could hardly bear hearing her sordid story. For one thing, it made me legally liable—I'm required to report cases of child abuse. I had no idea what to say to this woman.
>
> At last I asked if she had ever thought of going to a church for help. I will never forget the look of pure, naïve

shock that crossed her face. "Church!" she cried. "Why would I ever go there? I was already feeling terrible about myself. They'd just make me feel worse" (11).

As Yancey goes on to poignantly explain, the church as a whole has somehow achieved the reputation among those outside its ranks of being quick to condemn and slow to offer grace. Instead of being an oasis of unconditional love and acceptance, it is often fortified with judgmentalism that is so overpowering it keeps people like the prostitute from coming anywhere near. For many people, going to church seems to do more to expose and intensify shame than it does to heal it.

Early in my years in College Station, I used to visit some of the bars in town and just talk to the people there. I loved to listen to their stories, and I always found a way to invite them to church. In one particular bar I made friends with a cocktail waitress, and after much pleading and reassuring, I finally convinced her to come to church. I will never forget the Sunday she came in and sat down toward the back, only to have a lady behind her remark rather loudly, "I wonder what she thinks *she's* doing here!" It took me months to get her to come back.

While I am aware of many precious churches across the country that are filled with people who faithfully model grace in every sense of the word, I have also encountered many situations that seem to verify Yancey's regretful conclusion that the church as a whole seems to be dishing out "ungrace" right and left. One of the most memorable incidents happened years ago when I was pastoring in a small rural church in Texas. A man came to our church office one afternoon and explained that he was driving his family—his wife and three children—to another city where he had found work, and they had run out of money and gas. He told me he had already stopped at one church but had been turned away, and he was wondering if we could help. Without thinking too much about it, we gave the man enough gas money to get him where he was going, and we provided his family a place to rest for the afternoon as well as a good meal.

Later that week, I ran into one of the other pastors in town, and I asked him if the same family had come to his church looking for help. "Yes," he said. "They came to the church alright. We witnessed to them, but I didn't think it was a good idea to give them any money. The man had cigarettes in his pocket."

> *It* **is little wonder that people are not flocking to the doors of churches looking for grace and acceptance!**

Another incident that has haunted me happened just a year ago while I was visiting a friend down in Galveston, Texas. I was driving him around on my motorcycle by the beach, and we decided to stop for a drink at a little corner store. It was bright and clean, and the owner greeted us with a friendly smile. As we went to the back for a bottle of water, my friend told me that the shop was fairly new and that the owner and his family had recently moved there from Pakistan. They lived over the shop in a small apartment.

Not long after they had opened, one of the churches in town, disapproving of the family's religious background, had welcomed them to town by presenting them with a petition signed by many of its members. In effect, the statement said that since the family was not Christian, the members of this church would not shop in their store, and they would urge all of their friends to follow suit.

It is little wonder that people are not flocking to the doors of churches looking for grace and acceptance!

Religious Shame

As I read Yancey's book on grace, and as I have pondered the effects of religion on shame-based thinking, I have concluded that in many ways, we look to religion more in an effort to cover our shame than to heal it. We hope that somehow being in church will make up for our shortcomings. The result is that when we go to church, all we come away with is another helping of shame. Trying to be a "good Christian" simply gives us one more standard in life that we can never actually reach.

It works like this: Religious systems say, "Let us appease God for our sin by going to church, giving money, doing good deeds, memorizing scripture and writing a lot of rules and keeping them. Perhaps then we can earn enough points with God to erase our shortcomings." As Yancey says, "My visits to other churches have convinced me that this ladder-like approach to spirituality is nearly universal. Catholics, Mennonites, Churches of Christ, Lutherans, and Southern Baptists all have their own custom agenda of legalism. You gain the church's, and presumably God's, approval by following the prescribed pattern" (30).

"Doing" religion puts our relationship with God on the same kind of merit system that the rest of the world operates on—that is, you get what you deserve, and you deserve only what you can earn. This kind of spirituality makes for an interesting philosophy on prayer. I call it "religious praying." See if you recognize any of the guidelines:

1. To approach God, you must say the right thing. We will give you this formula when you join our church.
2. Pray for a long time. This is based on the principle that the more lottery tickets you buy, the better your chances of winning.
3. Suffer when you pray. Fast or cry if possible so that you can get God's attention.
4. Make sure other people see you praying. If God does not answer, maybe someone else will come through.
5. Keep copies of your tithing record handy as you pray so that you can wave it at God as you ask Him to bless you.
6. When possible, pray with someone who is ordained, who has appeared on television or radio, or who has written a book about God.

7. Pray at the altar of the biggest church in town.

8. Make a lot of noise when you pray, in case God is busy or distracted.

9. Memorize a very religious-sounding prayer vocabulary, even if you are not sure what all the words mean. Make sure that it is hard to understand and impressive to those who don't know it.

10. Most importantly, develop an elaborate system of interpretation so that you can always prove that God responded like you wanted Him to.

Religious prayer of this kind is usually performed more for the people who might be watching than for the purpose of really seeking to know God. Imagine a flagman on a navy aircraft carrier standing out on the deck waving his flags in a flurry of precise signals, with no airplane in sight. He could go through every motion with exactness and accuracy, performing every signal in the book. But if he is not signaling to an airplane, then all his efforts are wasted. I doubt his fellow flagmen would be too impressed.

Prayer is not just an exercise in standing and kneeling. It is not a performance of complicated rituals and scripts. How empty and frustrating this kind of prayer is! How ludicrous it is to think that we can please God with formulas and manipulate Him with good deeds! The whole display of religious routines evolving out of man-made systems of do's and don'ts is what the Bible calls self-righteousness, and it produces spiritual shame. The result: we fear God's rejection. We fear that we will do something wrong and He will turn us away, saying, "You are not acceptable."

Who Is Righteous?

The Bible says, "The prayer of a righteous man [person] is powerful and effective (James 5:16)," but how many of us really feel righteous? Whether we admit it or not, most of us feel dirty and delinquent when we assess our spiritual condition. "I really don't have my act together. I probably broke several commandments today. I haven't been to church in a few months, or is it years, and I'm not really sure if I even have a Bible. And you want me to pray? Yeah. Right."

So what are we to do? How can we overcome the fear of rejection? What hope do we have of ever being called righteous? Can we approach God with confidence in order to know Him and make our requests known? Will He really listen to us and answer our prayers? Yes! But we must be willing to look at prayer from God's perspective and understand the truth about our real identity. We must find a way to replace the rags of shame with a robe of righteousness.

Dear God,

   Is it true my father won't get in Heaven if he uses his Bowling Words in the house?

—Anita

(Hample and Marshall)

Chapter 2

Righteousness on You!

A couple of years ago, while I was doing some part-time prayer consulting for a dynamic church in South Houston, I had a rare opportunity to meet one of the church members—Evander Holyfield. Evander sometimes trains here in Houston, and when he is in town, he attends Windsor Village United Methodist Church. Windsor Village is a dynamic, 12,000 member African American congregation with a tremendous vision not only to reach people for Jesus, but also to raise the quality of life for all of the residents of the South Houston area. In fact, Evander is such an avid supporter of this church and its pastor that he donated one million dollars toward the construction of a prayer center that the church has in its plans for 1999.

During the time that I was working at Windsor Village, I was invited to Winnipeg, Canada, to do some interviews about prayer for a Christian television program called *It's A New Day*. In the course of the interviews, I mentioned the vision for the prayer center in South Houston and even suggested that perhaps

Evander might be willing to appear on the show and give his own testimony about how prayer has impacted his life. When I got back to Houston, the trip was arranged, and I was scheduled to accompany Evander Holyfield back to Winnipeg the following month.

> *Traveling with a person who has that kind of celebrity status was interesting and at times, amusing.*

Traveling with a person who has that kind of celebrity status was interesting and at times, amusing. We sat in first class on the airplane, and before we even left the ground, the flight attendant announced our presence on the plane and several people came asking for autographs—both his and mine! When we got to Winnipeg, I concluded that one of the airline personnel must have called ahead because another small group of admiring fans greeted us as soon as we got off the plane. After collecting our bags, we stopped in the restroom, and the second we emerged back out into the terminal, flashes began going off as several reporters had gathered to take pictures of the heavyweight champion. I have to admit, it was fun. When one of the reporters asked me who I was, I put my arm around Evander's shoulders and said, "I'm his bodyguard."

For the next couple of days, we did not go anywhere unnoticed. We went to Burger King, and they gave us our food for free, which would seem more impressive if you could have seen the pile of hamburgers and french fries that Evander ordered. He is a big man! We went into a nice restaurant, and without question they ushered us to the best table in the house. Within minutes, the chef appeared at our table to greet us personally. Everywhere we went, people smiled, pointed and asked for autographs. What amused me was that I received the same kind of treatment that Evander did. No one knew that I was just a preacher from Texas, and they did not seem to care. All they knew was that I was with a boxing legend, and that was enough. For two days, I was treated like royalty—no questions asked. Evander simply said, "He's with me."

Position Through Association

Had I gone on that same trip by myself, you can only imagine how different things might have been. No one would have greeted me when I got off the plane, no one would have given me free food, and I doubt anyone would have taken my picture. I did nothing to earn my celebrity status that weekend, and given a lifetime, I could never achieve what Evander has. But, because of my association with him, I was given all the same rights and privileges as the heavyweight champion of the world!

Shame and the fear of rejection from God are really matters of mistaken identity. The first step in building a prayer relationship with God is to come to an understanding of the difference between your spiritual condition and your spiritual position.

Your spiritual condition has to do with the struggle to conquer sin and live in holiness, which is very important. God is concerned about the choices you make and the way you live your life. He wants you to strive for holiness in response to His love for you, which is why the Bible tells us, "Awake to righteousness and sin not" (1 Corinthians 15:34, KJV). In other words, it is not all right to be a bum just because Jesus is going to love you anyway.

Your spiritual position, however, has nothing to do with conduct. It has to do with Jesus.

You see, since God was one of the main players in the Garden of Eden when Adam and Eve first blew it, He has known for a long time that we are weak and fallen creatures. Shame and sin entered the world when that first couple disobeyed God and ate from the wrong tree. God must have recognized quickly that if any of Adam and Eve's descendants, including you and me, were ever to be called righteous, that He was going to have to come up with a way to bestow that mantle upon us. We are simply not capable of achieving it on our own.

Therefore, your relationship with God might be defined as one in which you have position through association. When God sent His Son to the cross, He provided an opportunity for all mankind to enter into a new position with Him by associating with His Son. This new position with God is not dependent upon your own ability to keep your act together, but rather it is a free gift from Him for simply identifying yourself among the sinners Jesus died to save. You cannot earn it, and you do not deserve it. You can only accept it. It is a result of the blood that Jesus shed in His willingness to pay the price for your delinquency. If you have accepted Christ, then while your spiritual *condition* may fluctuate more than the stock market, your spiritual *position* will never change.

> *This* new position with God is not dependent upon your own ability to keep your act together, but rather it is a free gift from Him for simply identifying yourself among the sinners Jesus died to save.

The Bible says it this way, ". . . Be reconciled to God. God made Him [Jesus] who had no sin to be sin for us, so that in Him [Jesus] *we might become the righteousness of God"* (2 Corinthians 5:20b–21). Wow! The good news of Christianity is that God took all the sin and shame on the earth, past, present and future, and placed it on His Son so that you could enjoy celebrity status in heaven. Just take a look at the advantages of associating with Jesus:

"And God raised us up with Christ and seated us with Him in the heavenly realms in Christ Jesus . . ." (Ephesians 2:6).

"In this way, love is made complete among us so that we will have confidence on the day of judgment, because in this world we are like him. There is no fear in love. But perfect love drives out fear . . ." (1 John 4:17-18a).

"Praise be to the God and Father of our Lord Jesus Christ! In his great mercy he has given us new birth into a living hope . . ." (1 Peter 1:3).

Notice the positional language of these scriptures. In Christ, you are in a whole new place, and it is from this place that you pray—seated next to Him in the heavenlies, just like him in some mysterious way, with a whole new identity through rebirth. No wonder John says that perfect love drives out all fear. You have no reason to fear rejection or embarrassment when you pray because you are accepted and loved unconditionally through Christ. No matter what you have done or what was done to you, you can have right-standing with God. Jesus' blood can remove any tattoo. You have received a new message from heaven: *"Righteousness on you!"*

Priority Mail

Suppose you have an urgent letter to mail, but you do not have a stamp. So a friend offers you a paid-for Priority Mail packet. You drop your letter inside, address the front, and send it off. Every postal worker that handles that packet will see that it has been properly addressed and paid for, and he or she will deliver it with haste to its destination, unaware that on the inside there is a letter with no stamp.

When you pray, you are placing your requests in Jesus. He has paid the postage to cover your insufficiency. The Bible tells us that He actually lives to commend you to God (Hebrews 7:25). What this means is that your prayers are heard based on Jesus' track record, not yours. The unworthiness, insufficiency and failures in your past are covered by the Son. You do not need to shuffle up to the throne of God, cowering in shame. You have no need for cover-ups or schemes. Just as I did in Winnipeg, you can receive special treatment because of who you know. You can approach God with confidence, knowing that when you pray, it is as if Jesus is ushering you straight to the Father saying, "She's with me."

Myth #1
God will not answer my prayers if there is sin in my life.

Truth #1
Your prayers are heard based on Jesus' track record, not yours.

It's Free

"Free" is a difficult concept for most of us to grasp. We are so programmed to believe that nothing in life is ever free, and in most cases, that is true. But God's economy is different.

I heard a story once about a man whose lifetime dream was to go on a cruise. Although he was not wealthy, he saved and saved for years until finally he had just enough money to pay for a ticket. When he arrived on the ship, he carried with him two large suit-cases, one containing clothes and the other containing a week's supply of cheese, crackers, peanut butter and bread. Having spent his last penny on the fare, the man was sure he could not afford the extravagant buffets that were served nightly on the deck.

Each evening, after strolling through the dining area watching the other travelers feasting on beautifully prepared appetizers, fresh seafood of every variety, choice beef, gourmet side dishes, outrageous desserts and fine wines, he would retire to his cabin and eat cheese crackers and peanut butter sandwiches. And although he was a bit envious of the other passengers who were eating on deck, he always reminded himself how fortunate he was just to be on the cruise. He felt lucky just to be afloat.

When the ship docked at the end of the tour, the captain stood on the ramp, shaking hands with many of the passengers as they left. As the man passed by, the captain extended his hand and asked, "How did you enjoy the cruise?"

"It was wonderful," the man answered, "everything I always dreamed it would be."

"What about the food?" the captain inquired.

Embarrassed, the man explained his mealtime ritual, saying he was sure that the food had been excellent, even though he had not actually tasted it himself.

In disbelief, the captain stared at the man a moment before replying, "Didn't you understand? When you paid for the cruise, all your meals were included in the price of the ticket. You could have dined with everyone else and eaten as much as you wanted."

One Degree

Not only is righteousness a gift which absolutely cannot be earned, but it is also given in equal measure to everyone who accepts it. It is the epitome of grace, which Philip Yancey describes as "scandalous" because it is neither fair nor just. Righteousness is a place God allows each of us to enter into despite the fact that not one of us can afford the cover charge. It is truly scandalous because it comes in only one degree—complete. A homosexual drug dealer receives the same robe of righteousness the moment he enters into a relationship with Jesus as a twelve-year old girl in Sunday school. Because they are both seen in the light of Jesus and the cross, they are granted the same position through association. All that goes along with righteousness is available at no extra charge to all who identify themselves with Christ.

Furthermore, there is no merit system for righteousness that awards some while punishing others. Your position does not diminish when you falter. Once you receive the gift, you are as righteous at that very moment as you can be. You cannot improve upon it, increase it or lose it.

I am convinced that unless we fully understand this truth about righteousness, we will fall into the trap of trying to earn it, which only leads us back to guilt and shame when we come up short. We must never forget that we have right standing with God because of Jesus' work on the cross. This realization should motivate us toward holy living.

Lawn Mower Ministry

Understanding that our acceptance by God is in Jesus should shed light on another important but often misunderstood facet of prayer: praying in Jesus' name. "In Jesus' name" is not just a little formula that we tack on to the end of prayers to make them sound spiritual; rather, His name is the key to our access to God Himself. To know His name, His essence, His desire is to be intimate with God. It is through Jesus' name that we are heard, based on who He is and His continuing life before the Father. But that is not all.

Praying in Jesus' name is also a way to keep us on target when we pray. It is a reminder to us to pray in light of God's will and to focus on those things that will advance His Kingdom. Jesus said, "If you remain in me and my words remain in you, ask whatever you wish, and it will be given you" (John 15:7). According to this verse, receiving what we ask for in prayer is guaranteed, provided that we are seeking to know the Father's heart and advance His cause.

I once had a neighbor who was not a Christian. She used every opportunity to make it very clear to me that she had no desire to go to church. But one afternoon, I noticed her having trouble with her lawn mower. It had apparently quit halfway through the job, and she was cussing and fussing, trying to no avail to make it start again. So, being somewhat of a "shadetree mechanic," I walked over to see if I could help.

However, after tinkering with it unsuccessfully for several minutes, I finally had the crazy idea to pray over it. I figured if God could raise the dead, surely He could start a lawn mower. So I prayed, "God, in Jesus' name, please start Sandra's lawn mower so she can finish her job and so she will know that you are real. Thank you." Then I opened my eyes, nervously grabbed the throttle, and pulled. "Vrooom!" It started like it was brand new. The following Sunday, Sandra visited our church.

I had never prayed for a lawn mower before that day, and I do not believe I have prayed for another one since. I am fairly certain that God did not give me some mysterious anointing over lawn mowers. I simply prayed a prayer that was in line with the will of God—that Sandra's eyes might be opened— and I sent the prayer to the Father through His Son. In Jesus' name, I invited the Kingdom to be established in that situation, and it was.

Jesus left us with a divine purpose on this earth and gave us the power of attorney to carry out His business in His name. That is an awesome thought. He told his disciples,

> ". . . anyone who has faith in me will do what I have been doing. He will do even greater things than these, because I am going to the Father. And I will do whatever you ask in my name, so that the Son may bring glory to the Father. You may ask me for anything in my name, and I will do it" (John 14:12-14).

The responsibility on our part is to pray in accordance with what Jesus would pray in every situation. We are to act on His behalf, in His name.

A Heavenly Hillbilly

I once knew an old farmer who had lived on the same piece of property almost all his life. He worked hard for a living, toiling

long hours in his fields, making just enough money to get by.
When I would go visit him, he always had on a well-worn pair
of overalls and a plain white T-shirt that was often torn at the
neckline. He was a content old man, but he was destined to die
with exactly what he had when he entered the world.

Then one day, he discovered a thick, black fluid seeping from
the ground in one of his fields. When they came and set the rigs
to drill in the ground, they discovered that underneath the man's
property was a huge untapped reservoir of oil. Within weeks,
the old farmer had several gushing oil wells on his land worth
millions of dollars. The irony of the story is that for years, he
had been living, working, plowing and sweating on some of the
most valuable land in that state, unaware of the potential fortune that lay just below the dirt.

Do not let shame or the fear of rejection rob you of the
reservoir that is yours—go to the throne in confidence! You have
friends in high places: God, who is a Father; Jesus, who is a
brother; and the Holy Spirit, who is a helper. Through Jesus,
your spiritual position has been secured and you have access to
God in prayer. You have been given the power of the name of
Jesus, and with it, you have the authority to invite His kingdom
to be established here on earth just as He desires it to be.

The teacher asks, "What is prayer?"

The child answers, "It's those late night
messages sent up when the rates are
cheaper."

Chapter 3

God Wears a White Hat

God is good. It sounds simple, and in a sense, it is. But sometimes this truth becomes a source of torment and confusion. Although God is good, not everything that happens in this fallen world is good. Crimes are committed, accidents happen—even good people suffer and die.

Because I pastored for several years, I had many opportunities to observe how people respond to God in times of crisis or tragedy. I concluded this: God often gets accused of crimes He does not commit.

Consider a true story about a couple I will call Joe and Martha. They had been married for eight years when Martha started feeling depressed. Being at home all the time with their two children had been rewarding at first, but she had begun to feel trapped and isolated, having given up most of her interests to be a full-time mother. Joe was a good man, but he worked long hours to support the family, and he was exhausted when he got home. He simply did not have the energy to give Martha the adult companionship she desperately needed.

Confused and restless, Martha reached out to a single man from their church, and they quickly became involved in an adulterous relationship. Within months, however, Joe found out that his wife was spending time with another man, and suddenly eight years of marriage were hanging in the balance.

> *But* the night Joe took Martha to the hospital to give birth to their new daughter, her world came crashing down with a few simple words.

When tempers and emotions subsided, Joe and Martha decided to seek help from a counselor, and within a year, they had repaired much of the damage and felt that their relationship was even stronger than it had been before the crisis. Joe was spending more time at home, and they were enjoying a new-found intimacy. They decided to have one more child.

The pregnancy was a happy, healthy one for Martha. Her world seemed to have turned completely around. She fixed up the nursery and brought all the old baby things down from the attic. She even got involved in some projects in her community which occupied some of her spare time and kept her house bustling with friends and activities.

But the night Joe took Martha to the hospital to give birth to their new daughter, her world came crashing down with a few simple words: "Your daughter is blind."

Naturally they loved the baby, and their family and friends were very supportive. They visited several specialists in the first few months, but the doctors all seemed to agree—there was nothing that could be done to restore the child's eyesight. Slowly, they embraced the challenge and began learning all they could to meet their daughter's special needs, but inside Martha was tormented. She just could not understand why God had allowed this to happen. Hadn't they been through enough already?

Unable to cope, she went back to the church counselor who had helped them through their marriage crisis. She just wanted to know one thing, "Why?"

Discouraged and afraid, Martha was not at all prepared for the answer she received. As if she did not have enough to cope with already, Martha heard the counselor speak words that destroyed her right where she sat: "Your daughter must have been born blind as a punishment for your sin. God is teaching you a lesson."

I have to believe God's heart breaks when He hears words like those. Consider another true story about a couple I will call Dave and Sabrina.

I attended a funeral once of a close friend's wife who had died at a fairly young age from injuries she sustained in a car accident. She left behind two young daughters for my friend to raise.

Funerals are never easy, but that was one of the hardest I have ever been through. My wife and I had known Dave and Sabrina for several years and had grown to love them dearly. They were precious people, always concerned about the needs of others, always willing to sacrifice anything they had to help someone else.

Sabrina was a model of goodness and purity. She was a patient, loving mother and a supportive wife. They had the kind of family people strive to build—close, strong and well-adjusted. They had many friends.

When the accident happened and Sabrina was hospitalized, dozens of people pitched in to help Dave with the girls, and people came daily to the intensive care unit to offer support. We enlisted people to pray around the clock for her recovery. For weeks this went on with little change in Sabrina's condition, but Dave remained optimistic. He believed God could heal his wife.

It was a crushing blow to all of us when Sabrina died. It seemed so unfair, so senseless. As I left the gravesite, I heard two well-meaning family members talking, and I was glad Dave was not there to hear.

"Well, I guess it was just meant to be this way. It must have been God's will."

"I don't know. Maybe if we had just had more faith, she wouldn't have died."

Why do bad things happen to good people? This is one of the toughest questions to answer, yet it is one that we must understand if we are to pray with any confidence. It is a question that inspects the very nature of God. Is He really good? Is He always inclined to our best interest? And if so, then why is life so difficult?

Why Do Bad Things Happen to Good People?

The stories about Joe and Martha and Dave and Sabrina illustrate four common misconceptions about the nature of God and His actions:

The first misconception is that God sometimes causes bad things to happen to punish us for sin. Suffering is a form of God's judgement. According to this view, He is a stern and merciless judge who keeps a record of all wrongs and then pronounces sentences accordingly.

Second, God sometimes causes bad things to happen to teach us a lesson. This is the ultimate "school of hard knocks"— Pain and Anguish 101. Or perhaps it is "Remedial Faith Building 103." Since you did not learn to trust Him in Sunday school, He zaps you with a serious injury or a financial setback. Your best chance for survival is to learn the lesson as quickly as possible.

Third, bad things sometimes happen because God arbitrarily wills them to happen. In other words, there really is not a reason for why bad things happen, except that God does not want life to be too predictable. He likes to leave some things to chance. Occasionally, He dishes out misery just because He is bored.

The final misconception is that bad things sometimes happen if we do not have enough faith when we pray. God only gives to the strong in faith. If one of your children has a drug problem, it is because you just do not believe hard enough in God's ability to help.

God is good. He is good all the time, in every way. In fact, He is incapable of being evil.

Each of these explanations suggests that God uses pain or suffering much like a lion tamer uses a whip—to keep us broken and in line, or worse, just because he feels like it. Yet what a tragedy it is for a mother to go through life feeling responsible for her daughter's blindness! How sad it is for a loving husband to feel as though he failed in some way because he did not have enough faith to see his wife healed. Such thinking produces incredible shame and guilt, the very things Jesus died on the cross to remove.

God Is Good

The problem with these misconceptions is that they all overlook this one very important aspect of God's character: God is good. As simple as this truth is, it will revolutionize your prayer life if you can grasp its full meaning. God is good. He is good all the time, in every way. In fact, He is incapable of being evil.

Jesus revealed to us the nature of God when a leper came to Him wanting to be healed. The Bible says,

> *"A man with leprosy came to him and begged him on his knees, 'If you are willing, you can make me clean.' Filled with*

compassion, Jesus reached out his hand and touched the man. 'I am willing,' he said. 'Be clean!' Immediately the leprosy left him and he was cured" (Mark 1:40-42).

Interestingly, the Greek word used for "compassion" in this story is the same Greek word that means "angry." Taken literally, the verse says, "Filled with anger. . . ." What would Jesus have been angry about? I believe He was stirred to righteous indignation when the leper presupposed his request with the phrase, "If you are willing." I imagine Jesus looked back at the leper, and thought, "*If* I am willing!? What do you mean '*If* I am willing?' Of course I am willing. I love you."

> *A*lthough God may instruct us in the midst of a crisis, He does not inflict pain for the purpose of teaching us a lesson . . .

God's very nature is love. He does not punish sin with suffering. To be sure, some sin does bring about natural consequences—if you rob a bank you might get arrested and thrown in jail—but not all bad things are a result of divine punishment. And although God may instruct us in the midst of a crisis, He does not inflict pain for the purpose of teaching us a lesson any more than a loving father would press a hot iron to his little boy's face and say, "See, son. This is hot. Don't ever touch." He is not moody or unpredictable; He is the same yesterday, today and forever, and He is always good. Furthermore, while our faith pleases Him, he does not withhold blessings from us when our faith is weak. As I said in the previous chapter, our prayers are answered based on the person of Jesus, including His faith, and not on our credentials. Otherwise, how would Lazarus have been raised from the dead? I am fairly certain that he had no faith at all!

Another strong New Testament theme which gives us insight into the nature of God is His Fatherhood. All throughout Jesus' life, He demonstrated the Fatherhood of God. He taught us to pray saying, "Our Father" (Matthew 6:9), and in the Gospel of John, He refers to God as "Father" over one hundred times. He taught that all good things come from the Father (John 6:32), and that all the good things that He did here on the earth originated with the Father as well (John 10:25). He knew that the Father listened (John 11:41–42), and protected (John 10:29). Paul also underscored the Fatherhood of God when he said we could call Him "Abba Father," meaning "Daddy God" (Romans 8:15–16).

Jesus did not just call God "Father," He also reflected God's loving nature as He traveled and taught. He was everything good—patient, kind, merciful, forgiving. He was truth incarnate. He was never spiteful or violent, and He never inflicted pain or injury, even to His enemies. He taught and encouraged; He did not tear down. He was a teacher and a builder of lives.

The goodness of God is a powerful theme throughout the Bible. In Genesis 1 God made good things. In Deuteronomy He wanted His people to live in a good place (11:7). He rejoices over us to do us good (Deuteronomy 28:63). Over and over in the Psalms, God is praised for His goodness. Psalm 145:9 says, "The Lord is good to all." In the New Testament, Jesus went around saying and doing good things (Acts 10:38). God's goodness is reliable and trustworthy.

Consider these verses:

"Draw near to God and He will draw near to you" (James 4:8).

"For you did not receive a spirit that makes you a slave again to fear, but you received the Spirit of sonship" (Romans 8:15).

"Call to me and I will answer you and tell you great and unsearchable things you do not know" (Jeremiah 33:3).

"Ask and it will be given to you, seek and you will find, knock and the door will be opened to you. For everyone who asks re-

ceives, he who seeks finds, and to him who knocks, the door will be opened. Which of you, if his son asks for bread, will give him a stone? Or if he asks for a fish, will give him a snake? If you, then, though you are evil, know how to give good gifts to your children, how much more will your Father in heaven give good gifts to those who ask him!" (Matthew 7:7–11).

"Do not fear . . . , do not let your hands hang limp. The Lord your God is with you, he is mighty to save. He will take great delight in you, he will quiet you with his love, he will rejoice over you with singing" (Zephaniah 3:16–17).

Imagine! God delights in you as a person, not for what you can do, but for who you are. He watches over you while you sleep and says, "What a beautiful creation." When you are hurting, He wants to hold you and quiet you. And this is a most awesome thought—He sings to you!

You can approach God in prayer because He is willing and eager to welcome you into His presence. He is on your side, and He cares deeply about you. He is your "Daddy God." Etch the words on your heart, "God is good."

Enter Stage Right: Smutface

So why do bad things happen to good people? We are back where we started. And here is my answer: Satan. If life were an old western movie, God would be wearing white and Satan, or Smutface, would be wearing black. As much as God is incapable of being evil, Satan is incapable of being anything *but* evil. His mission in life, as Jesus states, is *"only* to steal and kill and destroy . . ." (John 10:10).

Bad things happen because we live in a fallen world where sin abounds and Satan has been given permission to create whatever havoc he can stir up. But remember, it was not God who invited Satan to the party; it was Adam and Eve. God never intended for bad things to be a part of this world. In fact, He never really intended for us to pray.

When God created Adam and Eve, He gave them a place to live—Eden. He also created a beautiful garden inside of Eden as a special place where Adam and Eve could meet with Him and fellowship together. It was a magical place, filled with extraordinary flowers of every kind, exquisite fruit trees and clear, flowing streams. They spent much time in the garden, walking with God in the cool of the evening in a paradise of discovery and delight. Face-to-face, they fellowshipped with their creator. They were one—Adam, Eve and God—partners and co-regents over the heavens and the earth. It was an open and wonderful relationship, just the way God wanted it to be.

God **never intended for bad things to be a part of this world. In fact, He never really intended for us to pray.**

But when Adam and Eve sinned against God, everything changed. The introduction of sin into the earth brought with it many consequences, the most serious of which was death. It also meant that because God was perfectly holy, He could not continue to co-exist with Adam and Eve in the garden as He had. The partnership had to be dissolved. Because of their decision, they were no longer one with God and they could no longer enter the garden to enjoy face-to-face contact with their maker. Adam and Eve had chosen to become autonomous and self-governing. With one juicy bite, they fell from a place of total satisfaction into a pit where they would constantly be searching for more.

Of course, God was saddened. This arrangement was not what He wanted. He missed His creation, and He longed to fellowship again with Adam and Eve, despite their rebellion. So He initiated another form of communication—prayer. He created prayer as an open line to Himself, one that Adam and Eve could use anytime they wanted to talk to Him. He laid the lines and prepaid the toll for an eternity of time. It would be His conduit of grace and love. Through prayer, God could once again walk and talk with His people much like they had in the garden. The partnership could be re-established. Prayer became the new point of contact between heaven and earth. The only problem was that He had to wait for Adam and Eve to pick up the receiver.

The Power of the Tower

The good news buried in this unfortunate story is that prayer is God's idea. This is important because God, as the one who designed it and put it into place, is the one who makes it work. He powers it. When we want to talk to Him, all we have to do is pick up the receiver, and He is already there, waiting to listen. We do not have to do it well, we simply have to do it.

If you have ever used a cellular phone while traveling, you are probably aware that it requires less cell to receive calls than to make them. In other words, even when the phone registers very little or no cell in a particular area, it will still ring if someone calls you. The reason for this is that the tower which transmits the signal for cellular communication is much stronger than your hand-held device. The power is in the tower, not in the phone.

In prayer, it is God's signal that makes communication possible. Our job is placement, not production. If we are in place and willing to pick up the phone, He will supply the energy needed to make the connection.

Local Call

A chief Rabbi went to visit the Pope in Rome. While in the Pope's office, the Rabbi asked to borrow the Pope's "red phone"—his direct line to heaven. Upon completing his conversation with God, the Rabbi asked the Pope, "How much do I owe you for the call?"

"Eighty-nine dollars," he answered.

Several months later, while in Jerusalem, the Pope paid a visit to the Rabbi. He, in turn, asked to borrow the Rabbi's "red phone," saying that he had several things he needed to discuss with God.

Some time later, when the Pope finally finished his call, he asked the Rabbi, "How much do I owe you?"

"Only a quarter," the Rabbi responded. "It's a local call."

Thanks to God's engineering, He is closer than you might think. The lines of communication to the throne of heaven are available to anyone who wants to talk to Him. Prayer was God's invention—His idea—and so He is faithful to maintain it and keep it in place. We do not have to create a way to reach God, nor do we have to produce it, promote it or achieve it. We simply have to use what is already there. For anyone willing to pick up the phone, prayer is a local call.

Myth #2
Prayer is like an international phone call—distance is extreme, the connection is shaky, the rate is high and the number is hard to remember.

Truth #2
Prayer is a local call. God designed it and He makes it work.

Dear Pastor,

Please say a prayer for our baseball team. We need God's help or a new pitcher.

—Alexander, age 10

Chapter 4

*L*earning to Be *C*o-Dependent

*L*abrador Retrievers are known to be among the most loyal of all animals, and my dog Murray is no exception. He is my constant companion when I am at home. Murray lies at my feet when I work, stares at me when I take a nap, and howls when I leave. He always wants to ride in the back of my truck wherever I go. When I send him outside to the yard, he sulks. From outside he follows me around the house, going from window to window, longing to be inside. One day I looked outside and saw him balancing on top of a bicycle—back paws on the seat, front paws on the handle bars—peering in the window at me while I worked! Murray has no life outside of me.

The truth is, Murray suffers from canine co-dependency. He has no idea how bad a shape he is really in.

Co-dependency, the human form, of course, is the disease of the '90's. Since its discovery, it has become the nemesis of all human relationships. Toni Braxton sings about it, "There's no me without you," and numerous twelve-step programs offer help with recovery from it. Innumerable books have been written about it, one of the first being Eric Berne's *I'm OK, You're OK*, and one of the most popular being Melody Beattie's *Co-Dependent No More.* It has emerged as probably one of the most widely recognized terms in the history of psychology.

> ℰhe gently brought it to my attention that I was not much better off than Murray.

As my wife was going through her course study for counseling, she gently brought it to my attention that I was not much better off than Murray. Although I would like to think I have come a long way down the road of self-examination and recovery—along with millions of other Americans—I was, for a period in my life, a living, breathing example of how an enabling, co-dependent person behaves. I was co-dependent on my wife and even on the religious institution which I served for 28 years. And although I understand the negative consequences of this condition, I personally believe that if we ever completely wipe it out, we might as well abandon all hope of anything ever getting done.

The possible symptoms or manifestations of co-dependency in any particular individual are endless, but co-dependents have some rather characteristic ways of relating to their "significant others" that seem to be common. Consider, for example, Rick, who has developed a very co-dependent relationship with one of his co-workers, Sharon.

Rick calls Sharon on the phone in the office at least three or four times a day. When he takes a coffee break, he always stops at her desk to drop a cup off for her, fixed just the way she likes it. He is always interested in how she is getting along, and he finds it hard to concentrate when he knows she is distressed or unhappy. They eat lunch together just about every day and sometimes Rick calls her at home. She is the first person he wants to talk to when anything significant happens in his life, especially if he has to make an important decision. He rarely does anything without Sharon's advice and approval. He is always willing to help her finish a last-minute project, even if it means he gets behind on one of his own. And Sharon can always count on Rick to bail her out or stick up for her when she misses a staff meeting or comes in a few minutes late to work.

Rick's behavior is typical co-dependent behavior because:

1. His whole identity is derived from Sharon—what is normal, what is acceptable, who he is. His ability to function is greatly hampered when she is not around.
2. In just about every circumstance, he responds or reacts based on her cues.
3. Spending time with Sharon is a priority. He cannot say "no" to her at all. He will make great personal sacrifices to be there anytime she needs him.
4. She is the first person he turns to when he has something important to share.
5. He is more concerned about her life than his own.
6. He is loyal to her at all costs, even when it might cause him trouble.

The truth is, Rick and Murray are two of a kind.

Needville, USA

The reasons people like Rick become co-dependent are even more numerous and complex than the symptoms. Assessing the causes of such a situation would require professional training and time. But from my own personal experience and from what I have gathered from my wife's bookshelf, I have learned that all human beings have a few very powerful basic needs that we strive to meet in whatever way we can. While I grew up in a small town that is actually named Needville, Texas, I have since discovered that many people live their lives in a place called

Needville, USA, driven by the desire to satisfy some very fundamental yearnings. Often, we choose to meet those needs in ways that readily fulfill the immediate longings, but are ultimately harmful to us in the long run, such as in co-dependent relationships.

The first need we have is to know who we are. We need an identity. We know our name, our address, our social security number, our phone number, our beeper number, our pager number and our e-mail address, but we have no idea who we really are. So we wrap ourselves in someone or something else, hoping to base our identity on the role we play—father, employee, friend, manager, boss, player, wife. We listen to how others talk to us and about us and we hang our life on their words.

> *We* make their life our life and live out of them.

A second need we have is to know that we have value. Some call it self-esteem or self-worth, and when it is damaged or absent, we may search for someone who will affirm us: "You're smart." "You are acceptable." "You make me happy." "You are important to me." We may actually deny other needs and interests of our own in exchange for a constant stream of validation.

Third, we have need for security. The idea of being alone is scary for most of us—we see solitude as a form of "time out." So to avoid any possibility of abandonment, we co-mingle our lives with someone else's and slowly tighten our grip. We make their life our life and live out of them. For some reason, we also seem to find some kind of false security in things: a BMW, a house, the latest, greatest computer system. Things give us a sense of belonging and permanence, insulating us from having to deal with disturbing realities of life.

Finally, and most significantly, we need to know we are loved. This is probably the most powerful force behind co-dependency. We "care-take" in the hopes of being taken care of in return. We rescue to be rescued. We accept to be accepted, and we love to be loved back. To be loved gives us life; it makes life worth living. We can survive almost any crisis we may face as long as we know we are loved.

"You're a Winner!"

Co-dependency is deceptive. Often it masquerades as dependability, selflessness, diligence or loyalty. It is an addiction that is easily justified because of its productivity and its harmless, even enticing appearance. But once unwrapped, the truth is evident. It promises happiness and fulfillment, yet delivers emptiness. It drives us to do for someone, to be someone, but we end up feeling like nobody.

Years ago, I received one of those pieces of mail that said, "You are a winner!" Something about it—perhaps it was the prize—kept me from throwing it in the trash. It said I had won a boat, and that all I had to do to claim it was make an appointment to see some lake property which was about an hour from my home. Although the letter did not exactly say what kind of boat I had won, the brochure had a picture of a beautiful ski boat on the front. I was convinced that this was no bathtub toy. It was a real floating boat that you could actually ride in.

My wife, of course, laughed at me, but I was sold. I called to make my appointment, feeling that an hour or so invested in looking at a condominium complex was a small price to pay for such a great prize. I even borrowed a pick-up and a trailer in case the boat was at the site, just waiting to be delivered.

When I arrived at the lake, I tried to be patient and act halfway interested in the building project. But I was relieved when the real estate agent led me back to the office. Feeling like I had paid my dues, I thanked her for showing me the property, laid the letter I had received on her desk, and said, "Aren't I supposed to receive a boat?"

"Yes," she said smiling.

My heart jumped. "What kind of boat is it?"

"A nine-foot inflatable raft."

I stood there silent for a moment, wondering how many different words there are in the dictionary that mean "stupid."

"So where's my raft?"

"Actually, we have had such an overwhelming response to our letter that I'm afraid we gave away the last one yesterday. But here's a nice sports watch instead. It's waterproof."

Angry and humiliated, I loaded the watch on my trailer and headed home.

Co-dependency is a disappointing substitute for the real thing. The casualty of it is the very thing it mimics—intimacy. Instead of feeling affirmed, secure and loved, people trapped in co-dependent relationships eventually end up feeling frustrated, angry and confused. Instead of gaining an identity, they lose all sense of where they end and others begin. They forfeit all personal boundaries and make themselves more vulnerable to the things they feared in the first place—rejection, abandonment and loneliness.

The reality is that we can never truly satisfy the needs in our lives that are designed to be filled by God. Although psychologists can list dozens of factors that contribute to co-dependency, few recognize this one critical fact: we were actually created to function that way. Yes, co-dependency is in our make-up. Our problem lies in the fact that we have a tendency to misdirect it.

A Healthy Dependency

If you ever went to Sunday school as a young child, someone probably told you about the "God-shaped" hole or vacuum inside of you. The illustration says that God created you with a void in your heart that cannot be satisfied by anything other than Him, and when you ask Jesus into your life, He comes and fills the emptiness. But your spirit cries out for more than just salvation. Not only are you designed to be incomplete apart from God, but you are designed to be one with Him, to live out of Him, to be wrapped up in Him—totally and completely "co-dependent."

1. He wants you to gain your identity from Him.
2. He wants you to seek His direction at all times.
3. He wants to be a priority in your life. He wants you to spend time with Him above anything else.
4. He wants to be the one you run to when you are scared, confused, happy or sad.
5. He wants you to understand His agenda and His plan.
6. He wants you to be sold out to Him, devoted and loyal at all costs.

Being co-dependent with God is more a matter of discovery than recovery. It is the healthiest place you can reside.

The difficult thing is learning how to let God meet those critical needs in your life even though people may seem more accessible. Looking to God for identity, self-esteem, security and love is not easy, but prayer is the key. The more you communicate with God, the more you will realize that He knows you best and loves you most because He created you! He is your Father; you are His child. He longs to relate to you, esteem you and cradle you. In fact, He created prayer for the very purpose of connecting Himself to you so that He could meet the deepest needs in your life. Defining yourself in Him is the very essence of why you pray.

Discovery Zone

As you begin to spend time with God, you will enter the "discovery zone." You are a creation of God and therefore your identity in all its manifold beauty is disclosed to you as you meet with Him. He made you a human *being*, not a human *doing*, and He created you for Himself. You will find that you are made in

His image and called into His purpose. You will start to understand where you have come from and who you are. He will reveal to you your gifts, your weaknesses and your uniqueness.

Every Thanksgiving when our children come to visit we get out our old home movies and spend a few hours laughing at polyester pants and wide lapels. Although we have seen them all many times, I think the kids enjoy watching them again and again because in those images from the past they see their heritage. While my children may laugh and joke through every one, I think they feel a sense of satisfaction in knowing where we lived, what they wore, where they played, and the kind of car we drove. They never get tired of seeing their first bath, their first bike ride, their first touchdown or their first date. It is all part of their lineage and it made them who they are today.

In prayer God will reveal to you your lineage. He will be there to affirm you and remind you that you were His idea. Just being in His presence will melt away false identities that you might have been fed and give you a new sense of destiny and purpose. You will discover peace unlike anything the world has to offer.

God will also meet your need to be valued and encouraged as you spend time with Him. He is the source of all self-worth. It is an amazing discovery to see yourself as God sees you. He does not look at you with critical eyes, but with the eyes of a loving Father. He wants nothing more than to help you be everything He intended you to be. He looks past the clumsiness of your humanity into that part of your spirit that He created and equipped for a special purpose. " 'For I know the plans I have for you,' declares the Lord, 'plans to prosper you and not to harm you, plans to give you hope and a future'" (Jeremiah 29:11).

My oldest daughter, Tina, was involved for several years with a singing group called "The Celebrant Singers." They traveled all over the world giving concerts in churches and performing at all kinds of special events. One of her most memorable experiences from those years was singing for the Pope. What an honor! It was thrilling just to be in the presence of such a dignitary, with all the fanfare and protocol. Not only did the group get to sing for the Pope, they were his invited guests, and they were treated with all respect and approval. Tina will never forget the feeling of standing in that Roman cathedral with the sound of their voices echoing the very majesty of heaven.

You have every reason to feel highly esteemed because someone of far greater position and authority than the Pope has made a way for you to be in His presence. In fact, not only are you able to enter into His court at any time, but in some mysterious way, He actually dwells inside you. You are a vessel of dignity and honor. Just imagine how Tina would feel if the Pope were to give her a call the next time he is in this country and ask if he could come to her house. She would need medical attention! To have an audience with God even once in a lifetime would be an unspeakable privilege. But you are so important to Him that He chooses to go beyond occasional visits and take up residency with you.

> *It* was thrilling to just be in the presence of such a dignitary, with all the fanfare and protocol.

Prayer is not an attempt to reach heaven; it is a much shorter trip than that. As you pray, the Spirit of the living God begins to work inside you, reaching out to you, eager to commune with you. You can realize His inner presence and partake of His divine nature. Your intrinsic worth is not in your garage or your bank account, it is in your heart by way of His presence. When you discover that you have been validated by the Creator of the universe, you no longer need to look for other people to make you feel important.

If you have ever been around toddlers, then you are probably aware that our need for security is high at a very young age. I was watching one of my grandchildren playing not too long ago, and I noticed a pattern. She would wander around for brief periods of time to explore a new toy or grab hold of something that caught her eye, but then rush back to Mommy or Daddy to sort of "touch base." It was as if she could only be secure for a few minutes at a time before she had to confirm that at least one of them was still there and still watching her. Most toddlers exhibit this same kind of behavior at a certain stage in development when they begin to get very curious about their world but still need desperately to know their caretaker is close by.

God loves it when we "touch base" with Him, just to make sure He is still there. He is like the most faithful father who gently reassures us every time we run to Him. You cannot go anywhere to be out of His sight—He is always watching over you, protecting you, ready to catch you if you fall. As you learn to crawl up in His lap and just rest in Him, you will find security and peace like you have never known.

Consider David, who was a man that loved God and spent time with Him. Listen to the confidence David had in knowing that God was always with him:

> O Lord, you have searched me and you know me.
> You know when I sit and when I rise;
> You perceive my thoughts from afar.
> You discern my going out and my lying down;
> You are familiar with all my ways.
> Before a word is on my tongue you know it completely, O Lord.
> You hem me in—behind and before;
> You have laid your hand upon me.
> Such knowledge is too wonderful for me,
> Too lofty for me to attain.
> Where can I go from your Spirit?
> Where can I flee from your presence?
> If I go up to the heavens, you are there;
> If I make my bed in the depths, you are there.

If I rise on the wings of the dawn,
If I settle on the far side of the sea,
Even there your hand will guide me,
Your right hand will hold me fast (Psalm 139:1–10).

As you become co-dependent on God, you will also discover, like David, an unshakable sense of security. You will begin to trust and know that He will never leave you or forsake you (Joshua 1:5). He has you in His grip, and He will not let go.

Finally, as you wrap yourself in God, you will discover how deep and how enduring is His love for you. God is love, and He is the author and source of perfect love. When you draw close to Him, He will draw close to you to touch you and bless you. He bonds Himself to you and loves you unconditionally—no strings attached. He will always be the same.

Country music singer George Strait sums up the love of God in the words of his song, "Love Without End, Amen":

Then one night I dreamed I stood outside those pearly
    gates.
Suddenly I realized there must be some mistake.
If they knew half the things I'd done, they'd never let
    me in.
But somewhere from the other side, I heard these words
    again:
"Let me tell you a secret about a Father's love,
A secret that my daddy said was just between us.
Daddy's don't just love their children every now and then,
It's a love without end. Amen."

The beautiful thing about intimacy with God is never having to apologize for who you are because God sees into the very depths of your spirit. He knows your thoughts and He loves you anyway. He is always patient, always eager to listen and reveal His own character to you as you pray. He wants to be known by you! The revelation of God living in you is the most profound result of spending time with Him.

Bitter to Better

A friend of mine named Betty, now in her 70's and full of grace, spent a lifetime finding her identity in Christ to a depth most of us will never comprehend. Placed in an orphanage as an infant by an unwed mother who chose not to raise her daughter, Betty did not have the identity and security of a birth family in which to grow up. Before she was even two years old, she was severely burned over much of her small body when a pot of boiling water fell off the stove. The accident scarred her deeply, both physically and emotionally. Her earliest memories are of rejection, loneliness and intense anger. She felt illegitimate in every sense of the word.

At pre-school age, Betty was shuffled in and out of several foster homes in an attempt to find an adoptive family, but no one seemed to want her. Her emptiness made her bitter and confused, and none of the couples who took her in could handle the raging tantrums and screaming fits she was prone to throw.

Finally, at the age of six, she was adopted by a couple I will call the Lindseys, and she went to live with them on their farm. The couple raised Betty as their only child, doing their best to manage her volatile personality with strict boundaries and severe punishment. Mr. Lindsey was a hard-working, resourceful man, but his crude, harsh mannerisms only reinforced the feelings of worthlessness that Betty had grown accustomed to. Her favorite place on the farm was a big tree where she would often go to hide from the world and talk to God. Based on what little she knew about God, she could not understand why He had been so unfair to her. She talked to God not because she loved Him or trusted Him, but because she thought He was cruel and distant, and she wanted an explanation. Sometimes she would yell, and sometimes she would cry.

As she got older, her tantrums diminished somewhat as she searched to get her needs met through relationships, parties and activities. When she met Frank, she was anything but modest.

Although Frank had a traditional church upbringing, he saw something in Betty that he knew was worth working for, and he eventually fell in love with her and married her.

Frank was patient and kind, even through the fits of rage that still exploded in Betty on occasion. He never forced his ideas about God on her, but his example and his steady tenderness sparked in her a deep interest in what the Bible might have to say to someone like her. One morning, alone at her kitchen table, she opened it up and began to read. Although she did not understand much of what she read, she understood all too well a verse in Deuteronomy that said, "No one born of a forbidden marriage nor any of his descendants may enter the assembly of the Lord, even down to the tenth generation" (Deuteronomy 23:2). Enraged, she slung the Bible across the room. Even God had no place for her.

> **Enraged, she slung the Bible across the room. Even God had no place for her.**

It was months before Betty could open the Bible again, but she could not shake the feeling in the depths of her spirit that there must be more to God than she knew. She either had to discover what it was or confirm her fear that there was really no hope. Slowly and tediously, she began sifting through the scriptures, searching for meaning and answers. Frank directed her to the New Testament, where she found promises that were literally too good for her to believe. For hours at a time, she read and reread the words, questioning God, challenging Him to make them come alive. It was there at her kitchen table, alone with Him, that she began to discover for the first time who she was and who He had created her to be.

Finding her identity in Christ was not easy, nor did it happen overnight. Betty had a lifetime of anger, rejection, shame,

fear and insecurity to overcome. Perhaps because she had nowhere else to look, she spent hours talking to a God she was not
even sure loved her. But the more time she spent with Him, the
more He revealed Himself to her, and the more she began to
feel the sense of belonging, the self-esteem, the security and the
love she had craved for so long. As she learned to be co-dependent on God, He met her needs over and above what she had
ever thought possible.

Our Father, which art in heaven, Howard
be thy name . . .

                                            —Joey, age 6

Chapter 5

Get Real

A dedicated prayer teacher and good friend of mine sent me a copy of this letter she received from a friend:

Does God answer prayer? I know He does. Our Heavenly Father recently answered the prayer of my 7-year-old son, Luke, and saved my life. Please allow me to share our recent witness to the power of prayer.

My son, Luke, is seven years old and in the first grade. Although not a strong verbal communicator yet, Luke participates in our family prayer time. Every evening during our prayers, Luke thanks the Lord for the same thing saying something like this, "Thank you God for helping Daniel and me to have a nice day at school, for helping Mom to drive home safely from work and for helping Daddy to have a nice day at work."

I must admit that I was concerned about the repetitiousness of his prayers. I had suggested to Luke that he offer thanks for all the other things or that he share other concerns with the Lord, but Luke continued his prayers in the same way every day.

Then, on Saturday, Dec. 14, 1996, I was driving home from work at about 3 p.m. I was heading north on the Black Canyon Freeway, just south of Camelback Road, when all of a sudden I saw a multi-vehicle accident involving about five cars unfolding in slow-motion about thirty yards ahead of me. One car had spun around the wrong way on the freeway and was facing me. A pickup truck was spinning around, across all three lanes, and crashing into other cars like a pinball.

My immediate response was, "Oh no! Help me, God. I'm not only going to be hit from the front but also from the cars coming up from behind."

I started thinking about my husband, Dave, and my sons, Daniel and Luke, who were out of town visiting family in Ohio. "Please God, don't let me get hit. Dave is out of town and I don't want to get hurt and have to go to the hospital without him. I don't want to ruin their trip and make them have to come home early. I don't want to get hurt right before the holidays. And please God, don't let them wreck my car. I can't afford an accident."

My natural reaction should have been terror. But instead of panic or fear I felt calm. I felt the heavenly Father's presence and assurance that He was in control.

As I was thanking God for His assurance, I felt that He was in control of my steering wheel. And in a fraction of a second, I scanned for traffic in the lane to my right and veered off to go onto the Camelback Road off-ramp.

As I veered towards the off-ramp, I saw the pickup truck crashing through the bushes in the little space separating the freeway from the off-ramp. I'm embarrassed to admit this, but I thought, "God, please stop that pickup truck or it is going to crash into me." (Like God couldn't see the truck). Immediately, the pickup truck crashed to a stop about three feet from the driver's side of my car.

I screeched to a stop on the side of the off-ramp. I knew that I must go over to see if the occupants of the pickup truck needed assistance. Then, just as I was about to get out of my car, another motorist ran up to the pickup truck. A passenger in the pickup truck rolled down the window and yelled, "We're okay."

I was stunned. I leaned back and realized that the Lord had answered all of my prayer requests as soon as I had asked. And

> *Immediately, the pickup truck crashed to a stop about three feet from the driver's side of my car.*

then, as if saving my life were not enough, the Lord poured out His blessings abundantly on me. The heavenly Father spoke to me—not loudly but emphatically, as if He wanted to make sure that I really listened so as not to miss a really big point. It was as if He wanted to make sure there was no doubt in my mind. He told me that yes, He had answered all of my prayer requests as things were happening on the freeway. He said that He was being faithful to answer prayers he considered of utmost importance . . . those of a little boy who prays with childlike faith . . . the prayers of my son, Luke.

I felt the Lord reassure me that He knows all of my son's thoughts and concerns, those unspoken and even those spoken not so clearly and that He will always be faithful to His son, Luke, whom He loves deeply.

I was truly humbled by the power of the prayers of my 7-year-old son. The experience was beyond profound.

How blessed I am that the Lord would speak to me and allow me to go through this experience. How blessed I am as a mother to have the Lord tell me how intimately He knows my son's concerns and how deeply He loves him.

Many motorists passing by probably felt it was all a lucky coincidence. How many times in our lives is God faithful to answer prayer, and we don't even realize it? Why does God have to speak as clearly as He did to me before we recognize His grace and the power of prayer?

—*Susan*

What could we say about Luke that would help us understand why his prayer was answered? Words like pure, innocent, unpretentious, childlike, trusting, simple and honest all come to mind.

Truly the prayers of children are of "utmost importance" to God. He rejoices over the little ones who come to Him, and He delights in answering their prayers. It should cause us to evaluate God's expectations with regard to prayer when the repetitious words of a seven-year-old boy move His hand in such a dramatic way.

Humanity, Humility and Heart

I have studied prayer for nearly thirty years. And as a result I have gained information from some of the most renowned prayer teachers in the world today. I have read hundreds of books on prayer that describe everything from the theological positions on what makes prayer effective, to dozens of different kinds of prayer, to detailed descriptions of how you should pray. I have studied the Greek and Hebrew texts in prayer passages of the Bible, and I have looked at the prayer lives of great men and women of God. And I have come to this conclusion: I already knew everything I really needed to know about talking to God when I was seven years old.

Prayer, as Philip Yancey said about grace, is a lesson of the heart more than the head. Although prayer can be cut open and examined from the inside out, it often dies in the process, and the last thing I want to do is to kill it. I would rather show you pictures of prayer and allow you to learn, as I have, from the lives of real people who had the audacity to pray without a seminary degree.

God responds to those who are real with Him. He is not impressed with degrees or theology. He is not swayed by position or location. He takes very little notice of eloquence or drama. But He pours Himself out where He finds humanity, humility and heart. Jesus told his disciples, "I tell you the truth, unless you change and become like little children, you will never enter the kingdom of heaven. Therefore, whoever humbles himself like this child is the greatest in the kingdom of heaven" (Matthew 18:3–4).

Like most parents, one of the qualities I valued most in my children was honesty. As they were growing up, I took every opportunity I could to teach them the importance of telling the truth, even when they had messed up. I do the same now with my grandchildren. If four-year-old Austen knocks a glass over in the kitchen and it breaks, I would much rather him come to me and tell me what happened than to try to hide it by sweeping the pieces under a rug. And I want him to be secure enough in my love to know I will not turn him away just because he did something he should not have done.

God is the same way with us. He would much rather you come to Him in all of your humanity—He sees it anyway—than to dress yourself up and try to hide what might displease Him. Besides the fact that it is impossible to hide anything from God, He values your honesty much more than he cares about your "warts." As your Father, He can handle sin much better than false pride.

Awareness of your humanity before God results in an attitude of humility. While self-righteousness usually leads to religious praying, humility produces true communication and intimacy with your Father. When you go before God with all your "garbage" in tow, you humble yourself and say, "Here I am, God. I know it's not pretty, but it's me. I want to spend some time with you." Just like I would with Austen, He will scoop you up in His lap and say, "Talk to me." He will listen to you, love you and teach you, if only you will be real with Him.

> "*Here* I am, God. I know it's not pretty, but it's me."

Mother Teresa said, "Prayer enlarges your heart for God"(4). It is your heart that He is most interested in. That is why the prayers of children are so effective, because their heads do not as often get in the way of what their hearts might say. Heart is about passion and desire—it is about really wanting a relationship with God over and above what He can do for you. It is about persevering and never giving up.

It is these three attributes, humanity, humility and heart, that move the hand of the Father. Anyone can be real with Him and know that He listens and responds. Prayer is an equal opportunity activity. In fact, if you look closely into the lives of many of the great men and women of the Bible, you may be surprised to discover that they were anything but saintly. In many cases, they were unlikely candidates to accomplish anything spectacular, but they were real with God. When He called them, they responded to Him with humanity, humility and heart.

A Barter of Betrayal

Consider, for example, Abraham. A "no-name" from a nomadic tribe in Ur, Abraham had the unsavory reputation of having sold out his wife to save his own skin. Genesis 12 tells the story:

> *Now there was a famine in the land, and Abram (Abraham's original name) went down to Egypt to live there for a while*

because the famine was severe. As he was about to enter Egypt, he said to his wife Sarai, "I know what a beautiful woman you are. When the Egyptians see you, they will say, 'This is his wife.' Then they will kill me but will let you live. Say you are my sister, so that I will be treated well for your sake and my life will be spared because of you.

When Abram came to Egypt, the Egyptians saw that she was a very beautiful woman. And when Pharaoh's officials saw her, they praised her to Pharaoh, and she was taken into his palace. He treated Abram well for her sake, and Abram acquired sheep and cattle, male and female donkeys, menservants and maidservants, and camels.

But the Lord inflicted serious diseases on Pharaoh and his household because of Abram's wife Sarai. So Pharaoh summoned Abram. "What have you done to me?" he said. "Why didn't you tell me she was your wife? Why did you say, 'She is my sister,' so that I took her to be my wife? Now then, here is your wife. Take her and go!" Then Pharaoh gave orders about Abram to his men, and they sent him on his way, with his wife and everything he had (Genesis 12:10–20).

Because he was afraid Pharaoh might kill him, Abraham actually gave up Sarai in exchange for a bunch of animals—the equivalent of a fortune in those days. He saw the Egyptians eyeing his beautiful wife, and he said, "Okay, honey, here's the plan. You go with the nice people and give Pharaoh whatever he wants. I'll stay here and take care of the house and the animals." Oh, to have been a fly on the chariot seat as they were leaving Egypt!

"Sarai?"

Silence.

"Sarai? I missed you."

Silence.

"Sarai . . . , Sweetheart? How 'bout that Pharaoh?"

No wonder they were almost one hundred years old before they had a child!

Despite the fact that he did not score big in the bravery or nobility categories, Abraham did exhibit incredible faithfulness and obedience to God throughout his life, indicating his humility before the Father. One verse says, "Abram believed the Lord, and he [the Lord] credited it to him as righteousness" (Genesis 15:6).

Abraham's faith was so strong that when God instructed him to take his only son, Isaac, up to the top of a mountain and sacrifice him, Abraham did not even question God. What he lacked in nobility he made up for in absolute trust. Of course, God did not allow Abraham to go through with the offering. An angel appeared and stopped him before he could harm the boy. The Lord said to him, ". . . because you have done this . . . , I will surely bless you and make your descendants as numerous as the stars in the sky . . ." (Genesis 22:16–17).

Abraham's humility and heart for obedience earned him favor with God, and as a result, God was very faithful to answer his prayers. Years later, another man, Moses, would also earn the favor of God because of his true humility and genuine spirit.

"B-b-b-but, God?"

In his moments of glory, Moses was the man who led the Israelites out of Egypt into the promised land and along the way, received the Ten Commandments from God. However, he was not without his own struggles of humanity.

Moses apparently had a bit of a temper that caused him, at age forty, to kill a man for beating one of his fellow Hebrews. Exodus 2:11–15 tells the story:

> One day, after Moses had grown up, he went out to where his own people were and watched them at the hard labor. He saw an Egyptian beating a Hebrew, one of his own people. Glancing this way and that and seeing no one, he killed the Egyptian and hid him in the sand. The next day he went out and saw two Hebrews fighting. He asked the one in the wrong, "Why are you hitting your fellow Hebrew?"

> *The man said, "Who made you ruler and judge over us?*
> *Are you thinking of killing me as you killed the Egyptian?"*
> *Then Moses was afraid and thought, "What I did must have*
> *become known."*
> *When Pharaoh heard of this, he tried to kill Moses, but*
> *Moses fled from Pharaoh and went to live in Midian.*

Moses also was believed to have a stutter, an interesting characteristic for a man chosen as leader for an entire nation. But perhaps it was this physical condition that caused Moses to be "a very humble man, more humble than anyone else on the face of the earth" (Numbers 12:3). When God called him to be the leader of the Israelites, Moses responded by saying,

> *"Who am I, that I should go to Pharaoh and bring the Isra-*
> *elites out of Egypt? Suppose I go to the Israelites and say to*
> *them, 'The God of your fathers has sent me to you,' and they*
> *ask me, 'What is his name?' Then what shall I tell them?*
> *What if they do not believe me or listen to me?" (Exodus*
> *3:11, 13; 4:1).*

He pleaded with God to choose someone else,

> *"O Lord, I have never been eloquent, neither in the past nor*
> *since you have spoken to your servant. I am slow of speech*
> *and tongue. O Lord, please send someone else to do it" (Exo-*
> *dus 4:10, 13).*

But God had chosen His man, probably in part because of the fact that he did not have a prideful bone in his body. Moses was humble and trusted God, and as a result, God made him a great leader despite his weaknesses. He had a heart for the Israelites—God's people— and he stuck with them even though they were weak at heart, self-protecting and at times down-right rebellious. Moses was special to God—he was the only person that God ever allowed to see Himself in the fullness of His glory.

Little Guys Can Do Big Things Too!

Another man that modeled humanity, humility and heart was David. The youngest of seven brothers, David was small in stature but big in heart. While he was still a young shepherd boy, he became a military hero and a well-known and well-loved leader in Saul's army. He won many battles and was successful in everything he did because the Lord was with him. Eventually, he was appointed king over Judah and then king over all of Israel. There was, however, one battle of the flesh in which David was anything but triumphant.

> *One evening David got up from his bed and walked around on the roof of the palace. From the roof he saw a woman bathing. The woman was very beautiful, and David sent someone to find out about her. The man said, "Isn't this Bathsheba, the daughter of Eliam and the wife of Uriah the Hittite?" Then David sent messengers to get her. She came to him, and he slept with her. (She had purified herself from her uncleanness.) Then she went back home. The woman conceived and sent word to David, saying, "I am pregnant" (2 Samuel 11:2–5).*

Oops! As David was well aware, the law prescribed the death penalty for both Bathsheba and him, so he devised a plan. Under the pretense of seeking information about the war that was going on, David called for Bathsheba's husband, Uriah, to come home, hoping that he would sleep with his wife and eliminate the possibility for suspicion regarding the child. But Uriah was very noble and would not lie with his wife and enjoy the comforts of his home while his brothers were still fighting on the battlefield. So David had to go to plan "B."

> *In the morning David wrote a letter to Joab and sent it with Uriah. In it he wrote, "Put Uriah in the front line where the fighting is fiercest. Then withdraw from him so he will be struck down and die."*

So while Joab had the city under siege, he put Uriah at a place where he knew the strongest defenders were. When the men of the city came out and fought against Joab, some of the men in David's army fell; moreover, Uriah the Hittite was dead (2 Samuel 11:14–17).

Not only did David commit adultery, but he had the woman's husband killed as well! He paid heavily for these sins. Yet through it all, despite some serious lapses in judgment, he was a 'man after God's heart" (Acts 13:22), passionate and loyal. God kept His promises to David and answered his prayers until he died.

All of these men—Abraham, Moses and David—were real people who walked with God in genuine humility. They were far from perfect, but they were not pretentious. My point is not to approve of their sin, but rather to emphasize that their humanity did not keep them from walking intimately with God. They were always honest and open with Him, and even in the midst of their sinfulness, they loved Him and revered Him. He dealt with their disobedience but continued to bless them throughout their lives.

Prodigal Love

Jesus told a parable about a father who lived on an estate with his two sons. One day, his younger son came to him and said, "Dad, I'm tired of living out here in the middle of nowhere. I want my inheritance now so I can go live in the city where the action is!" So, although he did not have to, the father gave his son his share of the estate, releasing him to go.

Almost immediately, the young son gathered up everything he owned and took off for a distant country. He was so glad to finally be out on his own—now he could really have some fun. But it was not long before he had foolishly squandered all of his money on parties and wild entertainment. To make matters worse, his new homeland was experiencing a terrible famine. He began to feel very hungry and very broke.

Still determined not to go running home, he hired himself out to one of the locals who sent him into the fields to feed pigs. The boy was so hungry that even the pig slop looked good! In desperation, his attitude began to change. He started to think, "My dad's servants live better than this. Maybe if I go back and grovel enough, he'll let me stay with his hired hands and eat the scraps from their table."

> *He celebrates when one of his kids —even a stinky one— comes home.*

So the son set off to return home, rehearsing as he traveled exactly what he would say to his dad when he got there, assuming his dad would even listen. But read what happened when the son arrived home:

> *But while he was still a long way off, his father saw him and was filled with compassion for him; he ran to his son, threw his arms around him and kissed him.*
>
> *The son said to him, "Father, I have sinned against heaven and against you. I am no longer worthy to be called your son."*
>
> *But the father said to his servants, "Quick! Bring the best robe and put it on him. Put a ring on his finger and sandals on his feet. Bring the fattened calf and kill it. Let's have a feast and celebrate. For this son of mine was dead and is alive again; he was lost and is found." So they began to celebrate.*

Jesus told this story to illustrate God's heart for all His children. Even when we sin against Him, He welcomes us back with open arms when we return to Him in humility. He celebrates when one of his kids—even a stinky one—comes home.

It is interesting that the parable goes on to explain the older son's reaction to the whole ordeal. He was angry and confused, feeling sure that his younger brother needed a good whipping, not a party! In fact, he refused to join in the celebration. When his dad came out to talk to him, I imagine he said something like, "Dad, how can you let him get away with that?! He humiliated you, spent his entire inheritance (and he's sure not getting any of mine!), and you're treating him like some kind of hero. It's not fair" (see Luke 15:11–32).

How right he is—it is not fair. It is scandalous grace. It is the unfailing, limitless devotion of a lovesick father.

God relates to us as imperfect people. He will not disqualify you from prayer for any reason if only you will humble yourself to say, "I want to pray. I want to know you and learn your voice. Please Dad, I'm ready to come home." He will respond by saying, "Let the celebration begin!"

Dear Father,

I enjoy making other people look good. Thank you for making me look good by giving me your robe of righteousness.

—the prayer of a hairdresser

Part 2

Overcoming the Fear of Failure

Chapter 6

The Time Bind

A faithful church-goer, Jim was the kind of man who seemed to model spiritual leadership and excellence in every way. He was committed to serving his church both with his time and money, and his generosity and integrity had earned him a very good reputation in the community. Also a successful business man and father, he was the picture of confidence and self-assurance.

Then one day Jim received news that a long-time friend had been hospitalized with the shocking prognosis that, short of a miracle, he had only a few months to live. Without hesitating, Jim canceled his appointments for the next day and put work aside so that he could spend some time visiting his dying friend.

When he got to the hospital, he went to his friend's room where he found several family members and a few flowers and cards heralding well-meaning but uncomfortably hopeful "get well" messages. Jim's presence always had a calming effect, and his friend smiled at him as he sat down on the side of the bed.

"I'm so sorry," Jim said, placing his hand on his friend's shoulder. "Is there anything I can do for you or your family?"

"Jim, I'm pretty scared. You know I don't go to church very often like you do; that's why I'm glad you came. Would you pray for me?"

> *We* do not like to do things unless we are fairly sure we can win and look good doing it.

Jim stammered a little as if he had been caught off guard, and then his gaze fell to the floor. After what seemed like a long silence, he said, "I can't. I don't really know how."

As Jim told me that story, tears rolled down his cheeks. "I wanted to pray for him more than anything, Terry, but I was terrified of doing it wrong. I wanted to somehow ask God to heal my friend, but I was afraid it wouldn't work. I just didn't know what to say."

The Fear of Failure

How angels must lament over prayers unsaid! How tragic it is that the fear of failing often keeps us from blessing those we love and from receiving a blessing ourselves. So many people, even those who love God and go to church, are paralyzed when it comes to prayer because they are afraid they will not be successful. We do not like to do things unless we are fairly sure we can win and look good doing it.

Many people wonder, "What do I say? How long should I pray? How do I know what's OK to ask and what's not OK? How do I know what the will of God is in a situation? What if God does not give me what I ask for?" And these fears are magnified one hundred times when we are called on to pray out loud in front of even one other person. I could list hundreds of names of people I know who would have reacted much like Jim did in that hospital room—they would have been completely overcome with the fear of failure. How would you have responded?

To fail at any endeavor can be seen from two different angles: not knowing how to do something or not accomplishing the desired outcome. If someone were to challenge me to a game of golf, I might fear failure either because I do not have the skills necessary to swing a club or because I do not like to lose. One has to do with technique, the other with result. In prayer, most people fear failure either because they do not know what to say or because they are afraid they will not receive what they ask for.

"Oops!"

I heard a story about a robber who broke into a house one night and was warmly greeted by a shrill voice, "Hello, nice to meet you!" Startled, the robber whirled around only to see a caged parrot who spoke to him again, "Who are you?"

"Never mind," he said to the parrot as he began surveying the room. As he was taking a mental inventory of the valuables, he noticed in one dark corner what appeared to be a large dog. He froze in his tracks and then very slowly inched toward the animal trying to get a better look. Sure enough, it was a full-grown Rottweiler, just lying there staring at him. The robber weakened a little, and his palms began to sweat. But as he gently moved back, the dog remained perfectly still, showing no signs whatsoever of aggression. The robber shrugged and went about his work.

Each time he re-entered the house however, the parrot would say something to him—"Polly want a cracker?" "Time for bed." "Wake up, sleepyhead." "My name is Jack." "Dog's name is Jill." "Want a kiss?" So the robber began taunting the bird by calling him names and tapping on the cage as he went by. In that manner, "Jack" kept the robber entertained as he loaded stereo equipment, computer parts, televisions and jewelry into the back of his van. As he went back and forth through the house, the robber never completely took his eyes off the dog, but not once did he ever see the animal do so much as twitch.

When he had finally emptied the house of everything he could find, the robber stopped one last time in front of the parrot's cage. He shook his head and laughed out loud. "You think you are so smart! But I have stolen everything of value in this house right in front of you, and you don't even know it. What do you have to say about that, stupid bird?"

> *He* really does not care whether you babble in incomplete sentences or speak forth an eloquent soliloquy.

Jack shifted his claws on his stick, cocked his head slightly to one side and said, "Don't call me names. Sic 'em, Jill."

From that night on, that robber had a healthy respect for what it meant to say the wrong thing! He probably thought twice before making fun of any more household pets. But when it comes to prayer, we never have to be afraid of letting the wrong words slip. As long as we are talking to God, we simply cannot mess up.

No Such Thing as a Bad Prayer

I have on my refrigerator a piece of artwork that is priceless. Sketched in purple crayon, I think it is a helicopter, while my wife thinks it is a flower. Regardless, since we both regard it as a beautiful masterpiece of impressionistic art, we have a hard time understanding why visitors to our home see it as just a bunch of scribbling. I have no doubt that in the mind of Annalise, my two-year-old granddaughter who drew it, it is a creative expression of her deepest thoughts. As far as I am concerned, she could never draw a bad picture.

In God's eyes, there is no such thing as a bad prayer when it comes from one of His children. He treasures every one of your prayers because He is your Abba Father. In fact, the Bible says that your prayers are kept in golden bowls and they are offered to God by the angels as sweet-smelling incense (Revelation 8: 3–4). He cherishes the very act of listening to you and communicating with you much as I take joy in listening to one of my grandchildren tell me about an exciting discovery or a recent achievement. God smiles and delights at the very sound of your voice.

God is not sitting on His throne with a giant score card, waiting to critique your prayer and analyze its flaws. He really does not care whether you babble in incomplete sentences or speak forth an eloquent soliloquy. He just wants to hear from you. Remember, prayer was His idea—it is not something He intended for you to have to make happen. He even gave you the Holy Spirit to be your teacher and helper in prayer. When you do not know what to say, the Spirit prays for you (Romans 8:26). God is always patient and eager to do anything He can to facilitate a relationship with you. You do not need to fear saying the wrong thing to Him.

Myth #3
Some prayers are better than others.

Truth #3
To God, there is no such thing as a bad prayer.
He just wants to hear from you.

Trick or Treat?

Although I will discuss how God answers prayer later in chapter twelve, for now I will simply say that you need not fear the outcome of your prayers. God will respond when we pray, and we must not let our own pride keep us from telling Him what we need. Trust Him to be God, and let Him be responsible for the outcome.

One afternoon a lady was driving down a small country road when she noticed one of her tires going flat. She pulled over into the grass, inspected the flat tire and found a large nail protruding from one side. Although she had a spare in the trunk, she did not have a jack, so she began looking around for where she might borrow some tools.

> *S*ometimes we are so fearful of not receiving what we ask for in prayer that we hardly give God the chance to answer.

She headed up the road toward a small farm house, thinking as she walked, "What if they're not home? Maybe they will be—but I'm such a mess. They probably won't even want to let me in. I'm sure they have a jack, but what if they think I'm going to steal their tools? Or worse, what if they think I'm crazy or something? They probably won't let me borrow anything. Nobody likes to lend a hand these days. People are so selfish—they won't even help someone who's stranded on the road!"

By the time the lady reached the farm house, she was on the verge of anger. When a smiling young man opened the door and said, "What can I do for you, Ma'am?" she clenched her fists and snorted back at the confused farmer, "Never mind! I didn't really need your stupid jack anyway!"

Sometimes we are so fearful of not receiving what we ask for in prayer that we hardly give God the chance to answer. Like the lady who needed to borrow a jack, we talk ourselves out of being disappointed by expecting the very worst. We say, "God, if you're not too busy, and if it's your will, would you please supply my need? But if not, that's fine. I don't really deserve any favors anyway."

The Purpose of Prayer

To overcome our fear of failure in prayer, our first step is to redefine the true purpose of prayer. Prayer is not some celestial athletic contest in which we sharpen our skills all for the purpose of winning a trophy. Success in this arena really has little to do with being the best or achieving a victory. Prayer is all about building a relationship with One who has already given everything He has to demonstrate His affection for you.

If the only time we ever go to God in prayer is when we want something, then we are setting ourselves up for a very shallow and disappointing relationship. Imagine how a close friend would feel if you never bothered to talk to him except when you needed a favor. Not that God will ever give up on you because you neglect to spend quality time with Him—He is probably the only one who will love you and be there for you no matter how long it takes you to come around. But He does desire to be more than just your "pulse" machine. He wants to give you something better than material things; He wants to give you Himself. He wants to be known by you.

We must replace our "crisis" mentality with a "Christ" mentality. In other words, we must pray to know Christ, not just to solve a crisis. We must desire above anything else to know Him and become like Him. We must learn to seek Him for His face and not just His hand. While God is a loving Father who takes great delight in blessing His children, and while He is eager to bestow on each of us His very best, as I mentioned before, giving us things was not the primary reason He created prayer.

God wants a relationship with you. When simply knowing God becomes your focus in prayer, then you cannot fail as long as you are communicating with Him. Wheeling and dealing give way to something deeper and more meaningful. Just being in His presence is so fulfilling, so peaceful and gratifying that crises seem to melt and urgent needs seem to lose their sting. Every time you get alone with God, you become a little more intimate with Him. As you see His heart and His mind, He presses Himself against you. What you can *get* from Him becomes less and less important than being *one* with Him.

Myth #4
Prayer is crisis-motivated.

Truth #4
We pray to know Christ, not just to solve a crisis.

Speed

You really cannot fail at prayer if you are willing to slow down long enough to be with God. Prayer is basically fail-proof. Time equals success—guaranteed. He will welcome you, listen to you, love you and answer you. The one thing He will not do is force Himself into your schedule. He will pursue you and follow behind you in anticipation, but He will not make you carve out even one minute to be with Him. That is entirely up to you.

I concluded several years ago that prayer, especially in our culture, is a time issue. Its greatest enemy is busyness—the never-ending rat race that we call life. We are like passengers on a speeding train with no brakes. With each new day, the train is going faster and faster, but we are so enamored with the amenities that we hardly even notice the acceleration. We work eight hours a day or more, do our best to keep family life going smoothly, socialize when we can and if we are really conscientious, go to church when we are not tied up with some other pressing Sunday obligation. Every minute of every day is as full as it can possibly be and our only regret is that we cannot fit more in.

I picked up a "national best-seller" while working on this book because the title caught my eye: *The Time Bind: When Work Becomes Home and Home Becomes Work.* In it, author Arlie Russell Hochschild gives a frightening account of the dilemma faced by many of today's working parents, particularly women, whose obligations have far exceeded their twenty-four-hour days. She explains the many ways in which we

> *Prayer, especially in our culture, is a time issue.*

have redefined our roles as husbands, wives, fathers and mothers in order to accommodate the ever-increasing demands of earning a living, getting ahead, and making our way to the top— of something.

Little House on the Freeway

One section of the book that I found poignantly humorous was Ms. Hochschild's discussion of various time-saving services that have cropped up all over the country to help parents squeeze more productive hours out of their days. I was somewhat amused and yet disturbed as I read about the creative options available to those who feel compelled to hire out those aspects of family life that used to be considered mandatory.

For example, she explains that many daycare centers now offer extended services to help busy parents with everything from meal preparation to Christmas shopping. Some provide amenities such as haircutting, activity planning and tutoring. KinderCare Learning Centers stay open late one Friday night a month so that for an extra fee, parents can leave their children and enjoy a night out.

In some parts of the country, a family can now phone in a dinner order to a child's daycare center in the morning and pick up both the child and the meal (in an ovenproof container) in the evening. Bright Horizons offers a dry-cleaning service based on the same principle. According to one news report, some daycare centers will schedule your child's extra time, arranging for and making sure that children get to swimming or gymnastics classes, for example. As the president of Bright Horizons notes, "At Christmas we even have vendors come in and set up displays so parents can buy gifts" (Hochschild 230).

She goes on to describe food services that will deliver a week's worth of flash-frozen dinners to your house, errand services that will do anything from grocery shopping to carpools, cleaning services that will do routine to extensive spring cleaning, and party planning services that will handle every last detail of your child's birthday from refreshments and favors to gift wrapping. A company in Washington D.C. called Playground Connections will actually find your child a playmate according to specifications you give them, much like a dating service. And, she states, "In several cities children home alone can call a 1-900 number for 'Grandma Please!' and reach an adult who has time to talk with them, sing to them, or help them with their homework" (231).

Aside from the obvious concerns *The Time Bind* raises about the changing mores of family life, it should raise concerns about the frantic pace of life in general and the effects the speeding train has on our individual spiritual well-being. Neither a mother who is so busy that she must hire someone else to talk to her daughter, nor a father who is so consumed with his job that he has no time to help his son with his science project is likely to have any spare time to spend getting to know God. In fact, it would seem that in the fast pace of today's work world, virtually no time can be spared for anything that does not somehow get us further ahead in the money game.

So, is our busyness strictly a result of increasing work demands, or are there other factors contributing to the "time bind"? What do we do with all 168 hours each week that keeps us constantly occupied?

Time is more than just money, it is a precious commodity that each of us is given in equal amounts every day. Once spent, it is gone forever. Sadly, we often squander more of it than we realize doing things that have no bearing at all on the aspects of life that we ourselves would probably deem most important if asked—family, personal growth, relationships and so forth.

The Time Bandits

I have identified ten activities and habits that can rob us blind when it comes to our time. I call them the "Time Bandits," and the good news (or bad news, depending on how you see it) is that we have at least some control over all of them. How much time they steal from our days and weeks is actually up to us.

In the fast pace of today's work world, virtually no time can be spared for anything that does not somehow get us further ahead in the money game.

1. Look Who's Talking – After a conference one weekend, a woman with whom I had visited gave me her business card for our mailing list. She had seven different phone numbers listed, each one of which would roll over to the next if the call were not answered within three rings. The last number on her card was her pager number which would accept a voice mail message in the event that she did not answer any of the six previous numbers! This woman was determined to never miss a call.

The technological developments in the communication industry have made you accessible to anyone anywhere at virtually any time. In addition to having multiple phones at home, you now can have a phone that you carry everywhere you go. A satellite pager can find you even if you travel out of the country. And with features like voice mail, call waiting, three-way calling and call forwarding, you can be "in touch" twenty-four hours a day, seven days a week.

2. Cable Guy – I heard a statistic just recently (on television, no less) that on the average, an American family watches about seven hours of television a day! That amounts to forty-nine hours per week, and over 2,500 hours per year. That means that in the eighteen years it takes to raise the kids, the average family has spent forty-five thousand hours staring at the TV screen! Most basic cable television services today offer subscribers at least fifty different channels to choose from, and if that is not enough, for a little extra each month you can most likely receive in the neighborhood of 200 selections through the same cable or by installing your own satellite.

3. Lost in Space – Or lost in cyberspace, as is the case for many avid Internet users. The world of the web has created a new addiction to the limitless amount of information that is available literally at your fingertips. With over one million registered web pages, the Internet has captured the time and attention of so many users that the volume of e-mail being bleeped across the country from modem to modem has already far exceeded the amount of mail delivered by the United States Postal Service.

4. Toy Story – Toys for grown-ups are big business these days, not only in volume but in dollars. Americans love to play and be entertained, and we spend hundreds of hours doing both. Boats, motorcycles, jet skis and sporting gear are just some of the "toys" that take up space in the middle class garage. Even remote control flyers, video and computer games, power tools and other cutting-edge electronic widgets can all qualify as time vacuums if they are overused. If you like to watch videos, Blockbuster offers over 21,000 titles in its catalog, or you can contribute to the billion dollar movie industry by going to see the latest release in a theatre. The restaurant business, which has become more entertainment oriented and less geared toward simply meeting physiological needs, is booming as countless high-dollar eating places open every day in cities across the country.

5. Planes, Trains and Automobiles – Within a few short hours, you can be on your way to literally anywhere in the world. Travel just for the sake of travel is a hobby that is within reach of just about anyone. Whether you drive to a nearby attraction for the weekend or fly off to a foreign country for an extended vacation, modern transportation has made seeing the world a reality—if you have the time. The ease with which you can jump in the car and run across town has also created yet another time bandit. Many times I have gone out at the wrong time of day for something that really could have waited, only to spend twice as much time running the errand as I should have. Poor planning together with a small compulsion leads to time wasted on the marginally important.

6. Parenthood – The blessing of having a family brings with it an almost endless opportunity for time investment into the lives and schedules of spouses and children. Ask any parents of teenagers how much time they feel they have to themselves and you are likely to get a puzzled reaction, "Time? For myself? I don't remember what that was like!" Keeping up with the activities of a busy household can drain every minute of a conscientious parent's day.

7. For Richer or Poorer – As I already mentioned, the challenge of making a living today can be totally consuming, even for two-income families. The work world is ultra-competitive, and to stay ahead you have to be willing to invest more of yourself, work longer and try harder. With second, third and even fourth occupations becoming more and more prevalent, education and training to keep up is also a serious time factor. Very few people are fortunate enough to be able to live on less than a forty hour per week job.

8. Godzilla – The monster of church related activities is one that many people overlook because the very idea that one could do too much for God is inconceivable. But the fact is, many churches offer such a wide array of opportunities for service that you can actually become terribly over-committed in trying to be a "good" Christian. While God does value our service, He does not want church work to take the place of our personal relationship with Him.

> *The* average female . . . would need thirty-five hours a day to do everything society requires of the "perfect" woman.

9. Dead Poet Society – I once met a man who was part of a commemorative Civil War fraternity that met together in various parts of the country to remember and reenact significant events of the war between the states. The man was not hard to spot because he was dressed in his character's attire—he played the role of one of the Confederate generals. After talking with him for several minutes, I realized that he did not just play the role, he had, in his own mind, become the general whom he represented.

As I travel, I meet all kinds of otherwise normal adults who have become so totally sold out to a common interest club or society of some kind that they can scarcely carry on a conversation about anything else. When a social group becomes your passion, it can be a very serious time bandit.

10. Pretty Woman – I read in a magazine not too long ago that today's man spends an average of forty-four minutes every day grooming himself. The average female, it said, would need thirty-five hours a day to do everything society requires of the "perfect" woman. Health and fitness clubs, beauty spas, hair and nail salons and fashion clothing stores all capitalize on our compulsive drive to look good. The problem is that society's definition of "good" is one that few of us can reach, even if we could spend thirty-five hours every day working at it. Although the beauty rituals are ever-changing, physical attractiveness has always been and always will be a time bandit that we have to struggle to manage.

Obviously not all of these habits or activities are inherently bad. While watching television may have virtually no redeeming value, spending time with your family certainly does. But if taken to extremes, they all have the potential to rob you of precious time. When they go unchecked, they become like thieves, stealing away the most valuable, irreplaceable commodity you have. The time bandits are only hazardous when you allow them to lay claim to more of your time than they deserve.

Could it be that we have given up our ability to muse in exchange for the temporal pleasure of amusement? In our obsession with Day Runners, are we running ourselves ragged to the point of being chronically fatigued, only to find that we still cannot be every place we want to be and do everything we want to do? Are we a generation that has become so addicted to speed and noise that we have totally lost the ability to sit still and be quiet, even for a few moments?

On this fast moving train, prayer is like the coupling that connects us to God. When we are speeding out of control, if we will just take the time to slow down long enough, He will reach out and grab us, pulling us into a life-saving union. He is waiting for any chance to break in.

I Brake for God

Not long ago, as I was returning home to Houston on a plane, I asked the flight attendant as we were in our final descent how fast the airplane is going when it first touches down on the runway. "About two-hundred miles per hour," was the reply. At two hundred miles per hour, a very coordinated, reliable braking system is necessary to slow down thousands of pounds of steel. As we touched the ground, the brakes against the wheels released a puff of smoke, the wing flaps extended toward the ground to catch the wind and the blades on the turbines roared as the pitch was changed to bring the MD-80 to a stop. "Thank God," I thought, "for brakes." An airplane without brakes would only fly once!

Slowing down long enough to connect with our Father is what I call "Braking for God," and the Bible offers us six brakes: **be still, rest, wait, sit, watch** and **stand.** Although they may sound very much the same, each of these biblical concepts gives us keen insight into making prayer effective and finding true friendship with God. In the next six chapters, we will look closely at each of these brakes, and I will offer you practical suggestions on how to implement them in your own life.

Many books have been written about prayer techniques and patterns. My shelf is full of them, and I teach from them often. But no amount of instructional material can help you until you slow down long enough to use it. When applied, these scriptural brakes will save you from crashing and burning. They are more than methodology; they are like stepping stones into the heart of God. To brake for God is to posture yourself to meet Him in a place called prayer. It is there that you can experience all He has to offer you, and kick the fear of failure for good.

If you are serious about building a prayer relationship with God, then you must learn to guard your time by calling the time bandits to task. You must learn to set limits, choose wisely and most importantly, say no to those things which steal time without leaving behind anything in return. Good time management requires strong, well-defined priorities.

What's in Your Jar?

A teacher of a time management seminar illustrated the concept of priorities in a very visual way. On a table in the front of the room, he set a large, empty pickle jar and then dropped in three fist-sized rocks that were each just slightly smaller than the opening in the jar. He asked, "Is the jar full?" The answer was obvious—there was still a lot of empty space in the pickle jar. So, he began to put handfuls of gravel in the jar until the rocks came right up to the top.

"Is the jar full?" he asked again. Most of the participants were still quick to say that something else could be put in the container.

Next he poured fine sand into the pickle jar, right up to the top just as before, and then he asked a third time, "Is the jar full?"

By this time, the participants, thinking they understood the point the teacher was trying to make, jumped a step ahead of him by urging him to put water in the jar, which he did, and then asked one final time, "Would you agree that the jar is now full?"

"Yes," they answered with certainty.

Then the instructor asked the deciding question, "What was the point of this illustration?"

Most of the students, eager to demonstrate their sense of time management, agreed that the point made by the rocks in the pickle jar was that even when you think you have done all you can do, you can always squeeze something else into your schedule.

"No," the teacher said emphatically. "The point of this illustration is that whatever is biggest and most important should always go in first."

What God has to offer you is the biggest, most important thing in your life. Put it in first. Do not let the time bandits steal away His provision. Learn to apply your spiritual brakes so that you can slow down long enough for Him to connect with you and bring you into His perfect love.

I will choose wisely what gets my attention and I will be in control of my own time. I will not be 'screened out' of God's wisdom, affirmation, direction, protection and assurance by the glitz and noise of a society that beckons me to sell my soul for material things. I am a spiritual being, not a spiritual doing, created to be connected to my heavenly Father. I am designed to touch that which is everlasting and life-giving. I will not let anything keep me from the threshold of prayer and the world of revelation and discovery.

Lord, thank you for my hands and the skills that you have given me. I like coming to a job site and shaping an unformed pile of lumber into a home. Create in me a home for your presence.

—the prayer of a carpenter

Chapter 7

Brake 1:
Be Still

_W_hen was the last time you came home to a quiet, empty house and did not turn on the television? When was the last time you drove somewhere in your car by yourself without the radio on? When was the last time you enjoyed an entire cup of coffee in the morning in perfect silence and stillness? If you are like most Americans, it has probably been a while—maybe even a lifetime—since you experienced true solitude.

The amount of stimuli which we encounter every day is mind-boggling. In the lives of most adults, moments of peace and quiet are few and far between. If we do get a minute to ourselves, we find it difficult to sit still for long before our mental list of "things to do" pushes us out the door. We are actually addicted to noise and motion, and without thinking about it, we are passing the addiction along to our children through heavy doses of television, movies, video games—anything to keep them entertained. Any country that launches an air attack against the United States in the next five to ten years will find out that this "Nintendo" generation of youth can blow to bits anything that flies!

I know that our children are growing up as "entertainment junkies" because I have had the enlightening experience of taking my grandchildren to places like Chuck E. Cheese's and Discovery Zone, only to return home several hours later and collapse on the sofa, my wallet empty and every receptor frazzled. I pay good money for these sensory overload encounters, and I am somewhat amazed that my grandchildren seem to thrive on them. The only sign that they show of duress is that they generally fall asleep within minutes of leaving the building (usually while the car is still in the parking lot). Otherwise, they appear to love it—racing from one activity to another in perfect harmony with the ear-piercing, motion-filled environment. For them, it is the pinnacle of excitement.

> *T*aking the time to be still and quiet is in direct violation to the overall spirit of busyness that dominates our lives.

Although I am not campaigning for families to throw their televisions out the window (maybe just the remote controls!), I do believe that with each generation of children, this particular influence takes on greater and greater magnitude and accounts for more and more childhood time. I know several pre-school children who could not only give you a run down of the characters in every motion picture made by Disney, they could also recite verbatim large sections of the scripts! One little girl I know, when her mother told her to leave the television off and find something else to play with, said with a sincerely puzzled look, "Why?" I could almost see her thinking, "With all that great amusement right here, why in the world would I want to do anything else?"

I realize that there are many excellent television programs for children, and to be honest, I enjoy taking my grandchildren to giant indoor playgrounds and watching them run and squeal with the best of them. But the way young children inhale some forms of entertainment might be a reflection of the way this society views stillness. Apparently, the very idea is uncomfortable at any age. Taking the time to be still and quiet is in direct violation to the overall spirit of busyness that dominates our lives.

Solitary Confinement

A teacher asked her class of elementary school children, "Why do you think twins are born into the world?" The students thought and thought, until finally one little girl said decidedly, "It's a scary world out there. Nobody wants to be alone!" It is interesting that in our society we equate solitude with loneliness. Perhaps that is why we go to such great lengths to avoid it. We keep ourselves on the fast-moving train, surrounded by the reassuring presence of other people. And if other people are nowhere around, then we accept the noise of radio or television as a substitute. When we feel lonely, we go to the mall. When we are faced with the quietness of an empty house, we pick up the phone or turn on the television, just to drown out the piercing sound of silence. We even consider solitude to be a form of punishment—for children it is called time-out; for prisoners it is called solitary confinement. We are frightened by the very idea of being by ourselves.

But the truth is, solitude and loneliness are not synonymous. The Bible teaches that men and women found strength and purpose, peace and direction, simply by being alone with God. Psalm 46:10 says, "Be still and know that I am God." Getting quiet before the Lord is fundamentally important if we are to learn how to relate to Him as His children. In fact, the word "solitude" comes from the word "sole" which means exclusive, individual, singular or unique. When you get alone with God, you discover just how special in His eyes you really are. Taking away the clutter reveals the beauty of simplicity. Being still allows you to focus on what is real and most valuable.

Solitary Refinement

The three men mentioned in Part 1, Abraham, Moses and David, all knew the value of being alone with God. I·do not believe it is a coincidence that all of them were shepherds by trade before they were called to take their places in history. Abraham was the father of faith; Moses became a wilderness tour guide for two million Jews; and David eventually became a great king. But before God got hold of their lives, their primary job each day was to sit with the sheep in the pasture and watch grass disappear.

> *I* do not believe it is a coincidence that all of them were shepherds by trade before they were called to take their places in history.

Think about it—no cellular phone, no pager, no Walkman, not even books to read—just sheep . . . and clouds and fields and trees and more sheep. I can almost picture David, heading out to the pasture early in the morning, lying back in the grass and looking up at the sky, saying, "Okay, God, what should we talk about today?" The time he and the others spent alone tending their flocks was like a giant window through which God revealed Himself to them. It was in their lifestyle of solitude that they came to know and trust the Father and receive His instruction.

Paul and John were also men who spent much of their lives in solitude. Called abruptly by God into one of the most dynamic ministries ever recorded, Paul spent a good part of his Christian life in prison for preaching about Jesus. When he was not spreading the gospel, he was sitting in isolation in Roman jails watching roaches scurry across the floor. Without the amenities of our modern day reform system, Paul no doubt had nothing but time on his hands to talk to God. Throughout his ministry, he developed a strong identification with the person of Jesus, an identity which probably grew during the time he spent in solitary confinement. The more time he did, the more time he spent focusing on Jesus, and the more his life revealed Christlikeness.

Similarly, John was sentenced to spend his life on a penal colony island. For him, much like Paul, being set apart in a place where he was alone with God was not really punishment. John thrived on being alone with God, so much so that he wrote the book of Revelation based on the things God showed him on the island. He received a profound revelation of Christ because he embraced solitude as an opportunity to seek the face of Christ.

Solitary Conformity

The lives of these men and the way in which they welcomed solitude should tell us something about how they received their strength and vision, even unto death, for the sake of Christ. Whether by choice or by chance, they carved out time to be with God, quiet and still. They practiced "solitary conformity"— spending enough time alone before God to conform to His image. Like a vine on a trellis, they grew into the shape of that which they pressed against.

Jesus Himself practiced solitary conformity, taking time to be alone with His Father. He "... often withdrew to lonely places and prayed" (Luke 5:16), even when He knew the people were looking for Him. He never let the demands of ministry steal His time alone with God. He knew the value of getting still. He even drew His disciples away as if to say, "Come apart before you fall apart." He taught them the value of being *with* Him instead of always *doing for* Him. When He chose them, "He appointed twelve—designating them apostles—that they might be with him and that he might send them out to preach . . ." (Mark 3:14).

We cannot really do for God until we have learned how to be with God. We cannot have a relationship with someone with whom we never spend time.

"But I have six kids and I live in a minivan! The closest sheep is in the downtown zoo. How can I ever get alone? And if I could, what would I do?"

Five Ways to Take Control

1. **Make a quality decision to get still.** It is a decision that will bless your life in immeasurable ways. Say this: "I will stop moving and I will be quiet. I will embrace solitude." It must be an act of your will because it does not happen in the natural course of events.
2. **Take courage and turn something off!** Close your day planner, unplug the phone, do whatever it takes to eliminate all distractions.
3. **As you begin to sense solitude, do not panic.** Resist the urge to break the silence or grab the car keys. Give yourself permission to unload, unwind, and undo.
4. **Schedule a time to practice solitary conformity each day, even if it is only for a few minutes.** Try gazing out the window as you sip your morning coffee. Or find a quiet place at work where you might sit for a few minutes during a break time. Be realistic with your expectations. Even five minutes of stillness a day adds up to two and a half hours a month.
5. **Try to still your mind, not just your body.** If you find yourself making a mental grocery list, ask God to help you clear your thoughts. You might whisper the name of Jesus, or hum a chorus or hymn that you know.

Speed Bump #1 – Scripture Praying

When you encounter a speed bump on the road, it forces you to apply your brake. And if you are like most people, you have probably gone out of your way more than once just to avoid having to negotiate one. But irritating as they may be, speed bumps have a noble purpose—to slow you down, generally for your own safety and the safety of others in the vicinity.

The speed bumps offered throughout Part 2 have a similar purpose—to slow you down for your own spiritual well-being. For each of the six brakes I will suggest a speed bump, a practical exercise that will help you apply that brake and make time for God.

Learning to Be Bilingual

One of the most common concerns I hear as I talk to people about prayer has to do with the basic matter of vocabulary. Many Christians, even long-time church goers, do not feel comfortable praying because they simply do not know what to say. That is why I believe strongly in scripture praying—using the language of the Bible to talk to God. It is so rich in variety and full of humanity that it yields an endless number of prayer models.

Scripture praying is a practical exercise that may help you apply this first brake and practice solitary conformity. It is a creative prayer pattern that can help you lay your burdens at the cross with confidence, knowing that God is not going to be shocked or surprised by what He hears. He is a big God and He has already seen it all! Placing your needs in the context of scripture is an excellent way to claim the promises of God, keeping your focus on His faithfulness instead of on the problems.

Story Praying

Many books have been written about how to pray specific verses or how to pray the prayers of the Bible, but none have touched on an idea I call "story praying." Story praying is simply a form of scripture praying that utilizes the well-known stories of the Bible instead of specific verses or passages. The advantage of this idea is that anyone can pray the Word, even if they do not have a thorough knowledge of the Bible. Young children and new Christians alike can pray the promises of God through familiar stories such as David and Goliath, Jonah and the whale, or the parting of the Red Sea.

For example, a husband/father going through an unplanned mid-life career change might pray this prayer:

> God, I remember a time when the disciples were in a boat in the middle of a raging storm, and you motioned for Peter to get out and walk on the water. As long as he kept his eyes on you, he was fine, but as soon as he began looking at the circumstances around him, he started to sink. Right now, I feel like I'm being forced out of my boat to walk on rough water. I didn't want to leave my old job, and I don't know if I can handle the new one. I feel uncertain and nervous about walking away from the security of what I know. Please help me to focus on you just as Peter did so that I will not sink. Thank you that you will uphold me when I falter and that you are my stability. Help me learn to trust you. Amen.

Or, a single mother who is struggling to make ends meet might pray this prayer:

> Dear Jesus, I don't know how I can ever pay all the bills I owe on what little salary I make. It takes so much money just to live, and I really want to be able to buy clothes and other things my kids need and want. I'm frustrated that I can't make more money to support my family. I feel helpless. Please, God, somehow multiply what I have just like you did when you fed the multitude with the little boy's lunch. You fed thousands of people with only a couple of fish and a few loaves of bread, and they even had baskets of food left over! I can't imagine having money left over! Give me the kind of faith that the little boy had. Help me trust you to provide for us. Thank you that you care about me and my children and that you are so able to meet our needs in abundance. Amen.

A high school boy facing pressure from some of his peers to sleep with his girlfriend might pray like this:

Hey, God. You know that story about the three guys that got thrown into the fire because they wouldn't bow down to someone else's God? Well, I know how they must have felt. Some of the guys are really giving me a hard time about trying to have sex with my girlfriend, and I just don't think it's right. I don't like being laughed at, but the truth is, I don't want to have sex with her. I really like Jini and I think it would hurt her if I pushed her to get physical. Besides, I know you want me to wait. I want to be strong like those guys in the Bible—strong enough to stay pure and even strong enough to tell the guys what I believe. It was cool the way they stood up for what they knew was right, even though it meant they might die. Please help me stand, too, even if it means getting hassled. Thanks, God. Amen.

> *The* characters in some of the most often told Bible stories were real people. They grieved over lost loved ones, struggled at relationships . . .

The possibilities for prayer are endless. The characters in some of the most often told Bible stories were real people. They grieved over lost loved ones, struggled at relationships, worked to make a living, suffered at the hands of enemies, and did their best to deal with ungodly political leaders and immoral societies. They tried to be holy, and sometimes they failed. They did not always obey God the first time, nor did they always under-

stand why things happened the way they did. But God was faithful, over and over. He will show His hand in your life just as He
did in theirs.

Here is a list of several Bible stories that can become the
basis for prayer:

The Creation Story ... Genesis 1–2 .... Goodness of God

The Fall .... Genesis 3 .... Redemption

Noah and the Ark ..... Genesis 6–8 .... Christ the ark of
                                            safety

The Rainbow .... Genesis 9:8–17 ..... Promises of God
   Promise

Abraham and Isaac .... Genesis 22:1–14 .... God's provision
                                            and faithfulness

Joseph and His .... Genesis 37–45 ...... Finding the good
   Brothers   in bad things

Moses and the .... Exodus 3:1–4:17 .... The call of God
   Burning Bush

The Passover .... Exodus 12 .... Forgiveness

God Parts the .... Exodus 14 .... Miracles
   Red Sea

Joshua and the .... Joshua 6 .... Faith that moves
   Fall of Jericho   mountains

David and Goliath .... 1 Samuel 17 .... Overcoming
                                            giants

Solomon's Wisdom .... 1 Kings 3:4–28 ..... God as the source
                                            of wisdom

Daniel and the .... Daniel 6 .... Protection and
   Lion's Den   courage in the face
                                            of persecution

Jonah and the Whale . . Jonah 1:1–2:10 . . . . . . The value of
obedience

The Birth of Jesus . . . . Luke 2:1–7 . . . . Small beginnings

The Temptation . . . . . . Matthew 4:1–11 . . . . Facing tests in life
of Jesus

Jesus Turns Water . . . . John 2:1–12 . . . . God's best comes
into Wine   last

The Woman at the . . . . John 4:4–42 . . . . Grace
Well

Jesus Calms the . . . . Mark 4:35–41 . . . . . . Faith
Storm

Jesus Feeds the 5,000 . . John 6:1–15 . . . . Provision

Peter Walks on . . . . Matthew 14:22–36 . . Stepping out
the Water

The Good Samaritan . . Luke 10:29–37 . . . . . . Selflessness

Jesus Raises Lazarus . . . John 11:1–44 . . . . Eternal life and
comfort

Zacchaeus Meets . . . . . Luke 19:1–10 . . . . Grace
Jesus

Jesus in the Garden . . . Matthew 26:36–46 . . Praying for
others

The Cross of Jesus . . . . Luke 23:33–56 . . . . . Redemption

The Resurrection . . . . . Luke 24:1–12 . . . . Hope
of Jesus

Paul and Silas in . . . . . . Acts 16:22–40 . . . . . . Perseverance
Prison

Paul's Shipwreck . . . . . . Acts 27:1–28:10 . . . . Finding the best
in bad circum-
stances

Divine Imprint

When I was a young man living in Bay City, Texas, I got my first real job delivering the *Bay City Tribune*. Sometimes I would arrive at work early enough that the last copies of the newspaper were still rolling off the presses. It was always kind of fascinating to me to watch the clean, white sheets of paper slide underneath the giant roller and come out imprinted with the day's news. It happened so fast, and the change was so dramatic.

Your life is very impressionable, and you are constantly being marked by the circumstances and people around you. Your job, family, friends, church and even advertisers battle for your attention so that they can stamp you with their message. Spending time alone with God is the only way to receive *His* imprint. As you get still before Him, He presses against you and leaves His mark on your spirit. He wants you to bear His acceptance, His affirmation and His thoughts. He wants you to be free to be a human *being*, not just a human *doing*.

Dear Lord,

As I hammer in shingle after shingle, I know that someday a child will sleep warm and dry in this house as a result of my labor. Bless and protect the people who will live here. Thank you for preparing a home for me in heaven.

—the prayer of a roofer

Chapter 8

Brake 2:
Rest

When General Patton took over the desert offensive in World War II, one of the first things he did was put a picture of General Rommel in his tent. He saw it every morning when he woke up and every evening when he lay down to sleep. It served as a constant reminder of why he was there by forcing him each day to look into the eyes of his enemy. He gave a face to his foe so that he could fight with purpose.

Know Your Enemy

In Christ, you have an arch rival—Satan. He delights in making you miserable, and he is the source of all evil. He hates anything in your life that draws you closer to God, which is why *his* number one enemy is prayer.

But how does Smutface attack? With what weapons and methods does he wage his war against us? How can an enemy we cannot even see steal from us and destroy our lives? Well-known author and theologian, C. S. Lewis wrote a classic book entitled

The Screwtape Letters in which he answers these questions. With riveting authenticity, he assumes the voice of Satan as he trains his army in the art of human hunting. The strategy goes something like this: We do not need any other weapon to destroy the human race outside of the human mind. Peoples' beliefs are so powerful that our goal can be accomplished simply by twisting, distorting and maligning the thoughts that are already there.

The evil one assails us through our own minds. Our enemies are the thought patterns and beliefs that rob us of the peace and joy God desires for us to have in this life. These enemies relentlessly attack our spirits and lay siege to our communion with the Father. They violate our sense of security and well-being, leaving us tired and confused, worried and depressed. They can cripple us emotionally, causing relationships to fail and dreams to die. In short, they keep us from enjoying life.

Enemy #1 – The Anxiousness of Uncertainty

I was traveling on an interstate through Mississippi several years ago when I encountered an intersection with what seemed to be hundreds of road signs. I felt sure that the Mississippi Highway Department had placed all of the state's directions at that one juncture! With cars moving fast on every side of me, I had only seconds to read the signs and make a decision about which way to go. I really could not slow down and I knew I could never read fast enough to take in all the information. As you might have guessed, about sixty miles later I realized I had made the wrong choice.

I think many people feel the same kind of anxiousness over the countless decisions we are called to make in life. We know that every turn we make eventually determines our destiny, and we do not want to go the wrong direction. "Where should I go to school? Where should I live? What job should I take? Who should I marry and how many children should we have? How do I plan for my future? Should I buy or rent? How should I respond to aging parents? How do I train my kids?"

Important crossroads come flying at us from all directions and we are forced to read the signs and choose a path. Life all around us is moving too fast for us to slow down, so we often feel like we are making choices on the run, unable to carefully weigh our options. As people and opportunities go whizzing by us on every side, we may even feel as though we are the only ones who are not sure of which way to go. We feel pressured to make good decisions, all the while being unsure and uncertain about the outcomes. The tension created by the maze of life's unpredictability can shake or altogether destroy our sense of peace.

> *We* often feel like we are making choices on the run, unable to carefully weigh our options.

Enemy #2 – The Pressure to Perform

When my two sons were young, I coached several years of little league baseball. Although I was never a star athlete myself, I was the kids' top choice for a coach—their only choice. The first game we played, we lost 33–0. Our only batter to actually make contact with the ball hit a respectable fly ball into the outfield and was so excited that he ran to third base instead of first.

I did not particularly like losing ball games, but I never lost any sleep over it because I was under the delusion that little league was all about learning teamwork, having fun and spending time with the kids. Apparently, however, many of the other parents did not share my idealistic viewpoint. At every opportunity, they lined the field, excited and at times irate, shouting instructions, encouragements and corrections. They not only wanted us to win; they expected it. And in the process, they wanted to see their own child outhit, outrun, outthrow and outdo every other kid on the field. We re-enacted the World Series each Saturday afternoon.

The pressure to perform is another message that, in our own dysfunction, we send to our children at a very early age. The adult job world thrives on winning, earning and achieving. We want to make it to the top, and we want to earn a lot of money doing it. We are told to "make something of ourselves," whatever that means, and there are usually plenty of people around us who will let us know if we have not.

Enemy #3 – The Feelings of Failure

As I have already discussed at length, every time you make a mistake or do not quite measure up in some way, feelings of guilt or shame are likely to creep in and set up camp. Since mistakes in this life are unavoidable, this enemy can do serious damage to us if we do not learn early how to handle failure without necessarily thinking we are failures.

Enemy #4 – The Stress of Maintaining

Have you ever tried to call the bank to ask a question about your account only to find that they do not know who you are? Have you ever spent three days on the phone trying to locate a part for your refrigerator without ever talking to a real person? Do you dream of having a whole day just to mow the yard, change the oil in the car, fix the leaky faucet, clean out the gutters, pick up the dry cleaning, iron some clothes before you need them, sew on all your missing buttons, catch up on some phone calls, get your thank-you notes finished from last Christmas, organize your photo albums, and of course, clean out your closets?

Not long ago the zipper on one of my favorite jackets broke, and I carried it around in my car for weeks trying to find someone who could fix it. I must have taken the jacket into at least twenty different tailors or cleaners, all of whom looked carefully at the zipper and announced, "It's broken alright. But I can't fix it." I was so frustrated I almost gave up. By the time I finally got the zipper repaired, I had probably expended several hours and a full tank of gas.

Sometimes the stress in just maintaining our lives is burdensome. Keeping up with insurance claims and tax information could be a full-time job in most families! As if the daily requirements—washing clothes, preparing meals, buying

Perhaps we do not want to lose what we have because we have allowed our possessions to define who we are.

groceries—are not enough, those irritating extras seem to pile on, none of which ever turn out to be easy. We simply do not have enough hours in the week to put in our time at work, spend quality time with the family, invest in a few personal friendships and still keep up with the busywork of life.

Enemy #5 – The Fear of Loss

Probe into anyone's personal finances and you are sure to find a large percentage of their income dedicated to one thing—insurance. It is one of the biggest businesses in America. Perhaps because we watch the evening news, we realize how vulnerable we are. Everything we have can be taken away in mere seconds by fire, tornado, car accident or deranged criminal. We go through life with the ever-present awareness that we could be the next victim, and so we spend thousands of dollars in an attempt to somehow protect our things and our loved ones.

With all that we know about medicine and illness today, we are also terrified of losing our health. It is almost as if the more we see and hear and read, the more we are afraid. Television pipes a sort of medical paranoia into our homes by constantly making

us aware of all kinds of new diseases that we are likely to con-
tract. I wonder how many people have rushed to the doctor with
a bad case of "documentary-itis" and a wild imagination.

Perhaps we do not want to lose what we have because we
have allowed our possessions to define who we are. We all have
a kingdom, be it big or small, and we do not like for it to be
threatened.

Enemy #6 – The Imminence of Death

In Nederland, Colorado, there is a shed that houses the body
of a man who, upon contracting some incurable disease, decided
to have himself frozen in the hopes that he could be thawed out
when the cure was found. He actually left behind a small fortune—all to be used to buy ice!

Death is a sure thing in life, and most of us are not too eager
to experience it for ourselves or anyone we love. We do not like
to think about it or talk about it—it just looms out there in the
distance as our inescapable fate. We are, as a culture, afraid of
both aging and dying, but we all suffer from the incurable condition of mortality.

Place of Immunity

However, it is from these enemies that God promises us rest.
He offers us immunity of the spirit, even in the midst of the most
difficult circumstances. The concept of rest is a strong theme in
both the Old and New Testaments. It is a brake that we need to
apply to keep from being arrested by our unseen foes.

*And God blessed the seventh day and made it holy, because on
it he rested from all the work of creating that he had done
(Genesis 2:3).*

*But you will cross the Jordan and settle in the land the Lord
your God is giving you as an inheritance, and he will give you
rest from all your enemies around you so that you will live in
safety (Deuteronomy 12:10).*

When the Lord your God gives you rest from all the enemies around you in the land he is giving you to possess as an inheritance, you shall blot out the memory of Amalek from under heaven (Deuteronomy 25:19).

Remember the command that Moses the servant of the Lord gave you: "The Lord your God is giving you rest and has granted you this land" (Joshua 1:13).

The Lord gave them rest on every side, just as he had sworn to their forefathers. Not one of their enemies withstood them . . . (Joshua 21:44).

My soul finds rest in God alone; my salvation comes from him (Psalm 62:1).

In that day . . . , his place of rest will be glorious (Isaiah 11:10).

Come to me, all you who are weary and burdened, and I will give you rest. Take my yoke upon you and learn from me, for I am gentle and humble in heart, and you will find rest for your souls (Matthew 11:28–29).

. . . for anyone who enters God's rest also rests from his own work, just as God did from his (Hebrews 4:10).

The rest that God provides is a state of being as well as a place. It is rest for our souls, and it can only be found in the person of Jesus.

Rest Stops

In Christ you can have victory over all of these forces. Smutface is rendered powerless by the name of Jesus (Philippians 2:10) because in His death and resurrection, He defeated evil once and for all (Colossians 2:15). As God's child, you can rest, knowing that your enemies cannot prevail over you.

1. **When the uncertainty of life makes you anxious, rest in the Word.**

You do not need to feel arrested by tough decisions in life because God has provided for you a road map—the Bible.

Your word is a lamp to my feet and a light for my path (Psalm 119:105).

I will instruct you and teach you in the way you should go; I will counsel you and watch over you (Psalm 32:8).

I will lead the blind by ways they have not known, along unfamiliar paths I will guide them; I will turn the darkness into light before them and make the rough places smooth (Isaiah 42:16).

If you seek God by spending time with Him, then you can make important decisions with confidence. As you pray the Bible promises, your Father will clarify your thoughts and speak to you about His will for your life. You find victory over confusion as you learn to let His precepts guide your actions.

2. **When you feel the pressure to perform, rest in your position in the kingdom.**

You can let go of any kind of performance-based acceptance because in Christ, you have already received the highest position you can achieve. You have been adopted into a royal family and made co-heirs with Jesus.

Now if we are children, then we are heirs—heirs of God and co-heirs with Christ . . . (Romans 8:17).

If you belong to Christ, then you are Abraham's seed, and heirs according to the promise (Galatians 3:29).

And when the Chief Shepherd appears, you will receive the crown of glory that will never fade away (1 Peter 5:4).

You have no need to gain the approval of man through position or status because in Christ, you have a crown of glory! You are heir to an inheritance that is out of this world, beyond compare even to all the wealth of the earth. Remember—you have position through association with Jesus.

3. **When you are stressed out over the task of maintaining life, rest in the help of the Holy Spirit.**

God sent the Holy Spirit to be your helper in time of need and your strength in times of weakness. He is your inner resource for energy, and He is an expert problem solver. He is a comforter and a friend.

And I will ask the Father, and he will give you another Counselor to be with you forever—the Spirit of truth. The world cannot accept him, because it neither sees him nor knows him. But you know him, for he lives with you and will be in you (John 14:16–17).

In the same way, the Spirit helps us in our weakness. We do not know what we ought to pray for, but the Spirit himself intercedes for us with groans that words cannot express (Romans 8:26).

Not only does the Spirit live within you to comfort and guide you, He also prays for you. He will be your cheerleader when you need encouragement and your voice of reason when you need to slow down.

4. **When feelings of failure attack, rest in God's grace and forgiveness.**

God knows you are a messed-up creature, but He loves you anyway. He extended to you divine forgiveness in the unfair exchange at the cross—His righteousness for your sin. In Jesus, you are completely accepted and loved in spite of your weaknesses.

For as high as the heavens are above the earth, so great is his love for those who fear him; as far as the east is from the west, so far has he removed our transgressions from us (Psalm 103:11–12).

Therefore, if anyone is in Christ, he is a new creation; the old has gone, the new has come! (2 Corinthians 5:17).

*If we confess our sins, he is faithful and just and will forgive us
our sins and purify us from all unrighteousness (1 John 1:9).*

Why do you torment yourself over past mistakes when God
has removed them from his memory altogether? Do not accept
failure as final. Receive God's forgiveness, and let go of the past.
This enemy has no foothold in the light of amazing grace.

5. **When the fear of loss overtakes you, rest in God's loving provision.**

Fear has a way of causing you to lose sight of how God has
blessed you. But the force that undoes fear is love, and if you
could only grasp how deep the Father's love is for you, then you
would completely trust Him to meet all your needs.

The Lord is my shepherd, I shall not be in want (Psalm 23:1).

*So do not worry, saying, "What shall we eat?" or "What
shall we drink?" or "What shall we wear?" For the pagans
run after all these things, and your heavenly Father knows
that you need them. But seek first his kingdom and his righteousness, and all these things will be given to you as well
(Matthew 6:31–33).*

*And my God will meet all your needs according to his glorious
riches in Christ Jesus (Philippians 4:19).*

One of God's Old Testament names, Jehovah Jireh, means
"provider," and just like a loving father, He delights in taking
care of his children. Do not let an attitude of ungratefulness
give this enemy room to work—remember all that God has done
for you and the many ways in which He has blessed you. Rest in
His promises to meet all your needs.

6. **When death seems imminent, rest in the gift of eternal life.**

Although you cannot escape the reality of ultimate physical death, in Jesus you have an eternity in heaven to look forward to.

For my Father's will is that everyone who looks to the Son and believes in him shall have eternal life, and I will raise him up at the last day (John 6:40).

When the perishable has been clothed with the imperishable, and the mortal with immortality, then the saying that is written will come true: "Death has been swallowed up in victory." "Where, O death, is your victory? Where, O death, is your sting?" (1 Corinthians 15:54–55).

Since the children have flesh and blood, he too shared in their humanity so that by his death he might destroy him who holds the power of death—that is, the devil—and free those who all their lives were held in slavery by their fear of death (Hebrews 2:14–15).

Jesus conquered death when He died on the cross and then rose from the grave. Because He died for us, we will live on after our physical bodies give out.

Speed Bump #2 – Creating a Sacred Place

Just knowing about God's rest does not solve the problem of actually receiving it. You may know that you can rest in His provision, but until you carve out some sacred time to be with Him, you will not experience that rest. Applying the first brake is the first step—you must get still and let God catch up with you. He is the source of peace, but He will not thrust it upon you as you run here and there at breakneck speed.

Let me suggest that as you begin to set aside time to meet with God that you also apply this second brake by creating for yourself a special place of stillness—a resting place. While I recognize that you can talk to God anywhere at any time, there is something powerful about establishing your own unique spot that is designated as a place of solitude and refreshing. I call these little oases altars.

In the Bible, an altar was a "high" place, not necessarily geographically, but symbolically. Because physical peaks such as mountaintops were strategic when fighting against an enemy, the people understood and had respect for high places. Therefore, when they wanted to honor God and show their gratitude for His provision and protection, they built an altar to signify the high place He held in their lives. They went to the altar to pray and make sacrifices—it was a sacred point at which they could meet with Him.

Altaring Your Home

Building an altar in your home will give you an advantage over your enemies. It will be your high place where you can seek refuge from the forces that try to arrest you. It may be as simple as a favorite chair in a corner, a bench in a garden or a table by a window. Or you may be able to create your altar in a spare room, an attic or basement. Regardless, it will be special because it will be the sacred point at which you meet with the Father.

Once you have established a location for your altar, give some thought to what things you might put on or around it to remind you of the rest you have in Jesus. For example, a Bible might remind you of God's direction for your life. A chair could symbolize the position you have seated next to the throne. A laurel or some type of winner's crown might suggest the crown of life that you will receive in heaven, and a candle could remind you of the Holy Spirit who lives in you. You might include a table to signify God's abundant provision, and a cross to remind you of the victory you have over death. A kneeler or a pillow could prompt you to surrender to His grace and receive His forgiveness each day. You might want to somehow display the name of Jesus as a reminder that His name alone is powerful enough to tear down any strongholds and overcome any attacks of Satan.

Many people like to include prayer helps at their altar, such as photos of family members, a list of unsaved friends or a prayer guide. You might keep a favorite devotional book handy or a list of scriptures and stories that you can pray. Perhaps you have a picture or a special object that reminds you of a time when God answered a prayer in your life. If possible, allow flowers, trees and other forms of nature to signify the beauty and originality of God's creation. Always keep a note pad or journal handy so that you can write down anything you think God might be saying to you.

Building an altar in your home will give you an advantage over your enemies.

When you go to your altar, go there with faith, believing that God will meet you. He wants to have a relationship with you, and He will be eager to have your attention. Trust Him to give you rest and even confess out loud, "I will receive your peace. I will rest in your love and acceptance." You might even whisper the name of Jesus several times to quiet your spirit. Thank Him in advance for His direction, provision, forgiveness and help. Go to your altar with expectancy, but leave pretense behind. He wants you to come just as you are—happy or depressed, confused or angry.

As a matter of discipline, practice this speed bump every day, even if it is only for a few minutes. Do not be surprised when your altar becomes such an oasis that you want to spend more and more time there. The more you feel arrested by your enemies, the more you need to claim your rest in Jesus. The only power Smutface has over you is the freedom you give him to reign in your brain. Make your altar a place of eviction—tell Satan he has to go. God will give you victory as you meet with Him at the altar.

Jesus, waiting on tables is not easy. Sometimes people are very impatient and cruel. Help me to always serve as you did, with humility and love. Teach me how to remain positive, even when I get twenty-five cent tips.

—the prayer of a waitress

Chapter 9

Brake 3: Wait

I recently watched the movie *The Mask of Zorro*, about the passing of a mantle from a brave but aging hero to his eager, young successor. When the young man first encounters the master, he is full of adrenaline, ready to don the black mask and avenge his brother's death. But the older and wiser Zorro says, "No. You must wait until you are ready." He tells him, "If you go now, you will fight valiantly and die quickly without ever accomplishing your purpose."

So they train. The young man is an eager student, wanting to learn all he can as quickly as possible, knowing that in the end, he will receive the identity and corresponding invincibility of Zorro. Out of respect for his mentor, he waits, although not always patiently. At one point in his training, with his combat skills noticeably improving, he gets anxious and arrogant because he thinks he is ready. Waiting is not easy. But as he trains physically, he is also learning something of greater importance than skill—how to wear the mask with honor—so that when at last the time comes for him to receive the mantle, he will aspire to much more than just revenge.

Consider another story about Jesus and His disciples that involved waiting:

After his suffering, he showed himself to these men and gave many convincing proofs that he was alive. He appeared to them over a period of forty days and spoke about the kingdom of God. On one occasion, while he was eating with them, he gave them this command: "Do not leave Jerusalem, but wait for the gift my Father promised, which you have heard me speak about. For John baptized with water, but in a few days you will be baptized with the Holy Spirit."

Then they returned to Jerusalem . . . [and] went upstairs to the room where they were staying. They all joined together constantly in prayer . . . (Acts 1:3–5, 12–14).

> *Much* like the young pupil of Zorro, Jesus' disciples were eager.

Based on these two stories, what does it mean to wait? Is it the same thing you do when you stand in a long check out line or read a magazine in the lobby of the dentist's office?

Much like the young pupil of Zorro, Jesus' disciples were eager. Their master, who had died the death of a criminal just days earlier, was alive again, just as He had promised! They were ready to hit the streets and clear their names by spreading the news that He had risen. But Jesus told them to wait. Why? Because He knew the Father needed to give them something. He knew they could not be effective witnesses until they had received the power source—the Holy Spirit.

I wait for the Lord, my soul waits, and in his word I put my hope. My soul waits for the Lord more than watchmen wait for the morning . . . (Psalm 130:5–6).

Yet the Lord longs to be gracious to you; he rises to show you compassion. For the Lord is a God of justice. Blessed are all who wait for him! (Isaiah 30:18).

On Tip-Toe

When Jesus told the disciples to wait in Jerusalem, I do not think He meant for them to go in to the city, check out the entertainment scene, take in a good chariot race and generally "hang out." It was not a command to kill time. Instead, I believe Jesus' idea of waiting could be described as "lively expectation," or "eager anticipation." It was a mandate for action, not passivity. It was like He was saying, "Get ready!" as if the very exercise of waiting were the key to receiving the blessing. He wanted them to tarry or linger, postured on tip-toe, faces to heaven, knowing that something was about to happen.

Most of us hate to wait. We are the microwave generation that likes fast food, fast money, fast service and fast results. The idea of having to stand in line to wait our turn is almost unbearable. Perhaps we are afraid that we might miss out on something while we are waiting. Or maybe we can not stand to see precious minutes tick by when we have so much to do.

But the biblical meaning of wait suggests a groom pacing anxiously as he awaits his bride, or an expectant father wringing his hands outside the delivery room as he awaits the cries of his newborn son. It also implies a time of preparation, training and prayer. Though outwardly the person waiting may appear inactive, inwardly he or she is energetically hopeful, seeking to swallow up the blessing that is forthcoming. Waiting is the epitome of faith, because it requires an earnest belief that God is there and that He is about to speak or act.

I recently took a motorcycle trip to Colorado where I met a woman who lives on the side of a mountain close to Boulder. She told me that she had just seen a life-long dream come true— she had purchased a horse at an auction. She had been working hard every evening trying to make ready the area where the

horse would live. She was eagerly waiting, not by sitting around
daydreaming, but by fencing the pastures, raking rocks out of
the stable and buying the necessary supplies. She had faith that
the horse would soon be delivered, and she was doing all that
she could to be ready when it arrived.

As Good As It Gets

The Lord wants to bless you with life, wisdom, ideas, patience, strength, comfort, peace, assurance, direction, protection,
health, grace and much more. Look at Deuteronomy 28:1–14
and you will find a whole list of blessings that God wants to
bestow on all who will obey Him.

> *You will be blessed in the city and blessed in the country. The
> fruit of your womb will be blessed, and the crops of your
> land and the young of your livestock. . . . Your basket and
> your kneading trough will be blessed. You will be blessed when
> you come in and blessed when you go out. The Lord will
> grant that the enemies who rise up against you will be de-
> feated before you. They will come at you from one direction
> but flee from you in seven. The Lord will send a blessing on
> your barns and on everything you put your hand to. The Lord
> your God will bless you in the land he is giving you
> (Deuteronomy 28:3–8).*

Numbers 6:23–27 is another famous passage of blessing in
which God tells Moses:

> *Tell Aaron and his sons, "This is how you are to bless the Isra-
> elites. Say to them, 'The Lord bless you and keep you; the Lord
> make his face shine upon you and be gracious to you; the Lord
> turn his face toward you and give you peace.'"*

Jesus confirmed the Father's desire to bless us when He said,
"If you, then, though you are evil, know how to give good gifts
to your children, how much more will your Father in heaven
give good gifts to those who ask him!" (Matthew 7:11).

But the key to receiving the blessings of God is in learning how to wait. God wants us to tarry or linger in His presence with lively expectation, eagerly anticipating what He might say or do. He wants us to wait as the disciples waited, in fervent prayer, making ourselves ready in every way we can to receive His gift. Waiting is a brake we need to apply so that we do not miss out on what God has in store for us.

Speed Bump #3 – Biblical Meditation

So far, the description I have tried to give you of waiting might resemble the empty-headed sort of quivering thing your dog does when he sees you approaching him with the leash. But I would like to offer you a way to practice biblical waiting with more dignity than your canine—meditation.

Before you hit the floor in a yoga position and start chanting a mantra, or worse, write "pagan" across my picture and sling this book into the reject pile, let me explain what it really means to meditate.

The Holy Press

With all of the recent emphasis on New Age mysticism, meditation has received some bad publicity. But meditation, as Elmer Towns says in his book, *Biblical Meditation for Spiritual Breakthrough*, is a "lost art," and a "beautiful Christian discipline" (24). I define it as the act of pressing your heart against a divine theme or attribute with such intensity that you receive a lasting impression. Meditation is a "holy press."

If you have ever worried about something—I mean *really* worried—then you know what it means to meditate. Worry is nothing more than meditation upon a problem. You think about it night and day, turn it over in your mind, imagine every possible outcome and look at hundreds of possible angles. You talk about it, ponder it, dissect it and analyze it. Then you begin to live in it. You chew on the problem until it makes you sick. Finally one day you wake up and realize that the problem and the thought patterns surrounding it have cut a channel in your mind so deep that you can hardly think any other way. By meditating on the problem, you have created a groove into which all of your ideas and responses fall.

The longer you set your mind on something, the more you become like it in spirit. That is why Paul urges you to think about what you think about:

"... *whatever is true, whatever is noble, whatever is right, whatever is pure, whatever is lovely, whatever is admirable— if anything is excellent or praiseworthy—think about such things" (Philippians 4:8).*

Do not conform any longer to the pattern of this world, but be transformed by the renewing of your mind (Romans 12:2).

Set your minds on things above, not on earthly things (Colossians 3:2).

Imagine the power of applying the same mental energy it takes to worry to meditating on the names of God or something about His character. What would be the results of focusing your mind on the cross or the beauty and design of God's creation? How might it affect you if you spent an hour one day just meditating on the person of Jesus Christ and His love for you? What would God reveal to you if you were to take a specific passage of scripture and read it over and over until it sank deep into your heart?

Not too many years ago, an art form consisting of hidden images (often called Magic Eye pictures) became very popular. The pictures were made from a tight, repetitive pattern of squiggles and shapes that appeared, at first glance, to be nothing more than a colorful collage. But if you fixed your eyes in the middle of the design, gazing at it without looking away, you saw something more. An image "popped out" from the random design, and like magic you saw an amazing three-dimensional form. It might be an animal, a person's face, a spaceship or a jungle village. But the trick seemed to be in the ability to stare at the design for a long time. You could not see the hidden image with just a quick glance.

As you meditate on a verse or on some divine attribute, fixing your mind on it without turning away, you will begin to "see" an image that is the silhouette of divinity! As you ponder His words or His character, He will reveal Himself to you in a way you have never seen before. He will press His face against the veil of the spirit realm and allow you to see His loveliness, His goodness, His holiness and His majesty. But the trick is in gazing at God, not just glancing.

Meditation is not an easy thing to describe or talk about because it is an activity that happens somewhere between your mind and your spirit. To think about something and process it intellectually is one thing, but true meditation actually changes something about you. It leaves an impression that is the shape of that on which you have meditated. If you meditate on a problem, the impression will be problem-shaped; if you meditate on God, the impression will be God-shaped.

Some people confuse the act of studying for meditation, and although they may go hand-in-hand at times, they are not the same. Studying is a cognitive process—a quest for understanding. When you study, you are seeking the facts and the expertise of other people in order to enhance your own knowledge about a subject. Meditation, however, is an internal search, in which you ask the Holy Spirit living inside you, "What does this mean for my life? What is the significance of this passage or attribute?" Meditation requires no concordance, no reference material and no supplemental reading.

> *As* you ponder His words or His character, He will reveal Himself to you in a way you have never seen before.

If you were to study Jesus' crucifixion, for example, you might scan any number of books written on the topic, cross-reference it in a study Bible, look up Hebrew and Greek meanings of the words in the related texts and possibly even talk to a pastor or theologian about it. But if you were to meditate on the meaning of the crucifixion, you would simply focus your thoughts on it and perhaps imagine what it was like to be there. You might try to comprehend the enormous amount of love God must have for you to have made such a sacrifice by considering your own willingness to die for loved ones, friends, and even enemies. You could muse about the irony of an almighty God dying the death of a criminal. Perhaps most importantly, you could ask the Holy Spirit to reveal to you the full meaning of the cross—the divine exchange of your sin for His holiness. Meditation is not a fact-finding mission, but a journey into the heart of God.

> *Meditation requires no concordance, no reference material and no supplemental reading.*

Meditation comes very naturally to me because I love to be out in the middle of a lake on a boat with nothing to entertain me except my own thoughts. It has always played a key role in my life as a speaker and writer. As I wait on God and consider various aspects of His character, He blesses me with creativity, insights and direction.

I have found in my experience that meditation can take place at three different levels:

1. Capturing daily thoughts
2. Sanctifying the imagination
3. Sharpening your revelation

Capturing Daily Thoughts—Runaway Mind Train

When Paul exhorted us to "take captive every thought to make it obedient to Christ" (2 Corinthians 10:5), he must have known that we would occasionally have thoughts that God is not too impressed with. In this first level of meditation, you capture those thoughts by replacing them with new ones. As you work to renew your mind with the mind of Christ, select a verse of scripture or a divine theme that speaks to a need in your life and concentrate on focusing your thoughts on it throughout the day. If you are in need of strength, you might choose Isaiah 40:31 which says, ". . . but those who hope in the Lord will renew their strength. They will soar on wings like eagles; they will run and not grow weary, they will walk and not be faint." Or if you are facing physical illness, you might meditate on Jeremiah 30:17 which says, "'But I will restore you to health and heal your wounds,' declares the Lord." Instead of worrying over finances, set your mind on Luke 6:38, "Give, and it will be given to you. A good measure, pressed down, shaken together and running over, will be poured into your lap. For with the measure you use, it will be measured to you."

This type of meditation is somewhat spontaneous—it can take place just about anywhere your mind wanders momentarily. You might recall your scripture or thought for that day during a coffee break or while on hold on the telephone. You could whisper it several times in your mind while driving in your car, cooking dinner, waiting in line at the bank or lying in bed at night. Although this kind of meditation is characterized more by consistency than depth, it is important because it opens the door of our thought life for the Holy Spirit to work. Renewing our minds is a minute by minute, day by day process, not something we can do once a month or on our day off.

Sanctifying the Imagination – Musing

The second level of meditation, sanctifying the imagination, is a more deliberate activity that is aimed at a specific need, goal, problem or incentive. It requires a more concentrated amount of time to allow God to reveal something new to you. You might engage in this type of meditation when you are struggling with a major decision and you need guidance, when you are in the middle of a crisis and you need a solution or when you are facing a time of change in your life and you need assurance. You could spend thirty minutes or an hour just musing before God when you need a creative breakthrough or a new idea.

> **The Holy Spirit is our helper, our source for creative ideas and an expert problem-solver.**

I often engage in this kind of meditation early in the morning when I first wake up. I take my coffee cup into my office and just sit before God, not reading or working, but musing. As I am still in His presence, I sometimes say, "Lord, I am facing this situation and I need a breakthrough. Help me see the solution." And then I wait and listen, meditating on His Fatherhood and His worthiness. Often it is during these early mornings that He whispers in my spirit the creative answers I need.

It is good to spend time by yourself to sanctify your imagination because you need to be able to really listen to God. Your altar is a great place to meditate, although any place where you can experience stillness and solitude will work. This is what waiting on God is all about—He wants to impart His blessings to you if you will only sit with Him and listen.

As Paul writes to his friends in Corinth, "Now it is God who makes both us and you stand firm in Christ. He anointed us, set his seal of ownership on us, and put his Spirit in our hearts as a deposit, guaranteeing what is to come" (2 Corinthians 1:21–22). The Holy Spirit is our helper, our source for creative ideas and an expert problem-solver. That means that as Christians, we actually have inside of us the Spirit of the creator of the universe, the living God! While there is certainly nothing wrong with reading books and researching what others have to say, I wonder why we do not realize the divine resource we already have and spend more time allowing Him to speak to us.

Sharpening Your Revelation—The Silhouette of Divinity

The deepest level of meditation is where we press into the heart of God to discern the silhouette of divinity. It is the most difficult kind of interaction to explain because very few people ever experience it. When we meditate on the attributes of God, seeking His face and not His hand, He will sharpen our revelation by pressing Himself against the veil of heaven, allowing us to see Him as we have never seen Him before. This type of meditation is not about solving a problem or gaining insight into a particular situation; it is about knowing and becoming like Jesus. It is like staring into the eyes of a lover for the sheer pleasure of closely examining one so cherished.

People who experience this kind of meditation generally withdraw for days at a time to someplace away from the distractions of every day life. They seek refuge in a mountain hideaway or a lakeside cabin—anywhere they can be unmolested for extended periods of time. Although location is not most important, privacy does help facilitate waiting on God in a spirit-led way.

Consider John the Apostle, for example, who was exiled to the isle of Patmos. All alone, with nothing to entertain him, John meditated and communed with God. The result was the profound revelation which we now read at the end of the New Testament. When we wait on God long enough and listen for His voice, He will give us a sharper revelation of Jesus—His nature and His character. He wants to do more than just build our intellect; He wants to impart to us the spirit behind the Word.

Don't Hang Up!

Oswald Chambers, a great evangelical mystic and expositor writes,

> Wait on God and He will work, but don't wait in spiritual sulks because you cannot see an inch in front of you! Are we detached enough from our own spiritual hysterics to wait on God? To wait is not to sit with folded hands, but to learn to do what we are told (214).

To meditate is to abide in God with lively expectation as to what He might say or do. It is the key to receiving all that God wants to bless you with.

While reading a devotional book one morning, I ran across the following story that illustrated the importance of waiting:

> "Have you, perchance, found a diamond pendant? I feel certain I lost it last night in your theater," a woman phoned to ask the theater manager.
>
> "Not that I know, madam," the manager said, "but let me ask some of my employees. Please hold the line for a minute while I make inquiry. If it hasn't been found, we certainly will make a diligent search for it."
>
> Returning to the phone a few minutes later, the manager said, "I have good news for you! The diamond pendant has been found!"
>
> There was no reply, however, to his news. "Hello! Hello!" he called into the phone, and then he heard the dial tone. The woman who made the inquiry about the lost diamond pendant had failed to wait for his answer. She had not given her name and attempts to trace her call were unsuccessful. The pendant was eventually sold to raise money for the theater (Devotional 227).

Do you sometimes make requests of God without waiting around for an answer? How long are you willing to linger in His presence before you give in to other priorities? Try meditating throughout the day on a scripture that speaks to a need or desire in your life. Work at giving God time to speak to you in your weekly routine. Occasionally, plan to spend an entire day with God, and see what revelations He might impart to you! Make no mistake—He is waiting on you! Practice the discipline of waiting on God, and see if he will not give you just what you need.

Dear Lord,

So far today I've done all right. I haven't gossiped or lost my temper. I haven't been greedy or grumpy, nasty or selfish, or over-indulgent. And I am very thankful for that. But in a few minutes, God, I am going to get out of bed, and from then on, I'm probably going to need a lot more help!

Chapter 10

Brake 4:
Sit

While comparing notes with a friend and fellow pastor about the rigors of putting on a major event, he shared with me that his wife could definitely testify to the effects of pre-conference stress. Apparently, on the opening day of a conference at his church several years ago, his wife was so frantic about last-minute details that she made a rather embarrassing mistake. In between making final adjustments on the sound system and replacing the overhead at the front of the room with one that worked, she dashed into the bathroom, wishing she had stopped after just one cup of coffee.

As she sat down for the first time since that morning, her heart still racing and her mind busy calculating her next move, she hardly noticed the other deep voices in the restroom.

"My wife told me . . ."

Her mind was brought to attention by the sudden shot of adrenaline that rushed through her body at the sound of the man's voice. "No! This can't be happening," she thought. But as she glanced under the door at the masculine shoes that were shuffling in and out, her fears were confirmed. She had been in such a hurry and so preoccupied that she had navigated herself into captivity in a stall in the men's restroom. Snatching her skirt up off the floor, perched on top of the porcelain, she wondered if a dignified escape was even possible!

Your Assigned Seat

Sometimes in life it matters where you sit.

The Bible says that as a Christian, you have an assigned seat. "And God raised us up with Christ and seated us with him in the heavenly realms in Christ Jesus" (Ephesians 2:6). In God's supernatural scheme of things, you have been given a spiritual "seat" in heaven right next to the Father Himself. Like a child in his daddy's lap, you can "sit" beside the throne in Jesus even as you are living here on earth!

As I pondered this fourth brake and what it means to sit in Christ, I began to think of all kinds of very prominent seats—the chair in the Oval Office, the captain's chair on a ship, the chair at the head of a table, the director's chair. Where you sit is often an indication of your role or position. Even the very posture of sitting, as opposed to standing or lying down, denotes a kind of confidence or status. To be seated in Christ ascribes to us five things: privilege, honor, authority, encouragement and identity.

Seat of Privilege

Not long ago I boarded an airplane to find that my assigned seat was in the bulkhead—the first row behind first class. Tired from speaking and ready to get home, I struggled my bags past the wide leather chairs and crammed them in the already full overhead compartment above where I was to sit. My briefcase, however, would not fit, and since I had no intention of working on the flight, I turned to put it in one of the empty compartments in first class. But as she served a lady the drink she was holding, a cheerful flight attendant said, "I'm sorry, sir, but that space is reserved for first-class passengers." I went back to the bulkhead and collapsed into 7C.

I rested my head on the back of the seat and closed my eyes. As soon as we were in the air, the flight attendant, alias "overhead bin monitor," quickly closed the curtain that hung in the aisle and began serving dinner to the first-class passengers. It was grilled chicken, I think, with little roasted potatoes and a green salad. She had to move the fresh flower arrangements that decorated their trays in order to make room for individual baskets of hot bread. The smell of

> *The smell of fresh-baked, chocolate-chip cookies began drifting back from first class throughout the plane . . .*

food and the sound of silverware on china reminded me that I had not eaten. I closed my eyes again and tried to go to sleep.

I woke up several minutes later just in time to get a cup of lukewarm coffee from the cart. As I opened my very own bag of pretzels and poured all three of them onto my napkin, the smell of fresh-baked, chocolate-chip cookies began drifting back through the curtain. You could almost feel uprising in the main cabin. I have never been more relieved to get off an airplane as I was that night.

Being seated with Christ carries with it all the privileges of first-class treatment! We do not have to sit on the outside longing to share in the heavenly bounty. We are privileged in Jesus to be eligible for all that heaven has to offer. We have access to the throne twenty-four hours a day, every day. We never have to take a number or be put on hold to talk to God; He is available at any time. We also have the privilege of complete access to His promises, which are "Yes" for those seated in Christ. We can partake of the divine nature and realize blessings upon blessings in our first-class cabin in heaven!

Seat of Honor

Our seat in Christ, which entitles us to the privileges of heaven, is also a place of honor. I recently did a prayer conference in Jacksonville, Florida, for a dynamic young pastor of a fast-growing church. Although the church did not worship in a conservative style, they had a very strong sense of protocol that really struck me

Being **seated with Christ in heaven is a place of supreme honor.**

as unique. They knew how to honor a guest. In fact, they showed so much honor to me and my staff while we were there that we talked about it for days.

From the moment we first arrived, we did not lift a finger. They hauled in our boxes, helped set up our book display, served us juice and doughnuts—they met every need we had and some we did not have. I quickly noticed that a young man had apparently been assigned to be my personal escort because every where I went, he followed close behind, ready to take my jacket, carry my briefcase, pull out my chair or stir my coffee. As I spoke, he sat down to my left, watching me carefully, ready to spring into action at the slightest provocation. At one point in my talk, I referred to a book which I thought I had lying on the podium. It was not particularly important that I had it; I simply wanted to hold it up as a reference. But before I even noticed that he was gone, he took all the steps up onto the stage in one graceful leap and was standing at my side, book in hand. I was so surprised I totally lost my train of thought.

At lunch, we were led down to the fellowship hall of the church where several women were preparing a banquet for the pastors that were in attendance. I walked in behind my two associates and we sat down at the end of one of the long tables. Before our seats were even warm, one of the church leaders motioned to us to come to the front, where we had special seats reserved as the guests of honor. I was put at the head table, and my staff members were seated across from me at another table. It mattered where we sat!

Being seated with Christ in heaven is a place of supreme honor. God desires to honor you, just as that church so desired to honor us. You are His creation and His child, and He wants to bestow every spiritual blessing upon you. Ephesians 1:3 says, "Praise be to the God and Father of our Lord Jesus Christ, who has blessed us in the heavenly realms with every spiritual blessing in Christ." What is interesting is that the word used in this verse for "blessing" is the same Hebrew word that means "eulogy" or "eulogize." In other words, Jesus is blessing us by saying good things about us to God just as we would say good things about a loved one who has died. In that way, He honors us continually before the Father. To take our seat next to Him makes a difference.

Seat of Authority

Being seated with Christ is also a place of authority, since the throne of God is like the control room from which He rules and reigns over all the forces in the universe. He is the embodiment of perfect power and perfect love, and He is the final word. Because we are seated in Christ, we also have spiritual authority over our enemies and over Smutface.

I know a man who is a county judge in Mississippi. When he is not working, he is a fairly average guy. He mows his grass, carries out the garbage and watches little league. But when he puts on his robe and takes his seat in the courtroom, he has authority—authority that is given to him as a justice by the state of Mississippi. It sort of goes with the chair. When he is presiding over the courtroom, he has the power to make decisions and judgments that become law, but only in the courtroom. On the street, he has no more authority than you or I.

The Bible tells us that all of our enemies are a footstool to the feet of Jesus Christ seated in the heavenlies (Hebrews 10:13). As long as we are seated with Him, then we share in His authority over all the forces of darkness that work against us. Instead of praying to God, we can actually pray for God to address evil, and evict it when necessary. But we only have this authority in Jesus. That is why it is important that we understand our assigned seat.

Seat of Encouragement

My friend Mark Rutland tells the story of a tribe in Africa that has a very interesting custom for dealing with people when they mess up. As the custom goes, the one who has erred is seated in the middle of a circle of friends, who one by one begin to say something positive about their fellow tribesman. It may be a reminder of a past success or simply a statement of encouragement about the person's character. The goal is to build the offender up so that guilt or shame never has a chance to set in. Rather than inducing even more condemnation by tearing down their friend, they offer love and support in a tangible way. What an incredible idea!

When you brake for God and take your seat in Christ, He comes to build you up and encourage you to be hopeful and confident. If there is any message that I want to convey in this book, it is one of encouragement and support with regard to prayer. Prayer is the ultimate seat of reassurance from your Father. He wants to love on you and bombard you with positive thoughts and perfect love. He is not waiting to tear you down but to remind you of all that you are and all that He has created you to be.

Seat of Identity

Finally, being seated with Christ is where you will find your spiritual identity. It is critical that you know who you are in Him and that you understand your value as a child of the King.

One of the highest honors I ever had in my life was to serve as chaplain of the day for our Texas State Legislature. Basically, that meant that I was invited to sit in on the legislative session, and that I would open the session in prayer. It was very exciting to be a part of something like that— something so different from my normal routine. They printed my name in the daily program, took me to lunch, took my picture with the Speaker of the House and presented me with the Texas flag that flew over the capitol that day.

It is the highest point in the economy of God. It is the only identity that you can count on throughout your life.

In the Senate room where they met, a special chair was designated for the chaplain, and naturally, that is where I sat. As many of the representatives introduced themselves to me that day, they needed no explanation as to who I was, as long as I was in that chair. The seat itself gave me an identity, just as it had every other individual who had served before me as chaplain for the day.

When you are seated in Christ, your identity is realized in Him, not just for a day, but for an eternity. It is a seat of unlimited self-esteem—it is the highest point in the economy of God. It is the only identity that you can count on throughout your life. It will be an anchor to hold you in the storms of self-doubt and the rock that will not move in the currents of fads and trends. It is the one seat that will not collapse under the weight of criticism or failure because it is divinely supported and given.

I have a friend who is the president of a very large, successful corporation, and I asked him one day, "Joe, what would you be if you lost this company? Would you still know who you are?" He looked at me a little puzzled for a moment, and then he said, "I'd love to stay and talk, Terry, but I have to go. I have appointments this afternoon."

Oh, how I wish someone had warned me years ago about the dangers of wrapping your identity in an institution. I have seen dozens of people fall into a dangerous tailspin all because they lost a job, a relationship or a position from which they gained all of their personal identity and worth. The trouble with defining who we are through an occupation or even a spouse is that when the backdrop disappears, our whole life is turned upside down. If we fix our eyes on Jesus, however, we will not falter even in the worst kind of upheaval.

Speed Bump #4 – Forty Prayers to Take Your Seat

The issue here is putting your thoughts on Christ in the crucible of prayer. The Bible states, "For as he thinketh in his heart, so is he" (Proverbs 23:7, KJV), and this is the power point of prayer—setting your mind upon Him. Jesus is the power and full revelation of God. He is the complete picture. Being seated with Christ enables you to be completely surrounded by His affection and affirmation and to gain a new, heavenly vantage point over every situation in your life.

The phrase "in Christ" appears over 170 times in the New Testament! One practical way to apply this brake is to meditate on scriptures that will confirm all that you have in Jesus. This speed bump contains forty simple prayers of affirmation for you to pray daily. They will ignite a sense of profound love and true acceptance in you. As you pray through these prayers of identity, I believe you will begin to see yourself as God sees you, and what a picture!

1. Praise be to you, the God and Father of our Lord Jesus Christ, who has blessed me in the heavenly realms with every

spiritual blessing in Christ. Thank you for choosing me in Christ before the creation of the world to be special and blameless in your sight. Amen (Ephesians 1:3–4).

2. Lord, open the eyes of my heart that I may see clearly the hope I have been called to in Christ. In you, my future is secured! Make me ever aware of His inheritance and His incomparable great power that are mine as I believe (Ephesians 1:18–19).

3. You have made me alive in Christ even when I was dead in my sin! I praise you and thank you for demonstrating your great love for me in this way. You are rich in mercy and worthy of my adoration (Ephesians 2:4).

4. Thank you, God, that when you raised your son from the dead, you also raised me and have seated me with Him in the heavenly realms. I am honored to be placed in Jesus. Reveal your incomparable grace to me, expressed in the kindness you show me through Christ Jesus (Ephesians 2:6–7).

5. Dear Jesus, help me to accept myself the way I am, knowing that I am the workmanship of the Master Creator. I never need to doubt my abilities because I am created in Christ Jesus to do good works, and I have been perfectly prepared to fulfill my calling. Let it be! (Ephesians 2:10).

6. By faith, I believe that I am near to you, God, in Christ. Show this truth to me like never before—that the gap between us has been closed! Help me grasp the excitement of this concept and walk in it daily, especially when I feel discouraged or afraid (Ephesians 2:13).

7. Lord, like a giant oak tree, help me be so rooted and established in you that I may have power to grasp how high and how deep and how wide is your love for me. As I discover this love, I know I will be filled with all the fullness of God (Ephesians 3:17–19).

8. In you, Jesus, I am a new creation! I do not need to feel ashamed of the "old" me because through you I have been reconciled to the Father, and what I used to be is forgotten. You took my

shame and guilt and left it on the cross so that I could enjoy right-standing in heaven (2 Corinthians 5:17, 21).

9. Jesus, you said, "My grace is sufficient for you, for my power is made perfect in weakness." I claim this promise for every area of my life where I feel inadequate or unqualified. Thank you that I can do anything you call me to do through your strength (2 Corinthians 12:9, Philippians 4:13).

10. Let the name of Jesus be exalted! For in Him I have not been given a spirit of fear but of power, love and sound mind. The greater One lives in me (2 Timothy 1:7, 1 John 4:4).

11. I love you, Jesus, and I am proud to be called by your name. You are my source for everything I need, and you are a faithful provider. In you I have wisdom, hope for the future, encouragement and free access to the throne of God. In you I lack no good thing (1 Corinthians 1:30–31).

12. Because you knew that sometimes I would feel lonely, you came to call me your friend. When I feel isolated and alone, like no one understands my situation, make your presence real to me. Remind me by the Spirit that you will never leave me or forsake me (John 15:15, Matthew 28:20).

13. Heavenly Father, I know you speak to me. I want to hear and recognize your voice above all else. In Christ, I am one who can and does hear from you because I am your child, precious and loved in your sight (John 10:16).

14. Thanks be to you, O God—I know that in all things you work for my good according to your purpose. Take control of my life, especially these situations: _____, _____, and _____. I cannot fail when you are at work! (Romans 8:28).

15. Dear God, some days my physical body does not even feel like getting out of bed. I am glad to know that you made me whole in Christ and that you sent Him to be my healer. I ask you to heal issues of my past and my physical needs both known and unknown. In my savior I can walk in divine health (Isaiah 53, Matthew 8:17).

16. O Abba Father, you are my "Daddy God." Thank you for your many promises that through your Son are all "yes" to me. Because of this, I stand firm in you. I am honored to have your stamp of approval and ownership on me. Quicken my spirit to this: I am blessed! (2 Corinthians 1:20–22).

17. I can rejoice daily because you gave me the Holy Spirit who lives inside of me. Through Him, you empower me from on high and pour your love into my heart. Therefore, hope is my middle name, and I will not be disappointed. To God be all glory and praise (Romans 5:5).

18. How gracious are you, Lord! You made your abundant grace known to me through Jesus Christ, who was rich but became poor so that I could share in His inheritance. In Christ I am of great worth—I have supreme value because I am the child of the King of kings. Amen (2 Corinthians 8:9).

19. Jesus, sometimes I cannot see any good coming from my life—I see only mistakes. At times I feel as though I am beating at the air, but I know that you are the vine, and I am a branch, attached to you. In you I bear much fruit to the Father's glory. Show me that our union bears fruit that is eternal and not always known in this life (John 15:5, 8, 16).

20. Good and loving God, thank you that you will never leave me. Because you live, I will live. Peace—you have given me your very own peace. I receive it. In Christ, my heart will not be troubled, and fear will not prevail. I believe it! (John 14:18, 27, Colossians 3:15).

21. Lord, as I put my hand on my stomach, let your river flow from within me. You are my inner spring, welling up unto eternal life. In Christ my energy for life is at flood-tide. In all my relationships, teach me to give out of this river that flows from me so that I won't feel drained or depleted (John 7:38, Acts 1:8).

22. Jesus, in you I have been given new birth (John 3), a new life (John 10:10), a new mind (Philippians 2:5), a new purpose

(Ephesians 2:10), a new hope (Colossians 1:27), and a new home (Revelation 21:1–4). Thanks be to God.

23. When I am in despair or confusion, I will remember that I have access to the Father through Jesus by one Spirit. I don't have to take a number, leave a message or be put on hold. I can approach the throne with confidence and receive immediate help. Even in my time of need, I know that joy will come in the morning (Ephesians 2:18, Hebrews 4:16, Psalm 30:5).

24. Lord, I know that in you I can have peace at all times, even when things around me are anything but peaceful. I want to understand this with my mind. But until then, continue to guard my heart and mind in Christ Jesus. Amen (Philippians 4:7).

25. Today, I confess that Jesus is my CEO, my boss and my supervisor. He is Lord over all people, even those who do not recognize this fact. He is the Lord over my past, my present and my future. He is Lord over my work and my leisure. He is my living Lord, and because I am in Christ, I am rescued, saved and fulfilled (Romans 10:9–11).

26. I may not be wealthy by the world's standards, but in you, Jesus, I lack no spiritual gift. You enrich me in every way because all that you are is being confirmed and perfected in me. I can't wait for your return! (1 Corinthians 1:5–7).

27. God, I don't always look my best or have on the right clothes, which is why I am so grateful for the new wardrobe I have in Christ. He clothes me in joy, peace, patience, kindness, goodness, faithfulness, gentleness and self-control. Thank you for making me so finely dressed! I want to look good for your honor (Galatians 3:27, 5:22–23).

28. Since I received you as Lord, Jesus, help me to continue in you, being rooted and built up in you, receiving your strength as I trust. Encourage me in my faith, and allow my emotional cup to overflow with thankfulness (Colossians 2:6–7).

29. Almighty God, the Bible tells me that all things are underneath your feet and that you are head over everything. That

means that worry, fear, addictions, evil people, temptations—
everything is subject to you. My worst enemies are your
footstool (Ephesians 1:22).

30. God, you are my peace. When my life feels broken and frag-
mented, you somehow manage to put it back together, even
when I am not very cooperative. Because I am one with you
through Christ, I am whole in every way. It is very good—
and it is true (Ephesians 2:14).

31. Help! I just cannot seem to get my act together. I struggle
with the same temptations, the same bad habits and the same
sins over and over. Some days, I even do things I know are
wrong just because it feels good at the time. Thank you that
you became sin for me so that I might become righteous in
you. I want to live up to that gift! (2 Corinthians 5:21).

32. Jesus, thank you for giving me power in your name to overcome spiritual forces of evil that I cannot see but that sometimes come against me. When I feel depressed for no reason, overburdened because of something insignificant or
defeated by an unseen enemy, I will take authority over
Satan in your name, and he will flee (Philippians 2:9–11,
Ephesians 6:12, Luke 9:1).

33. Amazing grace . . . wonderful grace . . . awesome grace . . .
precious grace. Your grace has allowed me, because of my
hope in Christ, to be for the praise of your glory (Ephesians
1:12).

34. I speak against any force that has tried to lay claim to me,
wanting me to settle for less than who I am in you. With
your help, I will not buy into false hope and deceitful lies
about my identity. I am yours and only yours—you bought
me at a price! (1 Corinthians 6:20, 7:23).

35. Jesus, be my protector and my shield. Guard me and keep
me in your sight. When I pass through the rivers I will not
be swept away, and when I pass through the fire I will not be
burned, for you are my Lord and my God (Isaiah 43:2–3,
Psalm 3:3).

36. In Christ I am saved by grace . . . In Christ I am saved by grace . . . In Christ I am saved by grace. Let my life be a thank you card (Ephesians 2:5).
37. In you, Jesus, I am anxious to experience the fulfillment of all these good things I have in you. Thank you for sending me the Holy Spirit as a down-payment to verify what is mine. Glory! (Ephesians 1:9–10).
38. You are the lifter of my head. I will look up and not down. I will fix my eyes on you, for someday I will live with you in eternity (Psalm 123:1, John 14:3).
39. My savior and friend, I am steadfast in you. I will not be moved. I have surrendered to your good work and I know that anything I have given to you or done through you will not be lost (1 Corinthians 15:58).
40. Now unto the King eternal be honor and glory forever. Let my life be a never-ending melody to this tune. Amen and amen (Philippians 4:20).

(Keys to the Kingdom)

Dear God,

   I don't ever feel alone since I found out about you.

                                          —Nora

(Hample and Marshall)

Chapter 11

Brake 5: Watch

A story is told of a factory worker in Pittsburgh who had the important job of blowing the five o'clock whistle each day, notifying hundreds of workers that they could go home. He took this responsibility very seriously and therefore always wanted to make sure that his watch was exactly correct. Each morning on his way to the factory, he walked past a clock shop. He would stop in front of the store, pull his watch out of his pocket and set the precise time according to a big clock that hung in the window.

One morning, the owner of the shop, who had noticed the man's daily routine many times, was outside cleaning his windows when the factory worker came by. As he watched the man pull his pocket watch out for inspection he said, "Good morning. That sure is a fine-looking watch you have."

"Thank you," replied the man with an earnest look. "It is a very important watch, too, because a lot of people depend on it to keep the proper time. That's why I check it every morning by that big clock you have in the window."

"Yes sir," chimed in the shop owner proudly, "I keep all my clocks running perfectly. You can count on that. In fact, every evening before I close, I make sure each one is right on time with the five o'clock factory whistle!"

The Theory of Relativity

We all need a standard to live by—a compass that we can rely on to give us accurate direction in a world of complex choices. But what a predicament we get into when we choose to make decisions relative to anything other than the truth. Just imagine how far off the correct time these two men might be after years of setting their clocks against one another!

> *But what a predicament we get into when we choose to make decisions relative to anything other than the truth.*

We live in a "wordy" society, overrun with information and signs that point in every direction. We are literally bombarded with options. It seems there is no such thing as a simple choice, and we are surrounded by people who are eager to choose for us. But making decisions based on the opinions of people, current trends or the influence of advertisers will eventually lead us off the mark. The only standard we can rely on is the voice of God.

Matthew 26:40–41 says,

> *Then he returned to his disciples and found them sleeping. "Could you men not keep watch with me for one hour?" He asked Peter. "Watch and pray so that you will not fall into temptation. The spirit is willing, but the body is weak."*

This fifth brake, watching, is about knowing and hearing God. It is, in a sense, a culmination of the four previous brakes.

To be still and rest and wait and sit are all primarily for the purpose of disciplining yourself to keep watch—to listen for the Master's voice. They are simply ways of turning your heart to His heart and being quiet enough to hear His direction. To watch is to be alert to what He has to say so that His wisdom can become your standard.

When God Speaks, Even E. F. Hutton Should Listen

As I have already mentioned, prayer is God's idea. It is His method of communicating with His precious creation. But cultivating the ability to be silent long enough for the Father to speak to you is critical to the whole idea. God did not design prayer to be unidirectional—He wants to converse with you. The business of prayer is meant to be a two-way interaction— you speak; He listens. Then He speaks, and you listen. Talking to God without ever being able to hear His reply would short-change the overall process. It would make prayer into little more than a voice mail service!

God is a personal God who is concerned about everything in your life, big or small. He desires for you to be victorious in this life in every way. Because of His perfect love for you, he yearns to speak to you for five reasons:

1. He wants to communicate His affection for you. Sometimes, your Daddy God just wants to gush over you. He wants to tell you how precious you are and how beautiful you are in His sight.
2. He wants you to know Him. As amazing as it seems, God actually wants to be intimate with you—for you to know His heart and understand His mind toward everything He created.
3. He wants to show you direction. God did not create you with a purpose and a plan only to leave you in the dark about the whole thing! He wants to guide you through the

maze of choices to the place where you can become all you
are meant to be.

4. He wants to give you solutions. Look around—God is the
ultimate source of creativity and new ideas. He is also the
giver of wisdom. He has the answer to every dilemma you
face because He is a premier problem solver. He wants to
help you overcome the toughest challenges of life.

5. He wants to offer you protection. As one who has paid the
ultimate price for you, God does not want to see you hurt.
He wants to guard you from evil and comfort you when life
leaves you wounded.

Holy Hunches

Just about every Christian book that has ever been written
about prayer addresses the topic of "hearing God." I guess it is an
aspect of prayer that even the most noteworthy saints find difficult at times. The Bible indicates, however, that the most important qualification is something all of us can display—desire.

*You will seek me and find me when you seek me with all your
heart (Jeremiah 29:13).*

. . . he rewards those who earnestly seek him (Hebrews 11:6).

*Call to me and I will answer you and tell you great and
unsearchable things you do not know (Jeremiah 33:3).*

So how will God speak to you? Although God has, in the
past, used stone tablets or pillars of fire to communicate to His
people, I will go out on a limb to say that, in all probability, He
will speak to you most often in your own thoughts. I call these
thoughts "holy hunches." A holy hunch is nothing more than a
message from God that is whispered into your mind by the Holy
Spirit.

It works like this: Because God and the Holy Spirit are two
parts of the same divine being, and since the Holy Spirit resides
inside of you, God can speak to you from right inside your own

spirit. The communication is very intimate. Although you may have trouble discerning holy hunches from the other noise that rattles around in your head, with a little practice, you can learn the sound of the Father's voice. The more you listen, the more your heart and mind will become tuned to His frequency.

Years ago, during the depression when good jobs were scarce, a retired military naval officer saw an advertisement for a Morse code operator position at Western Union. Having become fluent in Morse code during his service, he went to apply for the job.

A holy hunch is nothing more than a message from God that is whispered into your mind by the Holy Spirit.

When he arrived at the telegraph office, he found a rather chaotic scene. The room was full of people applying for various jobs. Everyone seemed to be talking at once, and because the positions were few, some of the discussions were rather heated as tempers flared under the stress of the situation. He sat down in a chair to wait.

After a few minutes, the man grew discouraged. He had not seen any signs of progress—only frustrated interviewers shuffling through applications and trying with little success to maintain some kind of order. With so many people waiting before him, how could he ever hope to get the job? He was about ready to leave when he heard a faint tapping coming from a door across the noisy room. Immediately, his trained ears recognized the familiar sound of Morse code, and he listened carefully to the message.

Slowly, the man got up from his chair and made his way through the crowd. According to the directions that had been tapped out on the door, he slipped through it, closed it behind him and proceeded down a long hallway to an office. As soon as he stepped in, the woman seated at the desk said, "Thank you for coming in today. Your have just demonstrated exactly the kind of listening skills we are looking for. When can you start work?"

Earmarked for God

Sometimes it pays to be the only one listening when everyone else is talking. Being tuned in to the Father's voice will qualify you to receive blessings and instructions that others may miss out on. Hear what Oswald Chambers has to say about discerning and hearing God:

> God never speaks to us in startling ways, but in ways that are easy to misunderstand, and we say, "I wonder if that is God's voice?" Isaiah said that the Lord spoke to him "with a strong hand," that is, by the pressure of circumstances. Nothing touches our lives but it is God Himself speaking. Do we discern His hand or only mere occurrence? (30)

Let me suggest that you keep in mind the following guidelines as you train yourself to know and hear God:

1. **God's message will always be for your good.** His nature is good; the content of His word will be loving. He will not tell you something that will result in ultimate harm to you or any of His children. This does not mean, however, that God will always say what you want to hear—in fact, sometimes He will give you instructions that are not easy to follow. He may ask you to make a personal sacrifice or do something that makes you terribly uncomfortable. He will tell you what is best for you, not necessarily what is easiest.

2. **God's message will always be simple.** He does not use big words; only humans do that. Your heavenly Father is not interested in impressing people. He will not speak something that is too complicated for you to understand any more than

you would do the same to your child. God wants to communicate with you, not confuse you.

3. **God's message will be hard to ignore.** His words tend to have a lasting effect because they leave an impression on your heart. Even if you do not hear Him the first time, His words are not easily washed away by the day's activities. He will continue to prod you for a time, until you listen and understand.

Speed Bump #5 - Journaling

Bill Hybels is an extremely busy man. He pastors a church of 18,000 people in Chicago, many of whom make appointments to see him during the week. In addition to caring for the needs of his own flock, he is also a leader in the church community there and a nationally known and respected teacher and author.

On any given morning when Bill arrives at his office, he has numerous phone calls to make, meetings to attend, people to counsel, problems to solve and activities to plan. And of course, he has to have time to prepare fresh sermons for each Sunday. The demands on his time far exceed what he is capable of giving.

In an effort to keep his sanity intact and his eyes focused on the reason for his ministry, he has an interesting morning ritual. Bill Hybels applies the brakes. He engages in a practical discipline that slows him down long enough to maintain his focus and gives him an opportunity to hear from God.

Every morning when he arrives at his office, he goes directly into his prayer place, picks up a plain spiral notebook and turns to a blank page. At the top of the page he writes the word "yesterday." For the next few quiet moments, he reflects on the previous day and jots down decisions, feelings, important outcomes, high points, low points, frustrations, successes—anything that he remembers. It might be comparable to a post-game analysis. When he is finished thinking about the day before, he writes out a short prayer to start the new day. Then he closes his notebook and goes like crazy.

It is important to know that Bill himself says that nothing he writes in his notebook is profound. In fact, sometimes it is downright trivial. He even admits that he seldom flips back to days and weeks gone by to read what he has recorded (102–104). So why does he do it?

Logging Your Trip

Taking time to record your spiritual journey is a speed bump, meant to slow you down long enough for God to get a grip on your day. It will help you keep watch and tune in to the subtle ways He might be speaking to you. Many call this "journaling," but if that word makes your palms sweat or your eyelids droop, then think of it as a debriefing time or a progress check. Taking time to evaluate where you have been and learning from your own experiences is a valuable exercise in almost all of life's endeavors.

> *L*earn something from yesterday that might help you do a better job tomorrow.

Athletes keep workout logs; astronauts keep daily accounts; medical professionals keep patient records; repair technicians keep job reports. In all of these examples, the objective is the same: Learn something from yesterday that might help you do a better job tomorrow.

If you are serious about hearing from God, journaling can be a very worthwhile discipline. But the first thing I would encourage you to do is try to put aside any preconceived ideas about the whole activity. Journaling has nothing to do with writing your most embarrassing thoughts or your most intimate feelings in a flowery, perfume-scented book so that anyone who finds it has enough material to blackmail you for millions. Nor is it about the legalistic obligation to fill up eighteen pages every day with profound insights, lest you lose your salvation and be condemned forever.

Journaling is simply writing down important events, breakthroughs, thoughts and decisions. It might be something you do every day, or it might be something you do once a week. You can keep a journal in a special notebook that is designed for that purpose, or you can keep it in a plain spiral notebook, in the back of your day planner, on a calendar at your desk or a grease board on the refrigerator. Your journal is your record—your "epistle"—of your walk with God.

Regardless of what your journal looks like, where it is kept or how often it gets updated, let me suggest four categories for you to record:

1. Scripture Verses
2. Significant Events
3. Things God Says to You
4. Needs and Answers to Prayer

1. Scripture Verses

One afternoon several years ago, I was on my way out of town in my car, and I was troubled about a particular problem. I stopped at a small gas station to use the pay phone, and when I hung up, a middle-aged man wearing a ragged pair of overalls and a scruffy beard thrust a small New Testament in my hands and said, "You look like you need to read what's in here!" It was not until I had returned to my car that it hit me what had just happened—I had just been witnessed to! I almost laughed out loud because it seemed funny. After all, I was a pastor and I had already read every word of that New Testament. And I certainly knew I was saved.

I started to get out and give the Bible back to the man so he could give it to someone else, when I flipped through the pages and noticed that Romans 8:28 had been highlighted: "And we know that in all things God works for the good of those who love him, who have been called according to his purpose." Now I knew that verse. I had read it hundreds of times. But seeing it again at that moment gave me a peace about the problem I had been worrying over all day. God was not trying to save me; He was simply trying to tell me something.

When God gives you a verse of scripture, especially when you are not expecting it, record it in your journal. You may not understand its significance right away, but in time you will know where to apply it in your life. God often speaks to us through His written word, which is why it is so important for you to read the Bible. I never know quite what to say to people who tell me they really want to hear a fresh word from God, but they do not even take the time to read the ones He has already given us!

> *G*od was not trying to save me; He was simply trying to tell me something.

The Bible is His word to you, and it has meaning and relevance in every situation you face. The intriguing thing about it is that you can spend a lifetime studying it and never stop uncovering new truths. It is like peeling an onion—just when you think you have found the center, you discover another layer. It is rich and timeless, and as you read it, your Father will lead you to passages, and the Holy Spirit will lift them from the pages and bring them to life in your heart.

2. Significant Events

For much of the time I lived in College Station, the head football coach for Texas A&M University was a man by the name of Jackie Sherrill. Because of the enormous amount of attention given to the football program there, Jackie was every bit a home town celebrity.

During one particular season, when his team was getting more press than usual due to some alleged violations, I got the rather absurd idea that I was supposed to go to his office and pray for Jackie. Not invite him to church, offer him advice, evaluate his situation or push him into some esoteric spiritual experience—just pray for God to be with him through the heat.

So, one afternoon I walked into his receptionist's office, introduced myself as a local pastor and asked if I could see Coach Sherrill. She asked me what my visit was concerning, and I simply said, "I want to pray for him."

"Well," she replied, "Mr. Sherrill's appointment schedule is actually booked up months in advance—even for those who have *official* business. I'm afraid it would be impossible to see him today."

I knew I would not get very far by arguing, so I thanked the lady and walked down the hall to the restroom. "God, I think you told me to do this, but I've run into a snag," I prayed as I walked. "There is nothing more I can do unless you make something happen."

As I stood in front of the bathroom mirror washing my hands, thinking maybe today just was not the day, one of the bathroom stall doors opened and out walked Jackie!

"Hi, Coach Sherrill. I'm Terry Teykl, a local pastor. Could I have a minute with you?"

"Sure," he smiled. "Come on down to my office."

As we passed back through the reception area, the secretary to whom I had spoken just a few minutes earlier looked absolutely bewildered. "Please hold my calls," Jackie said to her, and we left her to wonder.

As if that incident were not enough to verify God's absolute ability to create divine appointments, several months later, He went to work again. I was on my way out of town when I stopped for gas. When I went in to pay the cashier, she nodded toward my car and said, "You'll have to find another ride." I looked out the window—my back tire was flat. I finished paying for my gas and headed outside to use the phone, when who should walk in the station but Jackie Sherrill.

He remembered who I was (probably not many people have offered to pray for him in the men's restroom) and immediately offered me a ride back to town. Not only was I able to pray for him, we had a nice visit as well.

I recorded those events in my journal as reminders of how God can provide a way when we cannot. An unexpected phone call from a person about whom you have been thinking, a chance meeting with someone who holds the key to a project on which you are working, a turn of events that changes the outlook of a long term plan—any of these occurrences could be recorded in your journal.

At times, God will speak through other people, nature, circumstances, even songs or movies. He created it all. Somewhere down the road you may look back at an unexpected event and know that God was orchestrating a miracle that you would not recognize for months or even years. What a tragedy not to see His hand working in your life simply because you have forgotten all the little happenings that He put together in order to bring you to the place of success.

3. Things God Says to You

When the church we started was in its infancy, still meeting in apartment buildings and school cafeterias, I used to go to a cabin about twenty miles outside of town to pray. One hot Friday afternoon, as I was praying for our little church and seeking God's direction, He spoke five words to me, "Build the church in prayer." I wrote them in my journal, totally unaware of the magnitude and influence they would have on my future. What I thought was a rather obvious mandate has turned out to be a lifelong mission.

Sometimes God will speak "little" things to you, and sometimes He will speak "big" things. This was a big thing, although I did not recognize it at the time. It was one of those rare times when God did not exactly whisper. Instead, His voice was so clear that I could almost feel the words being seared into my heart. I have spent the last twenty years trying to fulfill that single directive, and I will probably spend twenty more the same way.

When you get still before God and wait patiently in His presence, He will speak to you. It may not seem like a very important message at the time, but do not let it go without writing it down! Nothing God says to you is unimportant. Like the words He gave me in the cabin, a single idea or thought that He impresses

***

*S*ometimes God will speak "little" things to you, and sometimes He will speak "big" things.

***

onto your heart may grow with you and gain more and more meaning as time goes by.

Do not be afraid to "miss" God. We all have. One Sunday during a church service, I heard God speak the word "shingles" to me. I thought, "God must want me to pray for all the roofers that are here!" Only after humiliating myself did I discover that He was trying to tell me to pray for a young girl who had a rare case of the medical condition known as "shingles."

Hearing God is a skill that you must patiently cultivate, and recording both your successes and your messes will make the process much easier. Like any other ability, you may learn far more from a single failure than from a whole string of victories.

4. Needs and Answers to Prayer

This is probably the most important section you can include in your journal because I believe it honors God. One of the greatest sins we commit is taking God's goodness for granted. We wake up in the middle of a difficult time thinking, "God, you have forgotten me. You must not love me anymore because you have not answered my prayer in this situation." Then, because He is a loving Father, He supplies our need for that day, despite our complaining, and we rejoice for a short time. The problem is that when we do not keep a record of the times when God answers our prayers, then the next time we are in a crisis, we are likely to be whining again because we have a short spiritual memory!

In your journal, you might keep a list of friends or family members who do not know Jesus. Every time you pick it up, you will be reminded to pray for them. You might even try writing out a short prayer now and then. It is a powerful thing to see your own request in writing, and when the answer comes, you are much more likely to recognize it and record it. This section of your journal will become an endless source of praise and thanksgiving.

"Hay, God!"

Back in 1982, as our young church in was growing, we decided it was finally time to build. We secured some land, drew up the building plans and hired a contractor to do the work. I will never forget the day they poured the foundation. As we stood admiring the dark, wet cement that would soon become our church home, the weather took a dramatic turn.

December in Texas is not exactly what you would call winter, especially if you live a little farther north where snow is not classified as one of the seven wonders of the world. But the weather in Texas is known to change rapidly, and in the winter months, we occasionally feel the chill of what they call a "Blue Norther"—a cold air mass that actually makes it all the way down from Canada.

As we stood there in the wind, our excitement gave way to the harsh realization that if the temperature dropped below freezing over night, the foundation would not dry properly, and it would have to be demolished and poured again. My stomach sank. Not only would re-pouring delay the building schedule dramatically, it would also mean a tremendous increase in cost, which we could not afford. The loss seemed inevitable.

Not knowing what else to do, we called together some of our leaders to pray for God's intervention. We prayed for warmer temperatures and for the grace to accept whatever might happen. As our meeting was winding down, I called the contractor to see if there was anything else we could do. He said, "Terry, I was picking up the phone to call you. I just remembered something that might work. Up north, when they pour concrete, they cover it with hay until it dries. The hay holds in enough heat to keep the surface from freezing. I have already got some men working on it at the site. It's funny, though. I don't have any idea why I didn't think of that until just now."

As we stood admiring the dark, wet cement that would soon become our church home, the weather took a dramatic turn.

I did.

Sure enough, that night the temperature plunged into the twenties, but the blanket of hay was enough to save the foundation. Today, if you were to go to College Station, Texas, and pull up a piece of the carpet at the Aldersgate United Methodist Church, you would find a layer of hay embedded in the concrete as a reminder of God's faithfulness.

Look around you, and make note of all the ways in which God has blessed you. How many times has He provided for your needs, protected your children, given you wisdom or blessed you in some small way? Keeping a journal is much like keeping a family photo album. It becomes a legacy—a personal testimony to the memories and significant events in your relationship with

God. Imagine what it might mean to you months or years from now when you are facing a desperate situation, to look back over all the times when God demonstrated His love and His faithfulness in your life. I know it would affect the way you pray!

Instrument Rated

When pilots fly, they have no need to look out the windshield because they do not fly by sight. That is why neither dense fog nor darkness impairs their ability to navigate airplanes safely into the air and back down again. Pilots are "instrument rated," which means that they are trained to fly airplanes solely on the information they receive from the instruments in the cockpit.

As you learn to hear God's voice, you become "instrument rated" in life. You no longer walk by what you see but by the reading of your spirit. The Holy Spirit is your co-pilot. Circumstances around you may be bright and clear or dark and gloomy, but it will not affect your ability to navigate through choices and decisions. When you are receiving your direction from the Father, you can be at peace at all times because your course has already been charted and your destination secured.

Lord,

I have a lot of respect for you because I think we are in the same business. Thank you for giving me the skills necessary to rescue those who are seriously injured or in danger, and keep me calm in the midst of crisis.

—the prayer of an Emergency Medical Technician

Chapter 12

Brake 6: *Stand*

An electrician was working on a very steep house-top when he suddenly lost his footing and began to slide down toward the edge. Panic-stricken at the thought of the two-story drop, he cried out to God, "Lord, save me! Don't let me die!" But he continued to slide. The roof was too steep for him to recover his balance, and there was nothing for him to grab to stop his momentum. He was sure he was a goner.

But just before he reached the edge of the housetop, he felt the jerk of his belt on a nail protruding from the roof, bringing him to a sudden halt. He lay still for a moment, regaining his breath. "Thank goodness that nail was there," he thought. "God sure didn't help me!"

I have a feeling we will all be quite surprised when we get to heaven and see fully what God sees. I do not think most of us have any idea how many times He has guarded, shielded and protected us when we did not even recognize His hand. He is such a wise and loving Father that there are even times when

He answers our prayers before we have prayed them! I know in my own life that a band of unsung angels have been kept very busy diverting disaster from my family and me, all in the guise of natural events or "coincidences."

> *Therefore put on the full armor of God, so that when the day of evil comes, you may be able to stand your ground, and after you have done everything, to stand. Stand firm then . . . (Ephesians 6:13–14).*

Now What?

Nevertheless, when we do pour ourselves out before God, laboring in prayer over some important matter, then comes the most difficult part—waiting for an answer. Does he always answer our prayers? If so, then why do I not always get what I pray for? How long do I have to wait? Will I always know when the answer comes?

> *If* you pray at all, then you either must believe that God hears you, or you are crazy to engage in an activity that you believe is useless.

It is critically important that you have these questions resolved in your mind before you pray so that you know what to expect afterwards. In fact, if you pray at all, then you either must believe that God hears you, or you are crazy to engage in an activity that you believe is useless. At the very minimum, the act of prayer in itself demonstrates a level of faith that says, "God just might come through."

The Bible promises us that God does hear our prayers and that He is faithful to answer us.

Before they call I will answer; while they are still speaking I will hear (Isaiah 65:24).

If you believe, you will receive whatever you ask for in prayer (Matthew 21:22).

Therefore I tell you, whatever you ask for in prayer, believe that you have received it, and it will be yours (Mark 11:24).

So why is it so difficult at times to claim the answer? Why does it seem at times that God is deaf or uninterested?

I believe God responds to every prayer that is made. After all, He is the creator and initiator of the whole process, and He is not subject to mechanical failure. The difficulty in receiving the answers is on our end of the equation. Because of our limited perspective, like the man who was saved by the nail, we often fail to recognize the answer when it comes. Or, we may recognize it but not want to accept it because it is not exactly what we had in mind. Sometimes, we even fabricate our own answer when we are not satisfied with God's.

Consider the man who was determined to lose weight. He shared with his friends and co-workers that he was going to do whatever it took to shed a few pounds. He started to exercise every day and eat a healthier diet. Within a couple of weeks, he was rewarded to see several pounds less on the scale.

Then, one morning on his way to work, he passed by the bakery and saw in the window his very favorite thing—warm cinnamon rolls, fresh from the oven and heavy with icing. When he carried a box of them into his office, already half-eaten, his co-workers scolded him for having so little willpower. They reminded him of the promise he had made to himself to do whatever it took.

The man smiled and nodded, "I know, I know. But these are very special cinnamon rolls. As I drove by the bakery this morning, I could see them in the window, and I felt this was no accident. So I prayed, 'Lord, if you want me to have those cinnamon rolls, give me the parking space directly in front of the door.'

And sure enough, on the eighth time around the block, there it
was!" (Devotional 225)

Answers to Live By

If we really want to know God's heart about a matter, then
we must be committed to seeing and accepting His answer only—
nothing more and nothing less. We must give Him creative license to respond to us in His best way rather than praying with
hidden agendas.

As you learn to pray with an expectant heart and an open
mind, you will find that God is faithful to answer your prayers in
one of four ways:

1. Yes.
2. Yes, as soon as you meet certain conditions.
3. Yes, as soon as some other things fall into place.
4. Yes, but here is a better way.

Sometimes, God is able to answer us right away and grant
us exactly what we asked for. These answers are easy to recognize and celebrate. You pray for money, and a check comes in the
mail; you pray for rain, and you hear the thunder; you pray for
healing, and the report comes back clean. This is the type of
answer we probably hope for in most cases.

Second, God may in essence say, "Yes, I will grant your request, but there is something you need to do before I can fulfill
it." For example, God might respond, "Yes, I will heal your lungs
as soon as you stop smoking;" "Yes, I will help you reduce your
indebtedness as soon as you cut up your credit cards;" or "Yes, I
will grant you the advancement you deserve at work as soon as
you forgive your supervisor."

Our actions can be the key to releasing the blessings of God
in our lives. If we are simply not ready to receive what it is we
have asked for, then the action may involve a growth process.
Or, it may be a step of faith or an act of relinquishing control.
Like the little boy who gets his hand stuck in the jar because he

does not want to drop the quarter, we sometimes pray with our fists so tightly clenched that God simply cannot help us until we are willing to let go. This is a control issue—we may be asking God to intervene in a situation that we are not really ready to turn over to Him. As long as we are in control, He cannot be.

Third, God may answer our prayer by saying, "Yes, I am ready to grant you that, but there are some events and circumstances of which you are not aware that need to fall into place first."

> *Our actions can be the key to releasing the blessings of God in our lives.*

Since, as I mentioned before, God often answers prayers through everyday occurrences in our lives, I think when we pray He begins to scan the earth looking for someone to become the answer. He searches for people who are tuned in to His frequency and are willing to obey. I remember one time when I was in school I felt led to give ten dollars to another student in one of my classes. On that particular occasion, for some reason, I chose not to listen to the Spirit's voice. As the scanner passed over me, I had the opportunity to become the answer to that man's prayer, but I missed it. My own unwillingness delayed his answer to prayer, even though he had no idea I was even in the loop. Sometimes, the answer to our prayers depends on another person or event, and we must wait patiently for the best timing.

Finally, God can answer prayers by saying, "Yes, I will meet that need but in a way you are not expecting." This is the toughest answer and the one that is most often regarded as no answer at all. Countless times I have sat face to face with husbands, wives, children and friends of someone who has died and had to somehow answer the questions, "Why did God let my loved one die? Why didn't He answer my prayers?"

I think if any of us had even a glimpse of what heaven is like and the unimaginable gift of divine health that awaits us, we would readily welcome death as the most gracious answer to prayer possible! But let me share with you one woman's struggle with what she perceived as an unanswered prayer.

An Unexpected Answer

Evelyn's husband, Rex, was a pilot and the owner of two small businesses—Hattiesburg Aviation and a mobile home retail lot. They had two sons, ages ten and twelve, and a nice home. They felt blessed with money, family and health.

But in 1974, tragedy struck. Rex left on a cargo flight for Caracas, Venezuela, but his plane never arrived at its destination. Searches turned up nothing, and Evelyn had no choice but to pray and hope for a miracle.

She and the boys tried to remain optimistic. They prayed fervently and constantly, but weeks went by and nothing changed. She began to worry about how she could possibly raise the kids, pay off more than $450,000 of debt on her teaching salary and somehow manage the aviation and mobile home businesses. "Life would be impossible," she concluded, "without Rex."

One morning as Evelyn was praying and asking God for answers, she came across Isaiah 40:31 which read, "... but those who hope in the Lord will renew their strength. They will soar on wings like eagles; they will run and not grow weary, they will walk and not be faint." She held on to that as God's promise that He would bring her husband safely back. Every day she reminded God of the promise and of how badly she needed Rex to come home.

But months went by, and there were still no answers. Forced to make some decisions about financial issues, Evelyn took a hard look at her options. Teaching did not pay enough. The aviation business did, but it would take her miles away from her sons. The mobile home business was also lucrative, but she knew nothing about it. Finally, with the help of a local banker and an attorney, she decided to sell the aviation business, use the money to pay off some of the debt, and try to learn the mobile home business well enough to survive.

The next several months were stressful. She could not understand why God was not keeping His promise to bring Rex back. She began to feel abandoned and angry. Seasons came and went, and Evelyn knew nothing more than she had the day her husband disappeared. Finally, after two years, according to maritime ruling, Rex was declared legally dead.

> *Every day she reminded God of the promise and of how badly she needed Rex to come home.*

In her anger at God, Evelyn had all but stopped going to church. Occasionally, in times of great pain and confusion, she would sit through a service hoping for some comfort. But each time, she left more in despair and more angry than she came. The one time she ventured into a Sunday school class, the lesson was on Isaiah 40:31! She burst out of the room, tears streaming down her face. Instinctively, she cried out to God, yet she wondered if He even cared.

Over the next nine years, she continued to manage the business and raise her two sons. Eventually, all of the original debt was paid, and she was able to leave the business world completely. With all reminders of Rex brought to completion and the boys out on their own, Evelyn once again looked to God for answers. She picked up the Bible and read Isaiah 40:31, this time very slowly, as if trying to understand it for the first time. As she did, the Spirit began to reveal that the promise had not been about Rex, but about her! God had not abandoned her, in spite of her anger and resentment. He had heard her cries, and had been there with her every step of the way. He had indeed given her and the boys strength, lifting them up on wings of eagles, and carried them when they were too weary to walk. He had kept His promise—every word.

Evelyn gained a different perspective on prayer as a result of her trial. She learned that "life" happens to us all, but God is faithful to walk with us through whatever may get thrown our way. He may not always grant us the easy miracle we request, but He will always give us an abundance of grace when we are overwhelmed by life's challenges and circumstances. For Evelyn, prayer was the bridge that finally carried her from her own perspective into God's ultimate plan for her.

> *He* had kept His promise—every word.

Father Knows Best

I do not always know why things happen as they do, but I do know that God always answers prayer according to His promises. He is for you in every way and delights in you as a person of immeasurable worth. He does not play hide and seek, nor does He make it hard for you to call on His name.

Garth Brooks sings a song in which he recognizes that when God does not give us something we think we want, it might be because He has something far better in store. In the song, Garth takes his wife back to his hometown for his high school reunion. At the reunion, he sees his high school sweetheart and is reminded of how hard he had once prayed for God to let her be his bride. But years later, as he looks at his family, he realizes how thankful he is that God knew better. He sings:

Sometimes I thank God for unanswered prayer—
Remember when you're talking to the Man upstairs,

Just because He doesn't answer doesn't mean He's not
there.

One of God's greatest gifts is unanswered prayer.

God is in the business of answering prayer, but He is also
the original Father who knows best. He will bless us with every
good gift He possibly can, but because He loves us, He cannot
grant us everything we ask for any more than a loving parent
can give in to a toddler's every wish. Sometimes a higher wisdom has to prevail.

Standing

Waiting for God to answer is what the sixth brake is all about.
Standing is the mental posture you take after you have prayed
and while you are waiting for God's response. It is the brake
that gives God time to work out the process of prayer in our
lives. To stand is to trust in God's faithfulness enough not to
give in to feelings, silence, circumstances, problems or public
opinions. It is to pursue the sacred and to resist being influ-
enced by the negative or ill-informed. It is in standing that we
gain maturity in our prayer relationship with God. The principle of standing reinforces the idea that the cutting edge of
effective personal prayer is not in activism or technique, but
rather in stillness and surrender.

Heart Condition

Standing involves three attributes of the heart: honor, faith
and perseverance.

To honor someone is to pay that person respect or homage.
Just as you stand in honor when a dignitary enters the room,
when you stand before God, you are giving Him the adoration
and reverence He deserves. After you have prayed, affirm His
goodness, His holiness and all of His attributes. Esteem Him
for the work He is about to do and for who He is. To stand is to
honor God by acknowledging that He is the giver of all good

things and glorifying His name above problems, circumstances and needs.

Faith is, according to Hebrews, "being sure of what we hope for and certain of what we do not see" (Hebrews 11:1). Faith is the one ingredient that gives substance to the whole idea of being with God. Through faith, you know that God has heard your prayer and that He will answer. It allows you to see the situation as God sees it and agree with His perspective in the matter. To stand is to have faith. Stand, then, until His perspective has infiltrated every area of your life.

> *To* stand is to honor God by acknowledging that He is the giver of all good things . . .

Perseverance means that you never give up. It is a covenant with God, sealed in your heart, that will not allow you to turn your face from His for any reason. It allows you to patiently wait for an answer without being paralyzed while God works it out in your life. Perseverance is like a rudder that sets you on course and will not let you be waylaid or tossed about by every wind and wave.

When I was a little boy, I planted a bean in a pot. But I was so anxious for the sprout to poke through the soil that every day I would dig up the seed just to see if the thing was growing. Finally, after several days, my mother told me, "As long as you keep digging up the bean, you will never see the sprout. Leave it alone, and it will grow."

Although we can never "uproot" a prayer that has been offered up to the throne, I think God must, at times, want to shake us and say, "Leave it alone, and it will grow. Quit talking about it, worrying about it or trying to force something to happen. Just let me work. After you have prayed, stand, and you will soon see the answer emerge!"

If you have been praying and praying for some particular thing to come to pass, and there is something you can do to facilitate its happening, then you must do it. If, for example, you are praying for a job, then sending out resumes will almost certainly increase your chances of receiving what you have asked for.

But in Ephesians, Paul emphasizes, "after you have done everything," stand. When you have presented a request to the Lord and have been fully obedient to do anything He instructed you, then, having done everything, it is time to stand.

Speed Bump #6 – Praise

In her book, *Prodigals and Those Who Love Them*, Ruth Graham Bell, Billy Graham's wife, gives this personal account:

It was early in the morning in another country. Exhausted as I was, I awoke around three o'clock. The name of someone I loved dearly flashed into my mind. It was like an electric shock.

Instantly I was wide awake. I knew there would be no more sleep for me the rest of the night. So I lay there and prayed for the one who was trying hard to run from God. When it is dark and the imagination runs wild, there are fears only a mother can understand.

Suddenly, the Lord said to me, "Quit studying the problem and start studying the promises."

Now, God has never spoken to me audibly, but there is no mistaking when He speaks. So I turned on the light, got out my Bible, and the first verses that came to me were Philippians 4:6–7 (KJV): "Be careful for nothing; but in everything by prayer and supplication *with thanksgiving* let your requests be made known unto God. And the peace of God, which passeth all understanding, shall keep your hearts and minds through Christ Jesus" . . . .

Suddenly I realized the missing ingredient in my prayers had been "with thanksgiving." So I put down my Bible and spent time worshipping Him for who and what He is. This covers more territory than any one mortal can comprehend. Even contemplating what little we do know dissolves doubts, reinforces faith and restores joy.

I began to thank God for giving me this one I love so dearly in the first place. I even thanked Him for the difficult spots which taught me so much.

And do you know what happened? It was as if someone turned on the lights in my mind and heart, and the little fears and worries that had been nibbling away in the darkness like mice and cockroaches hurriedly scuttled for cover.

That was when I learned that worship and worry cannot live in the same heart: they are mutually exclusive (Graham 272-3).

Worship, or praise, is such an integral part of prayer that the two should never really be separated. It is the one act that, more than anything else, will open the floodgates for God to answer your prayers and work dramatically in your life. After you have prayed and done all that you can do, stand by offering praise to God in advance for the answer that is yet to come.

Praise is the physical manifestation of faith. It is your emotional expression of love, gratitude, reverence and adoration to your heavenly Father. It is the speed bump that will arrest your thoughts and enable you to honor God, build your faith and persevere as you wait for an answer.

The power in praise is manifold even though the evidence would seem to be intangible. Praise works in at least six ways.

Praise **P**reoccupies us with God. It draws our focus onto Him and away from ourselves and our problems. Like a telescope, praise enlarges the reality of God, causing everything else to diminish in comparison. By praising Him, we place Him in center stage.

Praise **R**ecognizes His deeds and nature. To worship and praise God is to verbally acknowledge His supreme goodness and His perfect nature. It builds in us a sense of awe at who God is and a sense of thankfulness for all He does for us. As Ms. Graham pointed out, He is much more deserving of our praise than we are even able to comprehend!

> *P*raise is the physical manifestation of faith.

Praise **A**grees with God's perspective. Much of the art of learning to stand is in developing the ability to see situations as God sees them, and then coming into agreement with Him. The act of praising God helps to bring our thoughts in line with His.

Praise **I**nvites the Holy Spirit to work. The Bible says that God inhabits the praises of His people, which means that praise creates the right atmosphere for the Spirit of God to work. I cannot tell you how many times I have seen prayers answered in dramatic ways in the midst of a time of praise and worship.

Praise **S**ilences the enemy. Probably one reason that answers to prayer flow more readily during worship is that praise is to Satan what Raid is to bugs—it makes him sick and drives him away, which opens more doors for divine intervention.

Praise **E**stablishes faith. We tend to believe what we hear coming from our own lips. Our words are so powerful that we can often speak things into being—either positive or negative things. Praising God reaffirms what we know to be true about God, which in turn builds our faith. Professing our adoration and commitment to God sets in concrete our position, enabling us to stand and persevere without being shaken.

From Rags to Riches

The Bible compares praise to an article of clothing, saying that God gives us "a garment of praise instead of a spirit of despair" (Isaiah 61:3). I like this analogy because it underscores that praise is something you "put on" as an act of your will. Praise cannot be worn simultaneously with despair, and praise can be adapted to fit any season in life.

When you get up in the morning, you most likely get dressed whether you feel like it or not. Wearing clothes is not optional. The only choice you have to make is which clothes to put on, and that decision may depend on your mood, the weather and your plans for the day.

In much the same way, we need to adorn ourselves with the garments of praise each day as an act of our will. If we fail to put on praise, we might get caught wearing nothing but the "spirit of despair" which Isaiah talks about. It seems to be the style of attire our human nature gravitates toward!

"So," you might be thinking, "does this mean that every day I have to get up and sing and dance a jig?" Of course not. Luckily, praise garments come in all shapes, sizes and styles, and they can be tailored to fit any season of life. Some days you might put on praise that is bright and loud, while other days might call for something quieter and more conservative. The Bible indicates that you have a multi-faceted, colorful wardrobe from which to choose. In fact, I think various kinds of praise might be described according to the cycles or seasons that we all encounter in life: summer, fall, winter and spring.

Summer Praise

The season of summer is a time of constancy and routine. It is a period of little change, when life tumbles along on a fairly even keel. But even when you have no victories to celebrate and no crises to handle, it is important to look your spiritual best every day by putting on the garment of praise.

The old French word for praise is "preiser," which means "to prize." When you truly prize something, you cherish it all the time, not just on certain occasions. It is a treasure that you value simply because of its intrinsic worth. By "prizing" God, you value, esteem and cherish Him all the time because of what He means to you. He is not just the God of excitement and miracles —He is a friend at all times, faithful even in the minute details of every day life. During these long days of summer, you can praise God for who He is and for His nature. This is the time to seek Him

> ⟨*P*⟩**raise garments come in all shapes, sizes and styles, and they can be tailored to fit any season of life.**

and praise Him for His face and not just His hand. Dick Eastman, noted author on personal prayer, reminds us to praise God for His name (Psalm 115:1), His righteousness (Psalm 35:28), His infinite creation (Psalm 150:2) and His Word (Psalm 56:10) (Eastman).

"Prize" God in the midst of the mundane. "Prize" Him as you drive to work, get the kids ready for school, fix dinner or take out the garbage. Acknowledge all of His divine traits and tell Him that you love Him. Just as in any relationship, highs and lows may draw you closer to God, but it is the daily, consistent affirmation of what He means to you that gives your relationship with God depth and strength.

The Lord is compassionate and gracious,
Slow to anger, abounding in love.
He will not always accuse,
Nor will he harbor his anger forever;

He does not treat us as our sins deserve
Or repay us according to our iniquities.
As a father has compassion on his children,
So the Lord has compassion on those who fear him. . . .
But from everlasting to everlasting
The Lord's love is with those who fear him,
And his righteousness with their children's children . . .
(Psalm 103:8–10, 13, 17).

Praise the Lord, O my soul.
O Lord my God, you are very great;
You are clothed with splendor and majesty (Psalm 104:1).

Fall Praise

Fall is a time of transition in your life when you are breaking new ground or coming into new territory. Changes—even happy ones such as marriage, birth, graduation or a new job—can create stress and uncertainty. With the harvest often come additional responsibilities and increased challenges. The garments of praise best suited for this season are those of thanksgiving and gratitude for God's abundant provision.

The attire of appreciation should really be our uniform. We should wear it often to honor God for all He has given us and done for us. The Hebrew words in the Bible used to describe this kind of praise are "shabach" and "yadah" which mean to be verbal about our blessings. We are to break the sound barrier and declare to God His wonderful bounty. The Hebrew words also indicate that we are to use our hands to signify praise and worship. Declaring praise and thanksgiving to God enables us to stand in prayer by keeping us ever mindful of how our heavenly Father has been faithful to meet our needs.

Shout for joy to the Lord, all the earth.
Worship the Lord with gladness;
Come before him with joyful songs.
Know that the Lord is God.

It is he who made us, and we are his;
We are his people, the sheep of his pasture.
Enter his gates with thanksgiving
And his courts with praise;
Give thanks to him and praise his name.
For the Lord is good and his love endures forever;
His faithfulness continues through all generations
(Psalm 100).

Winter Praise

The winter season is the hardest time of life to praise because it is the time when things look bleak or discouraging. You may be struggling with a difficult relationship, financial problems or physical illness. You may be depressed and emotionally drained. It is in these times that you probably feel anything but joyful, maybe having to muster up courage just to get out of bed in the morning!

But the Bible talks about a form of praise that is appropriate to put on during such hard times. Hebrews 13:15 says, "Through Jesus, therefore, let us continually offer to God a *sacrifice* of praise . . . ," indicating that at times, praising God may require a good bit of effort on your part; it will not always just flow right out of your being. A sacrifice costs something. When you are weary from the onslaught of life, you may have a hard time saying anything nice about anyone, including God! Be assured, you are not alone.

However, as things in the spiritual realm go, winter praise is probably the most powerful and essential form of praise to your overall well-being because, as Isaiah pointed out, the garments of praise simply cannot be worn at the same time as the spirit of despair. When you are at the end of your rope and you feel yourself slipping down into the abyss of desperation, the most miraculous, mysterious, momentum-changing thing you can do is to go into your prayer closet and shout to the Lord! Declare His majesty and power and claim His victory. Praise Him for what you cannot see or feel. The very fact that it goes against every desire of your flesh at that moment should tell you that it is the key to spiritual victory.

One of the biblical words used to describe praise is "barak," which means to kneel and bless. Sometimes the simple act of kneeling can be a form of praise when you are too burdened to sing and words will not come. Kneeling is a sign of surrender—by kneeling before the Lord you are saying, "I can't handle this one. You take over."

O Lord, hear my prayer,
Listen to my cry for mercy;
In your faithfulness and righteousness
Come to my relief.
The enemy pursues me,
He crushes me to the ground. . . .
So my spirit grows faint within me;
My heart within me is dismayed.
I remember the days of long ago;
I meditate on all your works
And consider what your hands have done.
I spread out my hands to you;
My soul thirsts for you like a parched land
(Psalm 143:1, 3–6).

Spring Praise

More than any other season of life, spring seems to put praise on your lips. It is a time of fresh beginnings, new life, victories and celebrations. The days of spring are filled with joy, excitement and contentment, and it is during these festive times that you probably feel most like singing a song of praise.

The Bible contains several Hebrew words to describe this set of praise garments: "halal" meaning to boast and enjoy, "yadah" meaning to lift the hands, "ruah" meaning to shout to the Lord, and "tehillah" meaning to sing robustly about His achievements. They all describe the exclamatory, gregarious,

Chapter 12: Brake 6: Stand 193

demonstrative sort of worship that you most often see at a sporting event! God likes it when we get excited in His presence. We are emotional creatures and it is this style of praise that appeals to our need to release our emotions to God. Springtime praise may even include a dance offered to the Father.

> *Praise the Lord.*
> *Praise God in his sanctuary;*
> *Praise him in his mighty heavens.*
> *Praise him for his acts of power;*
> *Praise him for his surpassing greatness.*
> *Praise him with the sounding of the trumpet,*
> *Praise him with the harp and lyre,*
> *Praise him with tambourine and dancing,*
> *Praise him with the strings and flute,*
> *Praise him with the clash of cymbals,*
> *Praise him with resounding cymbals.*
> *Let everything that has breath praise the Lord.*
> *Praise the Lord (Psalm 150).*

Putting on these various garments of praise will help you to stand in prayer as you wait for the answer. Clothe yourself daily in the beauty and splendor of worship so that you always look your best.

Thank you, God, for making nature so marvelous. Flowers proclaim your majesty with vibrant colors. Trees lift their branches to your glory. Let my life display your splendor and beauty.

—the prayer of a grounds keeper

Chapter 13

*O*WJB?

*I*n the first chapter of this section, we talked about two aspects of the fear of failure in prayer: the fear of saying the wrong thing and the fear of not receiving what you pray for. Both can make prayer seem like a risky endeavor. But remember, things are not always as they seem, especially when God is involved. His expectations and definition of success are different than those of this world.

Often the Christian faith is pitched as some kind of hyper-spiritual experience laced with miracles and supernatural works. However, in reality, it is a minute-by-minute way of life based on radical co-dependence on God. Prayer is the lifeline between us and the One we are designed to exist out of. Excitement and emotion are fine, but they are not the norm. We are designed to live on oxygen, not adrenaline. Sharing daily, intimate time with God through prayer is supernatural and miraculous beyond what we can comprehend.

Overcoming the fear of failure in prayer, then, is a process of taking on God's perspective about the purpose and nature of prayer and then applying some practical speed bumps which will in turn help you put on the brakes. It is an issue of time, not technique. Success in prayer is not measured by how many times you see the hand of God move in response to your petitions, although as you learn to pray in His will you will certainly see His faithfulness time and again. Rather, success in prayer is measured by whether or not you choose to participate. Carving out time to communicate with your Father yields a relationship that has enough value to make the whole venture worthwhile, even if you never ask for or receive a single thing.

WWJB?

Currently, a nationwide campaign is sweeping through bookstores and churches all across the country posing the question, "What would Jesus do?" The initials "WWJD," originally aimed at reaching youth, are being sported by people of all ages on bracelets, t-shirts, caps, socks, necklaces, stationery, Bible covers, bookmarks—literally anything that can be imprinted. The goal of the paraphernalia is to remind wearers to ask themselves in every situation, "What would Jesus do if He were in my shoes right now?" It is a good question to ask.

However, if I had been clever enough to start such a catchy trend, I would like to have posed a slightly different question: "What would Jesus *be?*" After all, does not being precede doing?

Perhaps it is just a matter of semantics, but I believe God is more concerned about who we are than what we do. He underscored the importance of His own being in this conversation with Moses:

> *Moses said to God, "Suppose I go to the Israelites and say to them, 'The God of your fathers has sent me to you,' and they ask me, 'What is his name?' Then what shall I tell them?"*
>
> *God said to Moses, "I AM WHO I AM. This is what you are to say to the Israelites: I AM has sent me to you" (Exodus 3:13-14).*

That is quite a statement if you can wrap your mind around it! It was like God was saying, "All they need to know about me is that I am—not what I have done or what I will do, but who I am. My very being encompasses all there is to know about my nature and authority."

Our actions flow directly out of who we are on the inside; they are an expression of our being and an undeniable reflection of our spiritual level of maturity. The cliché, "Actions speak louder than words," is very true because while we can pay lip

We simply cannot act in a manner that is contradictory to what we are made of — at least not for long.

service to just about anything, we simply cannot act in a manner that is contradictory to what we are made of—at least not for long.

Our ultimate goal in life, as well as in prayer, is Christlikeness (Romans 8:29). If we can become like Jesus, then we will never have to question or contemplate our actions because they will spill out of His Spirit being perfected inside of us. This is the reason we pray. We sit in the presence of God like an apprentice sits before his mentor, watching, listening, questioning and learning everything we can to make us a reflection of Him. We brake for God—getting still, resting, waiting, listening, sitting, journaling—in order to give Him time to mold us and shape us into the image of His Son.

When I think about Christlikeness, I think of a man named Tommy who lies in a V. A. hospital in Texas. Tommy was a Dallas police officer until he was seriously injured in a car accident. The tragedy left him completely paralyzed from the neck down, robbing him of any physical ability to "do" anything. And yet Tommy exemplifies Jesus more than anyone else I know. Lying for years in that hospital, he has committed himself to one thing—prayer. He listens to scripture on tape and he talks to God. The presence of God is so strong in Tommy's motionless world that you can feel it the minute you set foot in his room. Though his wife left him and his children rarely visit him, Tommy never gave up on his life because in prayer, he discovered that Jesus' life could reside in any body, even one that did not work quite right.

For Tommy, the question "What would Jesus do?" might not have much meaning. He can do little to validate his Christian life through actions, but he is one of the finest men I know. Through his hours and hours of prayer, God has stamped him with His impress. Tommy has exchanged his life for the life of Jesus.

This is the blessing that we have in prayer—that we become like Jesus, and out of that fullness, we act accordingly. When we focus on God, He will return our gaze and give us His complete attention.

Myth #5
The main goal of prayer is to get God's attention.

Truth #5
The main goal of prayer is to become like Jesus.

RPM Reduction

Most cars today have a gage on the dash called a tachometer that measures the revolutions per minute (RPMs) of the motor. If you drive an automatic transmission up a steep hill, you will notice that the tachometer will register very low RPMs. While cruising on the highway it will register higher RPMs. And only if you attempt to drive the car well past its limit will you see the RPM needle move into the red area of the tachometer indicating that the engine is in danger of serious damage. The motor can only go so fast.

The changes in RPMs on your tachometer illustrate a relationship between power and speed—the faster the motor turns, the less power it has. Conversely, the slower the pistons move, the more force they are able to exert with each motion. Every engine has an optimum running speed at which power and efficiency meet. This particular point is not located at either end of the tachometer; it is somewhere between the hill and the highway.

When you feel the squeeze of life's demands, when every area of your routine seems to be crying out for more of your time and energy, when you feel stressed by the tyranny of the urgent—stop.

We are put together in much the same way, meant to operate between the hills and the highways of life. Our maximum level of operation is achieved when we rightly balance the demands of today's fast-paced life with times of stillness and solitude. We can exert more power at lower RPMs than we can racing through every day, skirting the edge of the danger zone. Our engines run best when we make good use of our brakes, slowing down enough to make time to pray.

Do not allow Smutface to coerce you into being afraid to pray. He will do all he can, even keep you running, to prevent you from discovering the oasis that is the presence of the Father. When you feel the squeeze of life's demands, when every area of your routine seems to be crying out for more of your time and energy, when you feel stressed by the tyranny of the urgent—stop. With Jesus' robe of righteousness around your shoulders, go to God in prayer. It really is His idea, and He is waiting for you to pick up the phone. He wants to bless you, love on you and impart to you His thoughts and ideas. He is not interested in your technique, just your attention. From where you are seated, you cannot fail.

Dear Jesus,

As I answer phones today, help me to be patient, understanding and helpful. I want to be a good listener like you are. Thank you for giving me the privilege of talking to you any time night or day; help me learn to listen to you, too.

—the prayer of a receptionist

Part 3

Overcoming the Fear of Embarrassment

Chapter 14

Intimidation and the Fear of Embarrassment

One of my favorite stories in the Bible is David and Goliath. It is a story about intimidation, comparison and fear, and a young man, David, who had his eyes focused squarely on God.

David was the youngest of eight brothers, and though he was also probably the smallest in size, he must have been physically attractive because he was described with words like "ruddy," "handsome" and "fine-looking" (1 Samuel 16:12). He was a brave warrior, good communicator and talented musician. A shepherd by trade, he was also a gifted harpist and fighter, recognized widely enough to have earned him a place in King Saul's service as an armor-bearer. Even more significant, however, was the fact that not long before going to work for Saul, David had been secretly anointed by the prophet Samuel as God's chosen one to be the next king over Israel.

King Saul was the leader of the Israelite army and a very successful military commander. In 1 Samuel 17, the Israelite and Philistine armies were faced off across a valley, preparing to fight each other. David's three oldest brothers were among the Israelites under Saul, and though he had to stay home and tend the sheep, David was making regular trips to the camp site to serve Saul and take food for his brothers.

One morning, as David arrived at the battle lines, he saw Goliath, the Philistine champion, step forward from the ranks across the valley. Goliath was huge, over nine feet tall—he would have been worth a mint in the NBA! Just as he had been doing for the last forty days, he taunted the Israelites, challenging them to send out a man to fight him. And just as they had done every time, all the Israelites ran and hid in fear of the giant who towered above them, defying their God. David asked them, "Who is going to take care of this overgrown, arrogant big-mouth who is making fun of us and our God?" But they were all too terrified by his size and his athletic prowess.

So David went to Saul's tent and said, "Haven't we all had enough humiliation? I will fight the giant."

I imagine Saul probably laughed at first, saying, "You're just a kid; he's a trained soldier who has been in the business of killing people since before you were born. You must be joking."

But David had no fear of the Philistine because, as he told Saul, ". . . [T]his uncircumcised Philistine will be like one of them [one of the bears or lions which David had killed], because he has defied the armies of the living God. The Lord who delivered me from the paw of the lion and the paw of the bear will deliver me from the hand of this Philistine" (1 Samuel 17: 36b–37).

With that, Saul had little to do except give David his blessing and his armor. But when David put on Saul's armor, it was too big and heavy, and he could scarcely move. He told Saul, "Thanks, but no thanks. I'm not used to all this heavy metal." David was not interested in trying to be anything other than himself, so he took off the armor and headed toward Goliath with only his shepherd's staff, his sling and five stones.

You know what happened, of course. David hurled the first stone which hit the giant right between the eyes and killed him, causing the Philistines to turn and run. With one shot, David restored some pride to Saul and the Israelite army, saved the nation and catapulted himself into immediate stardom. The people began to sing his praises, saying "Saul has slain his thousands, and David his tens of thousands" (1 Samuel 18:7). Everyone was happy except for Saul, who suddenly felt an overwhelming urge to kill David!

Saul, recognizing that the Lord's favor was with David, became so intimidated by his success and so

> The Israelite soldiers all compared themselves to Goliath and came up short . . . David factored God into the equation.

threatened by his popularity that he had to wrestle with another giant in his heart—jealousy. In fact, Saul's heart became so poisoned with envy toward David that he spent the rest of his life plotting and planning ways to get rid of the young hero. David's victory over Goliath was the beginning of Saul's demise.

This story has in it several interesting elements of comparison. First, the Israelite soldiers all compared themselves to Goliath and came up short, causing them to hide day after day. The Bible says that the difference between them and David was that David factored God into the equation, which the rest of the Israelites failed to do. The entire army looked across that valley, saw the physical size and strength of Goliath, and trembled in fear. They could not see past the surface to recognize the crucial spiritual advantage they had in the situation—that God was on *their* side.

Second, Saul's attempt to dress David in his own armor indicates that some interesting things must have been going through his mind as well. Perhaps he thought he could fool the rest of the soldiers into thinking that he was the one fighting Goliath, since his armor would have covered every part of David's body and would have been easily recognized. Or maybe he just thought David would stand a much better chance in the battle if he tried to be like the person Saul admired most—himself. The idea of David simply being David, relying on his own abilities and resources, was ludicrous.

Finally, as David's popularity skyrocketed because of his heroism, Saul nearly went crazy comparing his own accomplishments and status to those of the young upstart. Although he was a well-respected and decorated soldier in his own right, he lost sight of who he was in the light of David. His jealousy was so strong and his identity crisis so severe that he eventually lost his throne and his life.

The Comparison Trap

We all fall into the comparison trap on occasion. Like the Israelite soldiers, we fail to factor God into our perspective of some task we have been called to, and we feel inadequate. Or we try to wear someone else's "armor" because we do not have confidence in the uniqueness of our own gifts and talents. And often we simply become jealous when our own achievements look small compared to another's. It is hard not to look around and evaluate ourselves according to what seems to be "the norm."

However, when we play the comparison game, we always lose because it is out of line with God's perspective. He sees us as unique individuals whom He has created with a special purpose in mind. We will always be faced with people who make more money, have bigger houses, wear nicer clothes, and achieve more success, which is why the comparison game playing field is quicksand—eventually everyone goes under. When intimidation, jealousy and embarrassment set in, we lose our sense of worth.

The Fear of Embarrassment

The comparison game ignites the third fear that we must overcome in prayer—the fear of embarrassment. Many people are just intimidated about prayer. They feel self-conscious about talking to God because they have heard some television preacher or seasoned intercessor pray eloquently for fifteen minutes without taking a breath, and they think, "I can't do that." They compare themselves to other Christians that they know, and if they do not match skill for skill, or if they seem to have a completely different outlook on the whole process, then they are likely to lose confidence and become convinced that somehow, they have missed the boat altogether.

The purpose of this final section of the book is to help you kick the fear of embarrassment by gaining an appreciation of your own personal prayer identity and the identity of others. Just as God gave you a unique personality and perspective on life, He also created you with propensities and traits that influence how you interpret and participate in prayer. He did not create you to be like everyone else; He created you to fill a vital place in the body of Christ and in your private world. He instilled in you certain interests, insights and passions that make you specially equipped to pray in a specific, meaningful way.

Myth #6

In order for my prayer life to be legitimate, it should look like someone else's.

Truth #6

God created you with a unique prayer temperament to fill a special role in prayer.

A Matter of Perspective

Many things about you, including your past experiences, the spiritual influences in your life, and your personality all somehow blend together, causing you to see life, and prayer, through your own scope. Thus, you may have a very different perspective on prayer than others, even those who are closest to you like your parents, your spouse or your friends. You no doubt have likes and dislikes about style and manner of praying, and there are probably some aspects of prayer that you feel very comfortable with and others that make you squirm. These preferences are not a result of some spiritual deficiency or irregularity—more than likely, they are a result of your prayer temperament. Your prayer temperament might be defined as your unique combination of traits and tendencies that determine how you view God and engage in prayer.

> These preferences are not a result of some spiritual deficiency or irregularity—more than likely, they are a result of your prayer temperament.

One reason that prayer can be difficult to study is that it is intangible; it is not something you can actually see or put your hands on. So, I would like to explain prayer in light of something that is tangible—a river.

Picture a river in your mind. What does it look like? Is it deep or shallow? Is it rushing swiftly or trickling gently? What about the bank? Is it rocky or green? Steep or flat? What else do you see along the river? Are there people playing in the water? Is there a hydroelectric plant nearby? If I were to ask you, "What is the best thing about rivers?" you might answer in one of several different ways, depending on your perspective.

Rivers Are Connected

They bond us geographically and historically to other people, giving us a place in the bigger picture of life. Year after year, they pour out of their headwaters and flow across vast regions of land, eventually tumbling back into the ocean to cycle again. Rich in history, rivers have a long and established past, speckled with important events that have shaped our nation.

Rivers Are Now

They are exciting and playful, meant to be enjoyed minute by minute. Their past and their future is not important—all that really matters is the pleasure they can provide in the present moment. They offer an unlimited supply of recreation and refreshment for people all up and down their banks. Perfect for swimming, fishing, floating or boating, rivers are fun—one of nature's best sources of entertainment. At any given time, hundreds of people could be experiencing the same river.

Rivers Are Life Giving

They infuse everything they touch with energy and vitality. They provide essential nutrients and water for plants and trees along their banks, drawing people to settle along their edges because of their effervescence. Civilization seems to prosper in relation to rivers, which provide much needed transportation for people and products.

Rivers Are Mysterious

Sometimes hidden under the earth's surface, and sometimes flowing on top, they are incomprehensible and esoteric. What lies beneath them is unknown. At their deepest parts, they hide treasures not yet discovered and profound puzzles not yet revealed. We can never completely understand what makes a river flow fast and then slow, wide and then narrow. We can never grasp how a tiny stream of water could cut a canyon of immense size and beauty. They are, by nature, mystifying.

Rivers Are Cleansing

Always flowing downstream, rivers are nature's own waste removal system. They eliminate contaminants from the earth and carry them into the ocean. The rushing water of mountain streams can be abrasive, smoothing and refining stones as it continually rubs against their jagged surfaces. Rivers have no discretion—they confront everything in their path, carrying away anything which is not secured.

Rivers Are Unpredictable

Twisting and turning at will, they cut a path across the land that is distinct at every point. Rivers are always dynamic, never static, changing constantly as the water flows. Even the same spot along a river's edge is made new moment by moment as the water runs continually through it. Rivers have the potential to be destructive without warning when they spill over their banks and run wild where they are not supposed to be.

Rivers Are Manageable

They have great power that needs to be harnessed to create energy and do work. They can be very productive if the right strategy is applied and implemented. Constant and ever-present, rivers create natural boundaries and geographical divisions that define who we are and where we live. They are one of nature's finest resources.

Although each of these viewpoints is different in its approach, none of them is wrong. They all hold valuable insights that have unique benefits and strengths. Imagine how silly it would seem to limit your understanding of rivers to just one particular perspective, discounting all the rest as invalid. Yet when it comes to prayer, that is exactly what we often do— define the whole journey according to our limited view from whatever square foot of ground we happen to be standing on at the time.

The River of Prayer

Prayer is like a river that flows out from God through time and space, ever changing yet always the same. It has force because it is energized by the Holy Spirit and it has power because the very life of God flows through it. Prayer affects everything it touches with life and refreshment, and it will certainly alter every situation through which it moves.

When you pray, you step into that river and it begins to flow in you. Jesus said, "Whoever believes in me, as the Scripture has said, streams of living water will flow from within him" (John 7:38). God wants His life to rush into you and move through you to others (John 10:10). He sent His son to demonstrate the life of God in the form of a person and then gave the Holy Spirit to energize and empower the river to flow in us (John 7:39; Romans 8:26). The river of prayer surges from the Father by His Spirit to us and then back to the Son to accomplish His will.

Just as there are seven different ways to view a natural river, there are also seven different ways to view this river of prayer. I call them prayer temperaments because they describe a person's inclination to experience prayer in a certain way. Each one has its own unique purpose and benefits, and all of them hold essential pieces to the complete picture of prayer.

Temperament of Tradition

The river of prayer is connected. Through prayer, the life of God has flowed from its headwaters through time and history. The big picture of personal and corporate prayer, and how they have affected individuals and nations, is vital information. Knowing about significant events in our past and how prayer played a part in getting us to where we are now will enable us to pray effectively today.

Temperament of Immediacy

The river of prayer is now. God is able and willing to help and bless us if only we will ask. Prayer is most effective when it is "on sight with insight," reaching out to the immediate, felt needs of all those around us. We must always be ready to pray at any time and any place so that God can pour out His refreshment and comfort in day-to-day situations.

Temperament of Love

The river of prayer is life-giving. It is the source through which the love and mercy of God flow. Deeply relational, prayer touches the heart of those who are hurting with the salve of God's grace and unconditional acceptance. The most meaningful expression of prayer is the act of intercession when we stand in the gap for those who are lost and plead their cases before the Father until His purpose is fulfilled in their lives.

> *Through the profound act of prayer, we can experience His presence and exalt Him for His majesty.*

Temperament of Mystery

The river of prayer is mysterious. To be able to communicate with the Creator of the universe despite our human condition is beyond comprehension. The being of God is so awesome and vast that it compels us to meditate on His nature and His works. Through the profound act of prayer, we can experience His presence and exalt Him for His majesty.

Temperament of Confrontation

The river of prayer is cleansing. God's desire is that evil should be evicted and sin washed away. Satan is a dangerous foe with whom we must contend. Through prayer, we have the power and authority to enforce the rule and reign of Jesus in the earth, setting captives free and establishing holiness.

It is our mighty weapon of war against the principalities of darkness.

Temperament of Perception

The river of prayer is unpredictable. The life and deeds of God are new every morning, and in prayer, we must seek to know His direction to stay on course. As we spend time with Him, He will reveal Himself to us through visions and dreams so that we may always be in line with what He is accomplishing. Prayer sometimes causes contention because it stirs up bold ideas and challenges the status quo.

Temperament of Order

The river of prayer is manageable. The key to effective prayer is consistency and planning. Implementing proven methods and organizing resources yields maximum fruitfulness because it promotes longevity in personal or corporate prayer. We must work to establish good prayer habits and organize prayer for the long term. Prayer without discipline will be emotionally driven and short-lived.

I always cringe a little when I hear someone say, "Prayer is a gift," because I think that statement is dangerously incomplete and misleading. If prayer is a gift, then it is given to everyone who calls on the name of Jesus. In the army of prayer, there are no ranks—only the enlisted. God did not give the privilege of prayer only to a certain group of people while leaving out others. He gave each of His children the same ability to talk to Him and hear from Him. Although some may pray with more eloquence, they do not pray better. While some may pray with more experience, they are not superior. And though some may attain more knowledge, they are not more important. The field of prayer is level ground, each one bringing his own needs to the Father and each one receiving the same consideration.

All of the prayer temperaments are given by God to enrich the body of Christ and bring personal fulfillment to our individual relationships with Him. Prayer is not the gift—the gift is our particular profile that makes us who we are in prayer and equips us to be a part of the big picture.

Each of the following seven chapters describes one of the prayer temperaments in detail. In each one, you will find these five headings:

1. **View of God.**   As I mentioned in the first section of this book, how we pray depends greatly on how we view God. The image we have in our minds of His nature determines how we approach Him and relate to Him. He is so magnanimous, and His character is so far beyond our comprehension, that most of us, whether we realize it or not, put Him in a box of some kind simply so we can grasp in some minute way who He is. We pick one aspect of His character—He has many—and we identify with it, defining Him according to that role which we find easiest to understand.

2. **Prayer Profile.**   Out of our personal understanding of God will flow our prayer life—tendencies and patterns of behavior that visibly demonstrate how we relate to our Father. We develop likes and dislikes, strengths and weaknesses, "hot and cold buttons." This profile describes what each temperament looks like from the outside and answers such questions as: What motivates this temperament to pray? Where do they like to pray best? In what manner and for how long? What type of language do they use to talk to God? What do they generally pray about?

3. **Biblical Models.**   All of the temperaments are demonstrated in the Bible by various characters. This section identifies a few examples in each temperament and illustrates that particular perspective in action.

4. **Benefits.**   One of the primary reasons for you to understand prayer temperaments, in addition to overcoming your own insecurities about how you pray, is to gain an apprecia-

tion for the way God created us as His children to work together and complement each other in the journey of prayer. None of the temperaments were intended to work in a bubble, isolated from all the others. They all have strengths and weaknesses, and they are made to work in complete harmony within the body of Christ as a whole. In any group setting such as a family, a small group, a church or a city, failure to at least acknowledge and accept other temperaments as valid will produce schism and division. Unless you have a clear picture of the way the puzzle pieces interlock, it is easy to judge others and even fear aspects of prayer that are outside your realm of comprehension.

5. **Primary Purpose and Contemporary Expressions.** Ultimately, each of the prayer temperaments has one primary purpose, one main tributary that it is most suited to fill. Not by coincidence, many of the current prayer emphases that have developed into worldwide movements are basically nothing more than corporate expressions of these seven temperaments on a really large scale. These movements have formed as people have gravitated toward others who share their same temperament, and as a group, they have devised creative ways to do what they do best.

As you begin to spend more time with God, claiming your righteousness in Jesus and applying the brakes, you will find that one or two of these temperaments will rise up in you and dominate your prayer time. You may begin to notice the various temperaments being expressed in others around you in a whole variety of ways. Rather than comparing yourself to them, you can encourage their strengths while looking for ways to partner with them. Be who you are, and thank God for who they are.

Before we examine each of the temperaments more closely, let me point out one more word of caution. The purpose of understanding the temperaments is to free you to be yourself and appreciate others. They are not meant to define or confine you in such a way that you are limited to a certain area of prayer and not challenged to grow.

As we will discuss more at the end of this section, all of the temperaments flow in the same river—the river that originates with God, was demonstrated by the Son and is carried by the Holy Spirit. Although one or two temperaments probably dominate your prayer life, at appropriate times, you may operate in any or all of them. Though you may feel uncomfortable with certain styles of prayer, the Holy Spirit certainly does not. As the initiator of all prayer, He can help you stretch out of your comfort zone and learn to pray in new and exciting ways. With His assistance, you can exercise your spiritual muscles by experimenting with prayer that seems to go against the natural tendencies of your personality. If you are willing to risk some initial discomfort, you can grow in prayer and enjoy all the fullness and variety the river has to offer.

God, each morning when I walk into my classroom, I feel the weight of the awesome responsibility I have to shape the minds and characters of young people. As the Master Teacher, help me fulfill my role. Enable me to impart more than just facts.

—the prayer of a teacher

Chapter 15

The Temperament of Tradition

Not long ago, I was taking care of some business and visiting a friend in a small town in southern Indiana called French Lick. Named, as I was told, for the natural salt blocks that used to attract horseback travelers, French Lick was a premiere vacation site for the wealthy in the roaring twenties, thanks to the railroad that ran through it and a couple of ostentatious resorts. One of these resorts, called the West Baden Spring Hotel, which sits on hundreds of acres of land including several golf courses and elaborately designed gardens, has been taken over by the historical society and is now undergoing major renovations to re-open it to the public.

Intrigued by the hotel's mammoth size and unique features, I paid the ten dollar ticket fee to take a guided tour. To my surprise, what I saw on the inside of that structure was worth every penny I spent to see it.

The architecture was phenomenal, especially considering that the building was erected almost one hundred years ago. The combination of intricate detail, beautifully hand-painted murals and immense size made the dormant hotel mysteriously breathtaking. I had a hard time taking it all in. The most spectacular part of the building, however, was the enormous domed atrium which had been the center of activity when the resort was in its prime. Our guide told us it was the largest unsupported dome of its kind in the country and that despite several extensive tests, the renovators could find no structural weakness in it at all. Encircled by rooms stacked five stories high, the dome stood, as it has for many decades, a silent testimony to the original architect's incredible vision and skill.

> *A*lways seeking to pray with the big picture in mind, these people have a high interest in the spiritual history of places and events . . .

View of God – A Master Architect

Those who pray in the tradition temperament see God as a master architect, creator and designer of the universe and everything in it. Just as each mosaic tile, each support beam and each stained glass window of that historical landmark in French Lick was included in the architect's original building plans, every person and every circumstance, as seen through the eyes of the traditionalist, is part of God's overall design. He is the architect of life, and He works in the earth through His children to bring all things in line with His grand scheme.

Genesis 4:26, ". . . at that time men began to call on the name of the Lord," marks the headwaters of prayer, and since then it has flowed through history and time. For these pray-ers, God has created and is creating, and His purpose for prayer is to reveal to us the destiny He has in mind for every person. What we see as one piece of the puzzle, He sees as critical to the completion of His plan. He does not make mistakes or produce accidents, but fashions every one of His children with a future in mind. His desire is to see us fulfill that future, and all of His deeds are directed toward that end.

Prayer Profile

Because of this view of God, those who are strong in this temperament approach prayer primarily as a means of mediating the Master Architect's design in the earth. They stand between God and man, in a priestly sense, ready to help convey and bring about His purpose in every situation. As mediators, they pray to implement and safeguard the plans of our Heavenly Father. They pray from God's perspective to birth His destiny among His people. They love nothing more than to hear from God regarding His intent for a situation. Always seeking to pray with the big picture in mind, these people have a high interest in the spiritual history of places and events, and they are always hungry for information. You are much more likely to find someone of this temperament in the local public library than conducting a door to door evangelism campaign. They love to get to the bottom of spiritual questions.

As their name might suggest, this temperament also seems to gravitate toward more traditional forms of prayer in long-established patterns. Those who pray from this perspective probably prefer to pray within the confines of a church building or other conventional locale. Their style might be described as conservative, since their approach may be grounded in the ways and methods set down by those who have prayed before them. They may recite written prayers, litanies and liturgies. They show a high interest in sanctioned times of prayer that are well organized and based on reliable research. At times, they may even be accused of being too academic or indifferent simply because they take the whole matter of prayer very seriously and will not jump into a prayer experience without first seeking background information.

The traditionalists' prayer language is characterized by repentance because they feel a need to take responsibility for the sins of the past in order to position themselves and God's people in a place where they are ready to receive. Their prayers of mediation often identify circumstances or occurrences which have grieved God and prevented His purpose from being accomplished. In response, they will seek forgiveness on behalf of those who were wrong in order to facilitate healing and restoration. This process of identifying with sins of the past is called "identificational repentance," and it is one of the hallmarks of the traditional temperament.

Another distinction of traditionalists' prayer language is their emphasis on the hundreds of promises of God and His faithfulness to uphold them. Because they know the Father has kept His word time and again in the past, they hold tight to the Word as it applies to everything from family life to finances, healing to eternal life, wisdom to victory over crises. They love to pray the scriptures, especially those which contain the prayers offered to God by saints of old. They have a high expectation for prayers to be answered because they see each answer as simply another step toward the completion of the ultimate structure—like mortar in the bricks. God is a covenant God who has made the way for us to enjoy a covenant relationship with Him.

Also, since they relate so strongly to the faithfulness of God and have a strong awareness of His past deeds, these history-lovers tend to be a thankful bunch. Their style of praise and worship flows from hearts of gratitude for all God has accomplished. They glorify Him for His provision and honor Him for His goodness. Psalms such as 100, 102, and 106 reflect their attitude of appreciation, as in this passage:

Praise the Lord.
Give thanks to the Lord, for he is good;
His love endures forever.

> *Who can proclaim the mighty acts of the Lord or fully declare his*
> *praise?*
> *We have sinned, even as our fathers did;*
> *We have done wrong and acted wickedly.*
> *When our fathers were in Egypt, they gave no thought to your*
> *miracles;*
> *They did not remember your many kindnesses,*
> *And they rebelled by the sea, the Red Sea.*
> *Yet he saved them for his name's sake,*
> *To make his mighty power known (Psalm 106:1-2, 6–8).*

Finally, to the traditionalists, church history has significance in prayer because it chronicles the workings of the Master Architect to bring about His plans throughout time. History demonstrates cycles and patterns and depicts real examples that can act as models for solving problems today. Those praying in this temperament might be inclined to pray out of Old Testament passages which illustrate the interaction of God with His people. They will frequently underscore the sovereignty of the Creator and His ultimate control over all events, and they will pray with a sense of history and truth, always hoping to avoid the mistakes of their forefathers and see the kingdom agenda become a reality.

Biblical Models

Matthew, one of Jesus' twelve disciples and writer of the first gospel in the New Testament, as well as Nehemiah, an old Testament prophet, and Mary, the mother of Jesus all prayed in significant ways from the traditional temperament.

As I read the book of Matthew, two characteristics in particular lead me to believe that Matthew's perspective, as he described Jesus' ministry on earth, was in the traditional temperament of prayer. First, Matthew started his account by listing Jesus' genealogy. The first seventeen verses of the book record forty-two generations beginning with Abraham and ending with the birth of Christ. In some sense, Matthew saw the lineage of the Savior as foundational to gaining complete understanding of His life and works. But more convincing is Matthew's frequent references to Old Testament prophecies. At least thirteen times, Matthew specifically notes that something took place in order to fulfill what had been prophesied (1:22; 2:5, 15, 17, 23; 3:3; 4:14; 5:12; 8:17; 12:17; 13:14, 35; 21:4). He saw Jesus' works in the light of a covenant relationship, and he had an obvious awareness of how current events were connected to the past.

> ℐf Nehemiah drank without keeling over, then the wine was safe for the king to consume.

Nehemiah had an interesting profession—he was a wine taster for the king of Egypt. Not the kind that swirls wine delicately around the bottom of a goblet, inhaling the aroma and evaluating the flavor; no, Nehemiah's job was not that glamorous. A trusted servant in the royal court, he had the austere privilege of sampling the king's wine to make sure it was not poisoned. If Nehemiah drank without keeling over, then the wine was safe for the king to consume. While his position in the court was actually considered quite an honor, I imagine he had a difficult time acquiring good life insurance.

This man, Nehemiah, demonstrated the traditional temperament of prayer when he learned from one of his brothers that his hometown, Jerusalem, was in trouble. The city wall was broken down, the gates were burned and the people were disgraced. Its purpose as the city of God, where the national temple was located, was in jeopardy. Look at how Nehemiah prayed:

> *O Lord, God of heaven, the great and awesome God, who keeps his covenant of love with those who love him and obey his commands, let your ear be attentive and your eyes open to*

hear the prayer your servant is praying before you day and night for your servants, the people of Israel. I confess the sins we Israelites, including myself and my father's house, have committed against you. We have acted very wickedly toward you. We have not obeyed the commands, decrees and laws you gave your servant Moses.

Remember the instruction you gave your servant Moses, saying, "If you are unfaithful, I will scatter you among the nations, but if you return to me and obey my commands, then even if your exiled people are at the farthest horizon, I will gather them from there and bring them to the place I have chosen as a dwelling for my Name."

They are your servants and your people, whom you redeemed by your great strength and your mighty hand. O Lord, let your ear be attentive to the prayer of this your servant and to the prayer of your servants who delight in revering your name. Give your servant success today by granting him favor in the presence of this man (Nehemiah 1:5–11).

Notice in this short but passionate prayer that Nehemiah hit three of the telltale characteristics of the traditional temperament. First, he practiced identificational repentance when he confessed the sins "we Israelites, including myself" had committed. He identified himself with the transgressions of the group, and admitted that as a people, they had offended God. Next, he reminded God of a promise He made to Moses because he believed God would carry out His promises. And third, He illuminated the deeds of God by emphasizing how God had redeemed them by His "great strength" and "mighty hand."

Nehemiah prayed out of the past to affect the future. He knew God had a purpose for Jerusalem and he acted as a mediator to implement and safeguard that purpose so that it could be fully accomplished. Not only did Nehemiah see God as the Master Architect, he went so far as to become the general contractor to get the job done! God heard his prayer and sent him home to Jerusalem to help repair the city.

Another Bible hero who exemplified this temperament was
Mary, the mother of Jesus. While still only engaged to be married to Joseph, Mary received a visit from the angel Gabriel
who told her that she had been chosen to give birth to the
Savior, the Son of God. Such an announcement might well
have caused most women to react with disbelief, fear or even
anger. But Mary, in complete humility and honesty, simply said,
"How will this be since I am a virgin?" And when Gabriel explained to her that the Holy Spirit would "come upon" her and
"overshadow" her (this was supposed to be comforting?), she
responded by saying, "I am the Lord's servant. May it be to me
as you have said."

The promise of such a Savior to be born into the world had
been in place for a long time. Mary accepted the Word in prayer
and became pregnant with God—not just pregnant with a child
but pregnant with His divine purpose and destiny for all of mankind! She became a mediator par excellence between God and
the man, Christ Jesus. She submitted herself and her own plans
in order to birth the greatest promise that was ever written.
Even the song of praise she sang after receiving the angel's
news heralded the faithfulness of God and His promise to save
the generations (Luke 1:46–55).

Benefits

I was watching a football game on television recently when
one of the announcers made some profound observation like,
"Wow! The last time a team with an animal for a mascot and a
left handed quarterback came from behind to win by more than
ten points in overtime on a Monday night in the rain was in
1967 when the. . . ." (Where do they get that stuff, anyway?) It
seems to be their passion—to put every play in perspective
against the backdrop of football history, to somehow connect
the current game and the players with past games and players.
Sixty-three home runs in a single baseball season is only meaningful because someone before hit sixty-two. Sports trivia, even

when it seems truly trivial, gives us a greater appreciation for any game by reminding us of the bigger picture.

The traditional temperament brings to the body of Christ this same kind of enhanced appreciation because of its perspective. By placing issues and circumstances against the backdrop of our spiritual history, this approach to prayer builds truth upon truth, always looking for a link to the past—always connecting the desires of God now with the deeds of God then. This line of thinking has several benefits:

1. **It keeps us rooted in history.** Our heritage as children of God is just as important as our heritage as a nation or as important as your family heritage is to you personally. History can be our greatest teacher if only we preserve and allow it to speak to us. To pray with a sense of history is to touch the themes of God's faithfulness over time.

2. **It acts as a guard rail to keep us from being sidetracked by fads or trends.** Since this temperament is generally cautious and informed, it is not easily swayed from the Architect's master plan by emotional events or crises. It will abandon the tried and tested ways of our forefathers only when God's purpose demands it.

3. **It prevents us from becoming too self-aggrandizing because it is connected to the greater purpose of God.** While many of us are tempted to pray only when we have a desperate need, this temperament prays out of a magnanimous vision of destiny. Therefore, it is not inclined to overestimate our importance in God's economy. Because it discerns the bigger picture, it promotes humility and a sense of honor in response to the opportunity to participate in the eternal sequence of events.

4. **It reinforces our corporate identity, policing our urge to "point the finger."** Since we are all part of one body of believers, representing only a minute section of the time line of history, we cannot ignore sins of our forefathers and pretend they have no bearing on societal ills today. This tem-

perament exhorts us to take responsibility for repairing situations around us in which God's intent has been preempted by sin, regardless of when the wrong was committed. The sins of racism that occurred decades ago grieved the heart of God, and to imagine that He does not hold us, the heirs of that estate, accountable for our inheritance is spiritually naïve.

5. **It focuses on God's agenda.** This school of prayer is God-centered and God-driven. The needs and desires of man do not dominate here. Their heart cry is, "Thy will be done on earth as it is in heaven."

Primary Purpose and Contemporary Expressions

The primary purpose of the temperament of tradition is to see God's plan fulfilled in lives, cities and nations. Isaiah describes well the nature of God that sparks these people to mediate His purpose:

Remember this, fix it in mind, take it to heart, you rebels.
Remember the former things, those of long ago;
I am God, and there is no other;
I am God, and there is none like me.
I make known the end from the beginning, from ancient times,
*   what is still to come.*
I say: My purpose will stand, and I will do all that I please.
From the east I summon a bird of prey; from a far-off land,
*   a man to fulfill my purpose.*
What I have said, that will I bring about; what I have planned,
*   that will I do (Isaiah 46:8–11).*

While identificational repentance is not the final destination of this school of prayer, it is the most visible sign of this temperament in action. Healing the past is like leveling the ground before you build—it must be done before the Master Architect can go to work. Even foundational defects unseen below the surface can eventually cause major structural damage to the building above it. The traditionalist knows that for God to move, the way must be made clear.

The person I consider the birth father of the reconciliation movement is a man by the name of John Dawson, who authored the book *Healing America's Wounds* in 1994. Since this book came out, and because of its message, many have taken it upon themselves to dig into the history of their town or region and identify events and attitudes that have hindered the fulfillment of God's sovereign destiny. *Healing America's Wounds* was the first book to really address the issues of corporate repentance of past

> *A* small, racially diverse town, Marion was the site of the last lynching in America.

sins, calling Christians to deal with the abuses of racism toward African Americans, Native Americans, Hispanics, Jews, women, Catholics and other ethnic people groups that were mistreated in the formation and development of this country. Today, John Dawson conducts city-wide and even world-wide services of reconciliation, and has inspired many others who feel the passion of this prayer temperament to start International Reconciliation Fellowships all over the country.

Not long ago following a prayer conference in Marion, Indiana, I had an opportunity to lead a brief, impromptu reconciliation service myself. A small, racially diverse town, Marion was the site of the last lynching in America. The people there relayed to me the all too familiar story of how several white men, in the late 1930's, had abducted two African-American prisoners from their second-story jail cell, dragged them across the street to the county courthouse lawn, and murdered them by hanging. Regrettably, even though everyone knew about the crime, nothing had ever been done to bring about healing.

Interestingly, there were two men at the conference that day who had both been touched by the legacy of the lynching—one was a young black pastor, a direct descendant of one of the men who was hanged; the other was an elderly white man who had witnessed the event as a small boy. It seemed that the stage was set for an act of repentance on behalf of those who had committed the act, as well as those who just stood and watched.

At the end of the day, several of us, including the two men, gathered at the courthouse where the grievous act had taken place. We anointed the ground with oil. There, in the shadow of the victims' jail cell, our little band of white people, led by the man who still had a memory of that day, stood before a group of African-Americans and prayed. We claimed the sin as our own, handed down by our forefathers, and asked to be forgiven. In turn, the black descendant spoke forgiveness and healing through the grace and power of Jesus' name, and together we sang a song of praise. This was the traditional temperament at its best. Incidentally, since then, Marion elected an African-American sheriff—the first in the county's history.

Another demonstration of this school of prayer—one of the largest and most publicized—occurred earlier this year (1998) when 1.5 million men knelt on the mall in Washington D.C. and together owned and sought forgiveness for the abuse of women and blacks in America. The prayer meeting, sponsored by Promise Keepers, was called "Stand in the Gap," and it represented a very significant movement that is calling men to become mediators of God's purpose for marriages and families today.

In fact, the whole Promise Keepers movement was birthed through a coach named Bill McCartney who heard God through this traditional temperament of prayer. Recognizing that God's plan for men as spiritual leaders, protectors and role models was in jeopardy, Coach McCartney received a vision for an organization that would challenge men to fulfill God's original design. The result is a nationwide Christian brotherhood that encourages men by upholding all values which could be summed up in a single word—Christlikeness.

When true corporate repentance happens, healing may not come all at once, but the door swings open for the love and mercy of Jesus to flow. God can heal even the deepest of wounds when someone steps forward to stand in the gap, because He is fully "able to do immeasurably more than all we ask or imagine, according to his power that is at work within us . . ." (Ephesians 3:20).

Dear God,

    My grandpa says you were around when he was a little boy. How far back do you go?

                                      Love, Dennis

(Hample and Marshall)

Chapter 16

The Temperament of Immediacy

Years ago, a rather unbelievable thing happened on a Sunday morning at our church that forever impressed upon me the true desire of our Abba Father to meet even the most trivial needs of His children, especially those who are lost. In fact, it was so unbelievable that I hesitate to write it for fear it might damage what credibility I have left.

At any rate, a lady named Marci, who proclaimed to be an atheist, visited our church with a friend. She sat in the back, responding very little to anything that happened during the service. Now because I taught often on prayer and always made it an integral part of everything we did, many of my regular members were trained to pray for people in spontaneous ways. So at the end of church that morning, a woman named Shirley greeted Marci to thank her for coming and then asked her if she could pray with her about anything.

Marci thought for a moment, and then admitted, "I don't really believe in that stuff."

"That's OK," Shirley said. "I do, and I'll be the one praying. Are you sure there isn't anything?"

"Well, this is pretty silly, but my dog ran away, and I'd really like to find him. He's been with me for a long time. I suppose you could pray for that."

Without batting an eye, Shirley prayed a short prayer for Marci's dog before they both filed out of the sanctuary to go home.

> **Without batting an eye, Shirley prayed a short prayer for Marci's dog before they both filed out of the sanctuary to go home.**

About fifteen minutes later, I heard an unusual commotion in the parking lot and saw a group of people assembled around a car. My mind ran ahead of me as I went to see what was going on, "Injury . . . church property . . . lawsuit." Pastors are real people, and we occasionally think really stupid things. But when I got to the scene, I found a dog, a blue Porsche and a teary-eyed *former* atheist. It seems that when Marci went to her car, she found her lost companion, tail wagging, waiting for her in the passenger seat. She was stunned. Although she admitted to having left her car windows down, she could not imagine how her dog could have even begun to find his way to our church parking lot, much less her car, since her home was several miles away! She was utterly amazed to discover that not only was God real, but He actually cared enough about her to bring home her missing pet.

View of God – An Able Provider

To those who pray in the temperament of immediacy, God is an able provider, ready and willing to meet the needs of His children. He is in the business of giving and healing in answer to prayer, because He wants to make real to us His love and compassion. He is "Jehovah Jireh," meaning "the provider" (Genesis 22:14), and He is called "the breasted one" (Genesis 49:24–25) because He cares for us as a mother cares for her newborn baby. He is good in every way, the giver of all good things, and He is interested and involved in our lives, even to the smallest detail.

These pray-ers identify strongly with that part of the nature of God that parted the Red Sea, commanded the universe, rent the veil and caused the bush to burn. The man Christ Jesus was God in the flesh walking on earth to give sight to the blind, food to the hungry, peace to the troubled and life to the dying. He is the answer to every problem right now. Immediacy people pray to a miracle-working God who is the same today as He was yesterday and will be forever more.

Prayer Profile

Those who pray in this temperament are especially good at becoming conduits of God's grace and provision—bridges between the hope of heaven and a hurting world. With one hand on a need and the other outstretched to the Father, they love to be the connecting wire through which His power flows. They are full of compassion, driven by the needs of people around them. They know God can touch, and so their response to everything is, "Let's pray!" Your car won't run? Let's pray over it! Your mother is sick? Let's pray for her! You need a job? Let's pray about that! Prayer is their way of releasing the ability of God into a moment. What they see is what pushes their buttons, so they are likely to feel empathy for a beggar on the street corner or to stop and pray at the scene of an accident.

I have a friend named Max who exemplifies this temperament as well as anyone I have ever met. Max is an artist who lives in the hill country of Texas and designs exquisite bronze sculptures. I stopped in to see him not too long ago and he wanted to take me to lunch. As I climbed in his Suburban, I

How to Pray After You've Kicked the Dog

had to negotiate with four big notebooks that were occupying the passenger seat. "What are these, Max?" I inquired as I heaved them into the back seat.

"Oh, those are my prayer journals. For the past eight years, I have kept a record of every opportunity I've had to pray for someone and the result of the prayer. Take a look."

I thumbed through the pages of one of the books. Max had prayed for trucks, tumors, financial difficulties, marriages, children, animals . . . you name it. I could not have begun to count the number of incidents he had noted. He was literally a prayer just looking for a place to happen! And even more amazing were some of the places in which he had prayed: truck stops, art shows, galleries, restaurants, hotels, grocery stores, parking lots...just about everywhere you could imagine. If I could simply introduce you to Max, I would not have to explain any further about this temperament.

Since immediacy pray-ers are motivated by sight, they are likely to pray just about anywhere—in the mall, at a gas station, in the check-out line or at a dinner party. Steve Hawthorne would say they like "praying on site with insight" (10). Spontaneity is their trademark and their battle cry is "Let's go!" While the traditionalists are still conducting research, these people are already out in the thick of it, praying with wild abandon in as many different ways as possible. Faith is in action and the action is prayer. In a church setting, they might be the ones organizing a food drive or a relief campaign, and they would be prime candidates for praying at the altar or for doing some other kind of personal prayer ministry during the services. However, do not expect to find these people sitting in one place too long. As soon as they hear God speak or reveal a need, they will be anxious to hit the streets and make something happen.

Because they like to pray on the scene, many people who operate strongly in this style of prayer are seen as risk takers. They may even be called reckless or pushy because they are not easily embarrassed or put off. They are not too concerned about the past because they believe prayer is for now, and they do not want to miss a single opportunity to invite God to be God. Because they are always poised and available to pray at a moment's notice, they may even seem to be scattered, flighty or disorganized, and they may not enjoy working under boundaries of a rigid prayer plan. Rules and methods might frustrate their desire to move on impulse and flow within a given situation.

Another characteristic of this school of prayer is a high level of energy and emotion. Prayer is exciting and refreshing! Nothing gives the immediacy group more of a thrill than seeing a prayer answered—immediately. Their joy and satisfaction over watching needs get met is often expressed in praise. On the other hand, because of their connectedness with

> *Nothing gives the immediacy group more of a thrill than seeing a prayer answered—immediately.*

the pain of humanity, they may also be inclined to cry when they pray. Wherever they are at the moment, they are fully there. But moments later, they can be at the other end of the emotional spectrum!

The prayer language of this temperament reflects their view of God as an able provider, supported by scriptures like Philippians 4:19, "And my God will meet all your needs according to his glorious riches in Christ Jesus;" and Matthew 7:11, "If you, then, though you are evil, know how to give good gifts to your children, how much more will your Father in heaven give good gifts to those who ask him!" They also might pray out of the miracles of God and passages that describe signs and wonders. For example, in Acts 3, Peter and John pray for a crippled beggar at the city gate and immediately he jumps to his feet and begins to walk. The immediacy pray-er might pray for a friend like this, "Lord, just as you healed the lame man at the Gate Beautiful, strengthen Gloria and restore her to perfect health. In Jesus' name I pray. Amen."

They read about the miracles in the Bible, and they say, "Do it again, God!" They pray bold, straightforward prayers in line with Jesus' own works, and they do it in His name, just as the disciples did. They love to see God release His blessings in response to their prayers. Since it is need-driven, prayer in this realm is specific and focused on individual lives as opposed to intangible visions or plans.

Finally, for those who pray in this temperament, visual aids or prompts are basic equipment. They have photographs stuffed in their Bible, lists of names and prayer requests written in their journal, and if they are really serious, they may have a collection of newspaper clippings or other such information. I heard of a man who went to his local courthouse and asked for a list of names of couples who had recently filed for divorce. He took the list home and actually prayed over every marriage for several weeks. Then he called the couples one by one, and asked for permission to pray with them over the phone! Remember—immediacy prayer-ers sometimes appear pushy. They are so convinced of Jesus' ability to fix, heal and make right that they often do things others would not even dream of.

Biblical Models

The author of the second New Testament gospel, Mark, was most likely of the immediacy temperament. In fact, since the word "immediately" appears nine times in the first two chapters of the book of Mark, it is from this gospel that the temperament gets its name. (The word "immediately" is used in the Revised Standard Version; other versions say "at once," which doesn't seem to lend itself to being the title of anything.) Although we do not know much about Mark, we can determine from his writing that he was not terribly interested in historical background information—he presented the facts, and nothing but the facts. He also leaned heavily on stories of Jesus in action, performing miracles, while he omitted things like the birth of the Savior, the Sermon on the Mount and several of the parables Jesus told. Unlike Matthew, he showed virtually no concern at all over fulfillment of Old Testament prophecy.

Another man who modeled a similar temperament was Stephen, one of the seven men chosen by the disciples in Acts 6 to help them minister to the poor and needy in Jerusalem. We are told that Stephen not only served in a very tangible way by helping distribute food to widows, but he also "did great wonders and miraculous signs among the people" (Acts 6:8). In other words, he prayed for the needs of those he was serving and saw many of his prayers answered. Appropriately, he is described as "a man full of God's grace and power" (Acts 6:8). Perhaps it was this boldness in prayer that threatened the religious officials enough that they eventually had him arrested and stoned. The zeal of the immediacy temperament has the potential to offend those who do not understand its motives.

> The zeal of the immediacy temperament has the potential to offend those who do not understand its motives.

Although she is not a biblical character, a final example of this temperament in action is Mother Teresa. Immediacy personified, Mother Teresa spent every moment of her entire life touching, healing and helping the needy. She had nothing because she spent everything on others. She was driven by a compassion that most of us can scarcely even comprehend. A genuine conduit of mercy, the life and love of Jesus poured from her being and flowed from the work of her hands. In her book, *No Greater Love*, she says this: "When you look at the inner workings of electrical things, often you see small and big wires, new and old, cheap and expensive lined up. Until the current passes through them there will be no light. That wire is you and me. The current is God" (67).

Benefits

Epinephrine, better known as adrenaline, is a hormone secreted in the human body under various conditions such as fear, danger, excitement and speed. Its role is to quicken the pulse and raise blood pressure to enable us to perform physiologically above and beyond our normal state of being. Used for medical purposes as a cardiovascular stimulant, this hormone is responsible for what scientists call the "fight or flight" response. In rare cases or extreme circumstances, when adrenaline has been secreted in large enough amounts, it has enabled people to perform superhuman feats of strength or endurance such as lifting a car off of a trapped loved one or jumping to safety from a third story window.

The immediacy temperament is the adrenaline in the body of Christ. It is the school of prayer that stimulates us to action and pushes us to reach out beyond our spiritual safety zone. We need this temperament to operate among us for several reasons:

1. **It is motivational and inspirational.**   It builds excitement within the church about prayer and makes praying for people fun. Unfortunately, in many churches today, we have allowed the whole business of prayer to become . . . well . . . boring. In some churches I visit, the most excitement they have had in the last year related to prayer was when they moved the Wednesday night prayer meeting out of the sanctuary into the fellowship hall and started serving cookies. However, when this temperament is in full swing, creativity flows and

emotions are released. It fosters in us zeal and passion for prayer that might just give a lost world the idea that knowing Jesus is exhilarating and worth sharing.

2. **It challenges our faith by calling us to action.** The immediacy temperament is the backbone of the social gospel, always stirring us to minister as Jesus did, never allowing complacency to set in. It is the antithesis of apathy, forcing prayer to move outside the confines of the church walls and into communities where the love of God needs to be demonstrated in visible ways.

3. **It keeps us in touch with the reality of broken humanity.** One of the dangers of "churchianity" is the ease with which we can turn our gaze inward, tuning out the desperate cries and pleas for help and hope. Sometimes it is all too convenient "not to see" that which we think ugly or dirty. Rather than trouble our own spirits, we simply overlook those words of Jesus that call us to reach, touch, feel and move in the hell-holes of our neighborhoods and cities. This temperament will not indulge such self-protection. As Mother Teresa wrote:

> The fullness of our heart comes in our actions: how I treat that leper, how I treat that dying person, how I treat the homeless. You can touch the sick, the leper and believe that it is the body of Christ you are touching, but it is much more difficult when these people are drunk or shouting . . . How clean and loving our hands must be to be able to bring that compassion to them! (69–70).

4. **It often leads to salvation.** Just like in Marci's case, when the needs of people are met through prayer, the door is open for the Holy Spirit to draw them into a saving relationship with Jesus. When God answered Shirley's prayer and brought home the lost dog, Marci realized that the love of God was real and she put her trust in Him as her savior. Often the

signs and wonders that follow this temperament are nothing more than harvest tools God uses to bring one of His lost ones home.

Primary Purpose and Contemporary Expressions

The primary purpose of the temperament of immediacy is to reveal the ability and willingness of God to meet the needs of mankind. It gives hands and feet to His compassion and power. Although God could certainly perform any miracle He wanted without our help, He has chosen, in His sovereignty, to allow us to partner with Him through prayer. Extending the love of God to those around us is a privilege we have as His children.

Over the last five years we have seen an explosion of movements based on the principles of on-sight prayer. Here are just a few:

1. **Prayerwalking.** Efforts are currently underway to organize prayerwalkers in every zip code of America. This is a simple and effective prayer strategy which encourages people to walk their neighborhoods praying for the families who live there.

2. **Drive-by praying.** A derivative of prayerwalking, drive-by praying allows for praying over an entire city or region. In many cities, high crime areas that would be unsafe for pedestrians are being soaked in prayer as partners or teams of intercessors drive up and down the streets.

3. **Prayer at the Flagpole.** Public school students are not waiting for the Supreme Court to give them permission to pray! Every year, thousands gather on designated mornings around their flagpoles to pray for their school, their friends, their community, and their nation.

4. **Marches for Jesus.** Marches for Jesus, where people of all denominations literally hit the streets with tambourines and banners, have caught on world wide. In 1997, an esti-

mated six million people involving over 100 nations paraded through city streets on May 17, singing and praising the name of Jesus.

5. **Doorhanger Campaigns.** In 1996, an independent church in San Francisco called off services for one month. Instead of holding church on Sunday mornings, they hung a prayer of blessing on every home in the city! Many churches and ministries are using these simple tools as a way to at least open the door for relationships and prayer.

6. **Houses of Prayer Everywhere.** This movement focuses on establishing small prayer groups in homes and businesses to pray for the needs of neighbors, family members, co-workers and friends.

Another emphasis that has emerged in the last decade, fueled by the immediacy temperament of prayer, is altar ministry—reopening the altars of churches as places where people can receive a touch from God. For too long, prayer has been overlooked in the church as a ministry, but it is just as vital as any other outreach. Nothing is more tragic than to know that week after week, thousands of hurting people, desperate for a personal touch, pass in and out of churches and receive nothing more than a bulletin and a handshake. They wear a painted-on smile, but inside they are dying, and they leave the premises in no better shape than when they came.

About one year ago I wrote an article on this movement for a Christian magazine. I told the story of a lady who came into my church office one Sunday morning after the service and pulled a handgun out of her purse. "The sermon wasn't that bad," I thought, but she had my full attention. She told me she had awakened that morning so depressed that she could think of no reason to go on living. She had come to church as a last resort. "If God did not care enough about me to give me some sign of hope," she said, "I had decided to end my life."

With tears running down her cheeks, she laid the gun on my desk and started to leave. But she stopped at the door and said,

"It wasn't the praise time or the special music or even the sermon (I knew that) that got through to me. Someone prayed for
me at the altar during the ministry time and they seemed to
know exactly what I needed."

Thank God that He had more to work with that day than
my twenty-minute message! Prayer as a ministry is more than
just a movement. It is, I believe, the single most critical thing
churches can do to emulate the ministry of Jesus. It is the immediacy temperament at its best.

Dear Lord,

Give me wisdom that surpasses computer
chips and wires so that I can fix these cars
in my shop. Cars are not what they used to
be! Help me locate the problems and know
exactly what to do. Thanks.

—the prayer of a mechanic

Chapter 17

The Temperament of Love

My colleague Steve Hawthorne, who I mentioned in the last chapter, once told me a story about a rather frustrating experience he had trying to help a friend I will call Sam. Sam was not from this country, and though he was a very intelligent, honest, hard-working man, his English was limited. He used his bicycle to get around, so when it broke, he immediately took it to a repair shop to be fixed. The repair shop asked for payment up front, which Sam provided, but when he went back to pick up his bike, it was still broken. When the shop owner refused to do anything to make the situation right, Sam filed a complaint which eventually led him to small claims court.

When the court date arrived, Steve offered to go with his friend to help him explain his case so that justice could be done. They entered the courtroom together, and when it was Sam's turn to tell his story, Steve stood next to him and started to speak for him. But just as he began to relay the problem, the judge interrupted him, saying, "I'm sorry sir, but in this court-

243

244   How to Pray After You've Kicked the Dog

room, both plaintiffs and defendants must speak for themselves. Your friend will have to do the talking."

"But your Honor, he does not speak enough English to be understood," Steve protested.

The judge shook his head, "I understand, and I'm sorry. But that is the rule."

Sam did the best he could to plead his case, but he simply was not able to communicate well enough. The complaint was eventually dismissed.

View of God – A Righteous Judge

Those who pray in the love temperament relate to God as a perfectly righteous judge. Long-suffering and merciful, He is the Redeemer and the champion of justice. He is good and fair, and supremely wise and omniscient. Unlike the courtroom Sam was in, however, God welcomes friends who have come to speak for those who can not speak for themselves.

Luke sums up this view of God in the parable of the persistent widow which he retells in his gospel:

> In a certain town there was a judge who neither feared God nor cared about men. And there was a widow in that town who kept coming to him with the plea, "Grant me justice against my adversary."
>
> For some time he refused. But finally he said to himself, "Even though I don't fear God or care about men, yet because this widow keeps bothering me, I will see that she gets justice, so that she won't eventually wear me out with her coming!"
>
> And the Lord said, "Listen to what the unjust judge says. And will not God bring about justice for his chosen ones who cry out to him day and night? Will he keep putting them off? I tell you, he will see that they get justice, and quickly" (Luke 18:1–8).

Luke's purpose is not to compare God to an unjust judge but rather to contrast Him. If even the unjust judge will grant justice to one who is persistent, how much more will God, who is a loving Father, administer justice to His children when they come to Him without giving up! He desires that none of His children be lost, defeated, hurt or broken. And because He has complete power over the universe, including Satan's evil forces, He is more than able to make every situation right. The world is His courtroom, and He has complete and total authority in it.

Prayer Profile

The people who pray in this temperament play the role that Steve tried to play for Sam. They go to God and plead the case for someone who, for whatever reason, cannot do it on his or her own. They are public defenders, if you will, fervently seeking justice for the defenseless, while receiving little in return. In the church world, we call these people "intercessors" because they intercede or "go between" the one with the need and the One who is the answer. In the real world, we do not know what to call them because they are a very "different breed."

> *They* go to God and plead the case for someone who, for whatever reason, cannot do it on his or her own.

The love temperament has some strong ties to the two temperaments we have already discussed, yet it has some very distinguishing characteristics as well.

Just as in the temperament of tradition, those who pray from the love temperament are mediators. They stand in the gap between God and man for the purpose of mediating His will into a given situation. The difference, however, is perspective. While traditionalists pray from God's perspective looking down, those of the love temperament pray from within a problem looking

246 How to Pray After You've Kicked the Dog

up. They plant themselves in the midst of desperation and then appeal to the righteous judge for justice. They experience what I call "vicarious identification," identifying themselves with someone else's suffering and then praying from that position. They become the voice for the helpless, and they plead in God's court saying, "This is your child whom you love and sent your Son to save. Do not allow evil to prevail over her, but redeem her and draw her back to you where she belongs."

I once used an illustration for intercession which I, too, had to fight to convince my editor to keep in this book. (That will only ring a bell if you happened to have read Max Lucado's new book, *The Great House of God*. Thanks, Max!) Here it is: "Intercessors stand between the 'friend in need' and the 'Friend indeed' to intercede." In other words, an intercessor bridges the gap between someone who is hurting and God, who is always there and always a friend.

Often they pray for no visible reason, when others might say, "Give up on him; he's not worth your time," or "She's living with her boyfriend and doing drugs. Why bother praying for her?" Intercessors have a gift for seeing people and situations through "grace-enhanced" lenses which allow them to see things not as they are but as God intended them to be. With that picture in mind, they pray. Like the immediacy group, they remind God of His promises, His love, His work on the cross and His desire for *all* people to be saved. They pray, "I know it looks bad right now, God, but don't let Satan have them. They belong to you. Whatever you do, don't let go!"

As the name indicates, this temperament is fueled by the love and compassion of Jesus, which is the characteristic that ties it to the immediacy temperament. Both of these groups are motivated by an empathetic response to the pain of life they see around them. The difference here is that while immediacy prayers sort of "touch and go," affecting as many people as they can possibly reach, intercessors tend to attach themselves in certain places for the long haul. Once they are touched by a need, they will pray for hours, days, weeks, even years until they see justice done. Justice may mean salvation for one who has not yet found Christ, or it may mean redemption for one who has simply gone astray. Regardless, these tenacious prayer warriors will not stop praying until God reaches in and makes things right. They are enduring, relentless and persistent.

Another distinction between love and immediacy is that those in the love temperament often intercede for something that represents an entire group of people, such as a school, a gang, a cult, a profession or even a nation. They might commit to pray for an extended time for the police force in their city or for a specific minority culture. Intercessory prayer has the potential to affect spiritual issues of global concern because it is frequently aimed at large people groups with the intention of inducing widespread breakthroughs and changes. It has a corporate component that is not normally in line with immediacy praying.

Those in the love temperament often intercede for something that represents an entire group of people, such as a school, a gang, a cult, a profession, or even a nation.

People who pray in this temperament are generally very selfless. They identify strongly with the rescuing, nurturing nature of God. They, too, are prone to be emotional pray-ers but not up and down like their counterparts. They might be accused of being too intense or too caught up in someone else's problem because they feel the anguish of those for whom they intercede. Many people who fall into this category are very good at hearing God's voice, and they will often say things like, "I woke up at 3:00 a.m. and felt impressed to pray for Jack. My spirit felt so heavy, I just knew he was in trouble. Finally at 5:00 a.m. the cloud lifted, and I stopped praying and fell back to sleep." They take the responsibility of prayer very seriously.

The love temperament also produces a very relational style of prayer. You might even call it "touchy." Love pray-ers like group prayer, holding hands and sharing feelings. They wrote the book on eye-to-eye contact, and they love to listen because it only gives them more information from which to pray. They do not really need to be on the scene of the need to pray effectively—they are happy with a few of their own kind, a long list of hopeless situations and a big pot of coffee. They can pray in a church or in a living room, for a family

> *They* can pray in a church or in a living room, for a family down the street or a tribe of natives half-way around the world.

down the street or a tribe of natives half-way around the world. It is all the same to them. They will storm the heavenly courtroom with their voices until God brings His gavel down and sets the captives free.

Biblical Models

Luke's gospel is sprinkled with evidence that Luke exemplified the love temperament. A physician by trade, Luke was familiar with the process of physical healing which sometimes requires a long term commitment to medicine or therapy. He was compassionate, and he understood the principles of intercession. The story mentioned earlier about the persistent widow is indicative of how Luke perceived prayer. In Luke 11:5–8 he also recounts another story that Jesus told that has a similar message about a man who is in bed sleeping at midnight when he hears a knock on his door. Without getting up, he yells, "Who is it?"

The visitor turns out to be a neighbor who has had some friends drop in, and he has no food in his own house to offer his guests. So he asks if he can borrow three loaves of bread. But his friend who was sleeping answers, "Go away. We're all asleep, and I don't feel like getting up just to get you some bread."

But the man will not go away, and Jesus explains, "I tell you, though he will not get up and give him the bread because he is his friend, yet because of the man's boldness he will get up and give him as much as he needs" (Luke 11:8).

Luke's motto: "Persistence pays off!" Both the widow and the neighbor were eventually granted what they needed because they would not give up, even when the preliminary answer appeared to be a resounding "No!" Their requests were answered, not based on their eloquence or their reasoning or their connections but simply on their tenacity and determination.

Another powerful illustration of intercession is found in Numbers 16 where Moses and Aaron plead for God to spare the lives of the Israelites . . . again. Some of the Israelites had become disgruntled with Moses' leadership and the selection process for the office of "priest," so they had decided to appoint some on their own. Because of this show of disrespect, 250 false priests were consumed with fire—sort of a cosmic barbecue—and the ground opened up and swallowed all of their families and followers and everything that belonged to them.

Now the Israelites must have suffered from a rare form of spiritual amnesia or a bad case of dumb because when those who remained saw this, they blamed Moses for the rebels' destruction just as they had on many occasions in the past. This time, in response to their rebellion, a plague came upon the people, and more of them died. It was at this point that Moses said to Aaron, "Take your censer and put incense in it along with fire from the altar, and hurry to the assembly to make atonement for them."

The visual image of the next scene is the best representation of intercession that I know. The Bible says that "Aaron did as Moses said, and ran into the midst of the assembly. . . . He stood between the living and the dead, and the plague stopped" (Numbers 16:47, 48).

It is hard for me to imagine the kind of love Moses and Aaron had for the Israelites that they would literally risk their own lives to intercede on behalf of those who had caused them so much grief. The picture of Aaron standing between the living and the dead, crying out to God to spare the people, is a powerful portrayal of physical intercession.

Benefits

As I have traveled around the country, I have had the opportunity to visit various military graveyards lined with rows and rows of markers bearing the names of men and women who fought and died for some privilege I now enjoy. It is a humbling experience if you take the time to think about the incredible sacrifices that were made and still are being made by soldiers so that you and I can live in freedom and peace. These courageous individuals gave their very lives for no personal gain, but only to secure justice for the thousands whom they represented. Even today, American soldiers fight to preserve safety and freedom in foreign lands, while we sit at home watching football or surfing the Internet, virtually unaware of their supreme commitment.

Intercessors who pray in the love temperament are much like soldiers who go to battle in behalf of another person or group. They are the defenders, fighting on their knees for justice for no other reason sometimes except that they know help is available, and they hate to see anyone missing out. This temperament has much to offer the body of Christ:

1. **It fosters an atmosphere of acceptance, mercy and grace.** If you cannot remember a time when God had to

reach down into the pit and pull you to safety, then you have forgotten what your life was like before you were saved. Most of us, in fact, have had to lean on the grace of God more times than we care to count. We may never know until we get to heaven who was interceding for us. Yet how quick we are to judge others and write them off as unacceptable.

This temperament sees through a person's current condition right to the image of Jesus that resides inside of him. When others are focused on the "warts," the love temperament is willing to pray past the exterior to uncover the inner beauty.

> *When* others are focused on the "warts," the love temperament is willing to pray past the exterior to uncover the inner beauty.

There is no such thing as the point of no return because the Bible says that God wants all people to be saved. The love temperament has no place for judgmental attitudes.

2. **It promotes a global perspective of prayer.** Since this temperament does not necessarily need to see its prayer target, it can produce a strong sense of responsibility to pray for world crises, national or international tragedies, government leaders or specific people groups. It keeps us connected to those outside our normal sphere of thinking.

3. **It frequently affords breakthroughs in seemingly hopeless situations.** Since "quit" is not in the vocabulary of the love temperament, it will keep going long after everyone else has given up. Just like with the persistent widow, "no" to an intercessor is simply God's way of saying, "pray harder." They will not stop anywhere short of justice.

4. **It often leads to salvation.** Although not always, the prayer focus of this temperament is often those who have not yet put their faith in Jesus. I could not begin to count the number of wives and mothers I have known who spent years on their knees praying husbands, children or friends into the kingdom of God. The love temperament is especially intent on seeing that no one misses out on the promise of eternal life with Jesus.

Primary Purpose and Contemporary Expressions

The primary purpose of this temperament is to reveal and implement the redemptive purposes of God. It wants to see lost ones find their way to Jesus and prodigals come home.

When my boys were young, they used to sit on the front row in church next to my wife. One Sunday morning while I was delivering my message, my youngest son leaned over and whispered to his mama, "Is Daddy telling the truth, or is he just preaching?" I say that because I am not really sure if this story is true or just a good preaching illustration, and I have to admit right up front that I have no verification. But I have heard that during an American military effort overseas, one of our soldiers was accused by the foreign government of a crime and sentenced to be executed. The American ambassador to that country, though he was disturbed about the situation, had no way to help the man. So on the day of the execution, in a desperate attempt to save the life of his countryman, the ambassador showed up at the scene carrying an American flag. Just before the firing squad was ordered to fire, he bolted through the crowd that had gathered, ran right up to the soldier and draped the flag around his body. The symbolism of the flag and the significance of all that it stood for was so powerful that the executioners could not bring themselves to fire at the red, white and blue. They set the prisoner free.

When intercessors pray, they wrap the truth of God's Word around the hurting and confused, as if to remind Satan, "This one is protected by someone much more powerful than you!" If the Accuser is going to have his way, he will have to do it through the visible covering of God's promises and Jesus' work on the cross—and that he cannot do.

Several corporate expressions of the love temperament have grown and flourished over the past decade. Among them are Walk to Emmaus weekends, prayer for pastors and leaders, prayer for unreached people groups and intercession as a ministry.

The Walk to Emmaus is a retreat geared at highlighting the love of God for individuals. Very personal and intimate, these weekend encounters serve to soak participants in heavy doses of prayer and compassion for an extended period of time. Each attendee is given letters of encouragement, bathed in 24 hours of constant intercession and pampered with individual care. The weekend also allows for plenty of quiet time to reflect and be still before God. Thousands have been refreshed and redirected as a result of experiencing such an intensive outpouring of unconditional love.

> The importance of praying for leaders has really come to the forefront throughout the past several years.

The importance of praying for leaders has really come to the forefront throughout the past several years and has been made a top priority by many Christian groups, including Promise Keepers. The church is seeing that the prayer of honor for all leaders—spiritual, political, judicial, even popular leaders such as athletes or performers—invites the favor of God. Intercessors' groups all over the nation are praying daily for this country's most influential men and women as well as those abroad, while local churches are learning to bless their shepherds instead of striking them down with internal fire.

In 1993, a prayer emphasis that reached global proportions was a campaign aimed at raising up prayer for a section of the world known as the "10/40 window." This relatively small region, defined by its latitude and longitude coordinates, contained over ninety percent of the world's unevangelized population. Efforts were made to raise up a mighty prayer force to pray for the salvation of the people living in the 10/40 window. Since the crusade began, the number of missionaries and churches in that area have dramatically increased, and millions have professed faith in Jesus. The 10/40 window and other initiatives like it are carried by this temperament of prayer that latches on to a cause and will not give up.

Finally, intercession itself as a ministry has exploded in recent years, with several books on the subject emerging and training programs developing. Intercession has become almost a buzzword in Christian circles as the interest in this special calling has skyrocketed. In fact, it has been talked about so much that I am afraid many have held it up as the standard for all prayer, which has caused some confusion. It has been called a "gift," which it might be, but only to the degree that the other temperaments are also "gifts" meant to encourage and build the body of Christ.

Dear God,

They say you love everybody. But you never met my sister.

— Bryan, age 8

Chapter 18

The Temperament of Mystery

*W*ithout hesitation I can say that the most awe-inspiring sight I have ever seen was the view I encountered standing on the south rim of the Grand Canyon. Words like vast, expansive, majestic and magnificent scarcely describe the natural beauty and design. The size and depth of the canyon is unfathomable unless you have seen it—reaching twelve miles across and two miles down. The different colors layered in the walls in some places rival those of a brilliant sunset. Sometimes jagged and sometimes smooth, the formations of the rocks are breathtakingly creative and unique. To call it one of the "wonders" of the world is appropriate because it is almost impossible to imagine how something like it could have been formed simply by the flow of the Colorado River. It is one incredibly big ditch.

View of God – An Exalted King

Through the prayer temperament of mystery, God is seen as an exalted King who loves us and reveals Himself to us, and yet can never really be completely known or understood. He is the King of kings and from His heavenly throne, He rules over all the nations. His majesty is unequaled by anything on earth. The beauty of His countenance is so brilliant that we are not able to gaze upon it. His power is so supreme that we dare not test it. He is the Holy One, the Beginning and the End, the "Great I Am."

For you, O Lord, are the Most High over all the earth;
you are exalted far above all gods (Psalm 97:9).
I will sing praise to your name, O Most High (Psalm 9:2).
Be exalted, O God, above the heavens;
let your glory be over all the earth (Psalm 57:5).

Yet, mysteriously, the man Jesus was the true revelation of God, fully man and fully divine. He was "the radiance of God's glory and the exact representation of his being, sustaining all things by his powerful word" (Hebrews 1:3). Though He walked on our sod and wore our clothes on His back, He was completely one with the Father, God in the flesh living among us. He said, "Anyone who has seen me has seen the Father" (John 14:9). In light of this, He was called "the mystery of God" (Colossians 2:2, 4:3).

To know Jesus now is to experience the life of God (John 10:10). To be in Christ is the profound reality of the supreme God living in us. The very idea that the Most High who spoke the universe into being wants to have a personal, intimate relationship with each one of us is mind-boggling to the mystic!

Prayer Profile

Because of their view of God, mystics are inclined to focus much of their attention in prayer on the attributes, character and nature of God. He takes center stage. What He can do is not nearly as important as who He is. His workings in the lives of people are to be praised, but their primary significance lies in what they demonstrate to us about His being. In other words, when God performs a miracle, it is exciting because in it, He has revealed a part of Himself to us in a tangible way. Ultimately, His needs and plans take precedence over ours, not because He does not care for us, but because He is so timeless and supreme.

Humility is a common characteristic among those who pray in this temperament. Their perception of God is so big that by comparison, they may feel small. This is not to say they have a self-image problem; on the contrary, their assessment of where they fit into the scheme of things is probably most accurate. The idea that the Creator of the universe dwells inside of us is inexplicable and causes mystics to be humbled by such an honor. Prayer is an awareness of the very life of God living in us. Therefore, our identity and self-worth are not externally given but internally released.

> *When* they pray, they may become so overwhelmed by the greatness of God that they fall to their knees or even lie on their faces before Him.

When they pray, they may become so overwhelmed by the greatness of God that they fall to their knees or even lie on their faces before Him. They would have no problem assuming a posture of complete submission as one might do to pay homage to a high ranking official.

Mystics are obsessed with knowing God and seeking a revelation from Him. They might relate to Him a little like you might have related to one of your childhood idols had you met one. They are mesmerized by His very presence, and nothing else seems to be quite as important as just being with Him. Spending time with Him and getting to know Him is the most exciting, worthwhile aspect of prayer, and the answer to every problem is to seek Him more earnestly.

Those who pray in this temperament experience God with their spiritual eyes more than their ears. While others want to *hear* God, mystery pray-ers yearn to *see* God. They are driven toward the full revelation of His face. God reveals Himself as the "bread of life" (John 6:35), and the mystic responds, "I will feed on You." God reveals Himself as the fountain of life (John 4:13-14), and the mystic responds, "I will be refreshed in You." God shows Himself to be "the resurrection and the life" (John 11:25), and the mystic responds, "I will not fear death." Their prayer vocabulary tends to be very praise oriented, flowing from the adoration and awe they have for His splendor.

> While others want to hear God, mystery pray-ers yearn to see God.

Probably the hallmark of the mystery temperament is its affinity for solitude. Of all of the prayer temperaments, these mystics have the least trouble applying the brakes discussed in part two because, for them, stillness and quietness are among the basics of life. They are "musers." They thrive on being alone with God, often retreating to isolated places to pray. Creating a sacred space or altar is easy for this group, and many of them are especially drawn to pray in places of natural beauty, where they can behold the handiwork of God, such as a mountain hideaway or a secluded park bench. They love to gaze at the stars or listen to the sounds of a trickling brook as they meditate on the character and nature of the Father.

Since they could be described as "loners," mystics are easily misunderstood as being aloof or indifferent. They might even be labeled "anti-social" or "out of it." The Wednesday night prayer meeting or Sunday morning intercessors' prayer group would have less appeal to them than a visit to the dentist. Do not expect those of this temperament to be extremely comfortable praying out loud in front of large numbers of people; they are probably more inclined to just sit before God and enjoy His presence without uttering a word.

Biblical Models

John, writer of the fourth gospel, is a premiere example of the temperament of mystery. A fisherman by trade, John must have been a patient man, willing to bait a line and wait. He would have spent many hours alone on the water isolated from the activity of the city or marketplace.

The account which he wrote of Jesus' life is quite different from the other three gospels. For example, of the thirty-four miracles described in the New Testament, Matthew and Luke both recorded twenty, Mark recorded eighteen, but John only seven. Instead of emphasizing the works of Jesus, John focused more of his attention on the Savior Himself, His relationship to the Father and His true identity. Another interesting pattern is John's use of the term "signs" which he always uses when he does refer to Jesus' miracles. He viewed the deeds as symbols of something deeper, perhaps depicting Jesus' glory and sovereignty. He states his purpose for writing by saying, "These are written that you may believe that Jesus is the Christ, the Son of God, and that by believing you may have life in his name" (John 20:31).

John depicts the deeper sides of God in simple ways: Jesus is the light (John 8:12); Jesus is the life (John 10:10); Jesus is the way, the truth and the life (John 14:6). In fact, the word "life" is used thirty-six times in the book, while the term "truth" is used twenty-five times. Both are closely linked to Jesus as defining concepts. Furthermore, John himself is described, both in his own gospel and in others, as "the disciple whom Jesus loved," indicating that he had a unique and special relationship with Jesus beyond that of the other disciples. John's final words in his gospel echo his awe:

Jesus did many other things as well. If every one of them were written down, I suppose that even the whole world would not have room for the books that would be written (John 21:25).

This "disciple whom Jesus loved" also wrote the book of Revelation, aptly named because of the manner in which it was given to him and the symbolic nature of its content. Exiled to the island of Patmos because of his faith, John was actually quite content to be alone with God. It was on that solitary island that he received the Revelation in an elaborate vision. Jesus appeared before him, "dressed in a robe reaching down to his feet (Revelation 1:13)." He instructed John to write down everything that he was shown for the benefit of the churches. He then unfolded for John an incredibly elaborate apocalypse describing the sequence of events surrounding His return.

> Exiled to the island of Patmos because of his faith, John received the revelation in an elaborate vision.

In chapter four, John tries to describe an open door to heaven through which he sees a great throne. The One on the throne is radiating brilliant light and color, and there are creatures all around singing praise to Him continually. The sight was overwhelming and inspiring! John's ability to see and record such things was due to the fact that he made it a practice in his life to get alone and meditate on God.

Another man in the Bible who demonstrated a strong tendency toward the mystery temperament was Moses. As I said earlier, Moses was known to be a very humble man, and he spent many hours alone in the fields tending sheep. But there are also several things in the story of Exodus that indicate he leaned toward this prayer style. For example, after the Lord parted the

Red Sea for the Israelites to cross, Moses sang a song to God, praising Him for leading them to safety (Exodus 15:1-18). But Moses did not just sing about the miracle; his song exalted the name of God and His power and majesty. Notice the references to the nature of God:

> *I will sing to the Lord, for he is highly exalted.*
> *The horse and its rider he has hurled into the sea.*
> *The Lord is my strength and my song;*
> *he has become my salvation.*
> *He is my God, and I will praise him,*
> *my father's God, and I will exalt him.*
> *The Lord is a warrior; the Lord is his name.*
> *Your right hand, O Lord, was majestic in power.*
> *Your right hand, O Lord, shattered the enemy.*
> *In the greatness of your majesty*
> *you threw down those who opposed you.*
> *You unleashed your burning anger;*
> *it consumed them like stubble.*
> *Who among the gods is like you, O Lord?*
> *Who is like you—majestic in holiness,*
> *awesome in glory, working wonders?*
> *The Lord will reign for ever and ever (Exodus 15:1-3, 6-7, 11, 18).*

Moses often drew apart to pray, as he did before the battle with the Amalekites and when he received the Ten Commandments (Exodus 17, 20). He also went up on a mountain where God revealed Himself to Moses, and Moses spent forty days and nights in the presence of God there (24:15-18).

Benefits

I was on an airplane once when the man sitting next to me pulled out a little electronic gadget and started playing with it. It was not anything I recognized—a computer, a Gameboy, a portable CD player—so I asked him out of curiosity what it was.

"This is a Global Positioning System," he told me.
Wonderful. That cleared things right up. "What does a Global Positioning System do?" I asked.

"It can tell you where you are at any given moment based on information from seven different satellites which it locks into."
I was pretty sure I was in seat 14D somewhere over the state of Arizona.

"See here, right now we're above Tempe. Here's a map of the streets we're crossing." He showed me the screen which looked a little like a key map. "And watch this," he said as he typed something on the keyboard. "My brother lives in Cincinnati at this address." He pushed a button and waited. Within seconds, the screen revealed that we were exactly 2, 831 miles from his brother's front door. OK, I was impressed.

When mystics pray, they are not terribly concerned about the past. And they do not need a vision of the future to keep them going. They are existentially now—living for the present moment and content just to be in fellowship with God. Their prayers verify their current location with exactness because they lock into the One who is immovable and ever constant.

This temperament plays a key role in maintaining balance, focus and proper positioning in the body of Christ.

1. **It emphasizes obedience over emotionalism.** With immediacy and love pray-ers on the loose, running here and there responding to every human need they see, someone needs to be stationary, focused on God just because He is God. He is worthy of our attention even when we do not see any pressing needs around us. He is worthy of our time even when we do not feel very inspired or excited. Because this temperament is anchored into the heart of God, it does not rock or tip with the waves.

2. **It emphasizes being over doing.** Since God's nature is more important than His abilities, who we are is also more important than what we do. The slogan for this temperament might be "back to the basics," or "simplify." It stands firm for the

ideals of solitude and stillness because if we just get quiet long enough, God will show Himself to us. The goal of all prayer is simple: to become like Jesus.

3. **It helps us retain a sharp and clear image of Christ.** One of the tragedies in many of today's churches is the loss of an accurate Christology. He is being called all sorts of things because we have allowed ourselves to entertain thoughts about Him that are not scriptural. For instance, some regard Him as a "good man" who went about teaching on ethical issues. The mystery temperament turns our attention back to the true revelation of God and inspires us to worship Him for his nature and character.

4. **It yields truths that are inspirational and timeless.** One of the greatest known mystics to impact this century is Oswald Chambers, author of *My Utmost For His Highest*. Clearly, Chambers was a man who spent countless hours alone with God, seeking the deeper truths of the faith. The devotionals published in this book based on his teachings have inspired and spoken directly to the hearts of millions of people since the early 1900's. Not all of us are destined to go to the mountain top and see God, but we are certain to glean something of significance from those who do.

> When God gets us alone—when He gets us absolutely alone, and we are dumbfounded, and cannot ask one question, then He begins to expound (Chambers 13).

Primary Purpose and Contemporary Expressions

The primary purpose of the temperament of mystery is to seek and safeguard the revelation of Jesus. Because of their inclination to be alone, those who operate in this temperament are often used by God as messengers for a specific time and place.

They press into the profound, divine nature and become impressed with the desires and thoughts of God.

This is the temperament that dominates my own prayer life more than any other, although I also demonstrate a lot of immediacy characteristics. I thrive on time alone to the point that if I am deprived of solitude for too long, I actually feel tired and depleted. Stillness charges my emotional, mental and spiritual batteries, enabling me to travel, teach and minister.

> *I* thrive on time alone to the point that if I am deprived of solitude for too long, I actually feel tired and depleted.

Perhaps this prayer inclination would help explain why, upon traveling to Korea several years ago, I was so impressed and ignited by places like Prayer Mountain, a facility designed to provide places where people could be alone with God and pray, even for extended periods of time. I had never seen anything like it in America and certainly not in my own church.

The concept quickly consumed me. It resonated with my spirit and sparked a desire in me to create these oases from the noise and clutter of society. I loved the idea of establishing places where people could sign up to spend an hour away from the television, away from the phone, away from the kids and the chores—just sitting in the presence of God. I got excited about the possibilities and power of a prayer ministry that was based purely on commitment and not fueled by emotion. I firmly believed, as I still do, that if people would shut out all distractions long enough, God would speak to their heart.

So when I came home, I embarked on what has now been a fifteen-year campaign to help put prayer rooms in local churches all across this country. Although this has been a major priority in my ministry for some time, it has only been in the past few years that the prayer room movement has mushroomed. This year (1998) in particular marked a milestone with the completion of the World Prayer Center in Colorado Springs. The multimillion dollar facility, built and overseen by Ted Haggard and C. Peter Wagner, is intended to serve as a base of networking, training, coordinating, resourcing and reporting for prayer centers worldwide.

Along with the explosion of prayer rooms, there has been a significant increase in the number of altars or sacred places being established in homes and even workplaces. Many people are recognizing the value of claiming sacred time amidst the chaos of life, and they are creating personal areas of refuge where they can go to be still. Other related trends include the emergence of various retreat facilities ranging from single cabins to complete resort-type accommodations where individuals can "get away" at minimal cost for the purpose of seeking God.

The secret of monks and desert fathers is out! Loneliness is not fatal. To those who will stop long enough, God will reveal Himself.

Dear God,

How did you know you were God?

—Charlene

(Hample and Marshall)

Chapter 19

The Temperament of Confrontation

In the recently released movie *The Apostle*, one of the most dramatic moments is a confrontation between the apostle and a man with a score to settle. Celebrating the growth of his newly formed church, the pastor and his congregation are enjoying a time of food and fellowship in front of their small, white sanctuary. The sun is shining; children are running and playing. The day seems to be picture perfect until a man drives a bulldozer right onto the front lawn, stopping directly in front of the renegade preacher.

This was not the two men's first encounter. In an earlier scene, the troublemaker had wandered through the church during one of the services and made some degrading, racial remarks, to which the apostle responded by taking the man outside and beating him senseless. Now, the man is determined to repay the apostle publicly for his previous humiliation. His idea of revenge: level the church and scare off the people.

He barks to the apostle to move or get run over, but the apostle stands firm between the bulldozer and the sacred little building.

As all the activity ceases and his people gather around him, the apostle opens his Bible and lays it on the ground at his feet saying, "If you want to destroy the church, you'll have to run over the Word of God to get there!" The tension mounts. It becomes evident, however, that even though the man continues to exchange words with the preacher, he is visibly disturbed by the position he has found himself in, and he begins to waiver. He climbs down from the bulldozer to move the Bible, but ends up collapsing, weeping over its open pages. Just the Bible's presence represented power and authority too big to challenge.

View of God – A Commander in Chief

The central issue of any confrontation is control—the right to set the standard or determine the parameters in a given situation. At the heart of every stand-off are the questions, "Whose way is going to prevail here? Who is really in charge?"

Those who pray from this temperament of confrontation tend to look at most circumstances in life as a struggle between the forces of good and evil. To them, prayer is a weapon to be used to enforce God's way over the enemy's schemes, giving God ultimate control in the earth. They are a militant group who feel that prayer is a battle, and they view God as their commander in chief.

While many choose to focus on the loving, nurturing part of God's character, confrontationalists identify with His warring nature described in references such as these:

> . . . but you give us victory over our enemies,
> you put our adversaries to shame (Psalm 44:7).
> Surely God will crush the heads of his enemies,
> the hairy crowns of those who go on in their sins (Psalm 68:21).
> The Lord is a warrior... (Exodus 15:3).

In the eyes of this temperament, God is the supreme leader of the forces of good, and He instructs and commissions His people to enforce His kingdom. He is perfectly holy, righteous in every way, and He has all power and authority over the heavens and the earth. He has no tolerance for sin or evil, the source of which is always his adversary, Satan. Although Satan must be confronted, God has already won the ultimate victory through the death and resurrection of His Son, so the battle is never about final outcome, but immediate control.

Prayer Profile

Those who pray in this temperament can be an intimidating group because they have an affinity for spiritual warfare. Something in them is attracted to the front line where the action is the hottest and the stakes are the highest. Energized by head-to-head combat, they see themselves as the enforcers of the kingdom of light, and so they gravitate to those places where they sense darkness.

The language of prayer for a confrontationalist is authoritative—they pray for God instead of to God. Like the traditionalists, they are mediators of God's pur-

> *S*omething in them is attracted to the front line where the action is the hottest and the stakes are the highest.

pose, but with a competitive edge. Prayer is their weapon, effective for evicting, driving out, taking hold or taking back. They use it to bless, heal, bind and loosen. Taking this perspective into account, it is easy to understand why their prayer style can at times be loud and aggressive. They pray using words like "command" and "order," and they generally do not say "please." They are sometimes accused of being "too radical" or "far out" because they tend to see every situation on the level of spiritual dynamics, fully expecting to find Satan or one of his twisted helpers at the source of every problem.

Since our spiritual authority lies in the name of Jesus and in
the Word of Truth, these warriors like to pray scriptures, especially those that speak directly of the power that lies in Jesus'
name. They might pray from passages such as:

> *. . . that at the name of Jesus every knee should bow, in heaven
> and on earth and under the earth, and every tongue confess
> that Jesus Christ is Lord, to the glory of God the Father
> (Philippians 2:10–11).*

> *. . . for it is written: "Be holy, because I am holy" (1 Peter 1:16).*

> *And having disarmed the powers and authorities, he made a
> public spectacle of them, triumphing over them by the cross
> (Colossians 2:15).*

> *With authority and power he gives orders to evil spirits and
> they come out! (Luke 4:36b).*

They are also inclined to pray prayers based on Ephesians
6:10–18 where Paul describes the spiritual armor we have in Christ.

Since Jesus defeated Satan once and for all at the cross, His
name is the key that unlocks the power of God to every one of
His children. It gives us access to God (John 16:23), the power
of attorney (Acts 3) and position in the family of God. And not
only does His name hold the power to defeat, it also holds the
power to defend, so when we go "in Jesus' name," we are protected by His blood.

Like expert marksmen, people of this prayer style identify
their target before they fire. Because they understand the tac-
tics of the enemy, they know that Satan often works through
our own sins of the flesh to rob us of complete peace in Jesus.
Whereas others may look only at the surface of a situation, unable to distinguish exactly what the problem is, these pray-ers
get right to the root of the issue. They often find themselves
working in tandem with traditionalists to isolate sins of the
past that have given Satan a foothold, and then make a way for
the kingdom of light to be established.

Praise is an important part of the confrontationalist's prayer life, both as a weapon of warfare and as an offering to God for His faithfulness. Their worship might focus on those attributes of God which they identify most with—His authority, power, strength and holiness. They sing as David did, "The Lord is my strength and my shield; my heart trusts in him, and I am helped. My heart leaps for joy, and I will give thanks to him in song" (Psalm 28:7).

Biblical Models

Paul is the primary example we have of this temperament in the Bible. A hard, earthy man, Paul was one of the Pharisees before he was converted—a group committed to purging the religion of the day of any impurities, including Christianity. They believed the followers of Christ were heretics, and they treated them accordingly. Paul was zealous about his beliefs, even before he became a Christian.

So when Paul was suddenly and dramatically converted on the road to Damascus, it came as quite a surprise to those who knew him. Almost overnight, Paul made what would have been considered a radical change in allegiance. With all the enthusiasm he had been persecuting the Christians, he was now preaching their message about Jesus. I imagine Paul was the kind of person you would definitely have wanted on your side in an argument because he threw every ounce of his energy into furthering whatever cause he took up. Paul was no cream-puff.

Perhaps it was due in part to this background that Paul became a very confrontational Christian. He took as hard a stand against evil as any of Christ's followers. In fact, his writings— Paul wrote almost half of the New Testament—indicate that he almost could have been called intolerant where issues of sin were concerned. As he wrote letters to the Christians in various cities where he had visited, he often confronted them about aspects of their lifestyles that were not pleasing to God, and he was not necessarily gentle about it. Consider these verses:

It is actually reported that there is sexual immorality among you, and of a kind that does not occur even among pagans: A man has his father's wife. And you are proud! Shouldn't you rather have been filled with grief and have put out of your fellowship the man who did this?. . . [H]and this man over to Satan, so that the sinful nature may be destroyed and his spirit saved on the day of the Lord (1 Corinthians 5:1-2, 5).

Do not be yoked together with unbelievers. For what do righteousness and wickedness have in common? Or what fellowship can light have with darkness? (2 Corinthians 6:14)

For of this you can be sure: No immoral, impure or greedy person—such a man is an idolater—has any inheritance in the kingdom of Christ and of God (Ephesians 5:5).

Finally, be strong in the Lord and in his mighty power. Put on the full armor of God so that you can take your stand against the devil's schemes. For our struggle is not against flesh and blood, but against the authorities, against the powers of this dark world and against the spiritual forces of evil in the heavenly realms (Ephesians 6:10-12).

Also very significant is the fact that Paul is the only person mentioned by name, besides Jesus himself, that we know cast out a demon. In Acts 16, Paul and Silas were going to pray when they met a girl who made money telling fortunes. The Bible says that she "had a spirit by which she predicted the future." The girl followed the disciples for days, yelling and making a scene, until finally Paul became so troubled by her presence that he turned to her and spoke to the spirit, "In the name of Jesus Christ, I command you to come out of her!" And immediately the spirit left the girl (Acts 16:16–18). While similar instances are implied in other places, this is the only passage that describes someone speaking directly to a spirit in this manner. Paul understood the power of the name of Jesus, and he did not see any reason to put up with Satan's presence.

Another Old Testament example of this confrontational prayer temperament is Elijah, a prophet who confronted Ahab, the King of Israel. Ahab was leading the people to worship Baal, while Jezebel, his cunning and deceitful wife, was killing off many of the prophets who would not follow their example. A famine had fallen on the land because of the people's rebellion and as a result, fear and hunger were sweeping the nation.

Elijah presented himself to the wicked ruler and proposed a showdown between God and Baal. The terms were fairly simple. Both groups of followers were to gather on Mount Carmel where each was to prepare a sacrifice to be laid on an altar. They would then call out to their gods to send fire from heaven to consume their offerings. Whichever god answered with fire would be named the true God.

> *Paul understood the power of the name of Jesus, and he did not see any reason to put up with Satan's presence.*

Ahab agreed. The next day, he and all of the prophets of Baal prepared their offering and then cried out to their god. The Bible says they "called on the name of Baal from morning till noon. But there was no response; no one answered" (1 Kings 18:26). They danced, shouted, prophesied and slashed themselves with swords and spears. Still no fire. Elijah, being the ruffian that he was, even taunted the people, saying, "Perhaps he is deep in thought, or busy, or traveling. Maybe he is sleeping and must be awakened" (1 Kings 18:27). Nothing happened.

When evening came, Elijah called the people over to him where he was repairing the altar of the Lord which was in ruins. He placed his sacrifice on the altar and then asked that four large jars of water be brought and poured over the offering and the wood. Then, in a bold act of simple faith, Elijah stepped

forward and prayed, "O Lord, God of Abraham, Isaac and Israel, let it be known today that you are God in Israel and that I
am your servant and have done all these things at your command. O Lord, answer me . . ." (1 Kings 18:36–37). And with
that, the fire of the Lord fell from heaven, consuming the sacrifice, the wood, the altar, the soil and even the excess water in the
trench! God did not want to leave any doubt, and the people of
Israel fell on their faces and cried before Him, "He is God!" The
prophets of Baal were captured and killed, and the drought was
broken with a heavy rain.

Elijah was not willing to ignore the sin of the Israelites. His
mission was to drive out the evil that was holding them captive
so that their hearts could be turned back to God. He knew the
power of God would prevail against the false prophets, and he
was willing to put his own reputation, and possibly his life, on
the line to declare it.

Benefits

Several years ago, I attended one of our denominational conference meetings during which we pastors were asked to vote
on several key programs that the leadership of our church was
proposing to implement. Unlike some agendas, the one that year
was particularly positive; that is, the proposed programs were
fairly middle-of-the-road improvements that left little room for
dispute. They were not controversial, nor did they bring up any
sensitive theological areas that always lead to enthusiastic de-
bate. The meeting went smoothly and all of the proposals received majority votes as expected.

I happened to notice one older gentleman, however, who did
not seem to be voting on any of the issues. He sat silently, looking on with a rather uninterested demeanor. Since I knew him
to be a pastor in the conference who usually had strong opinions about things, I was curious as to why he remained so silent.

After the meetings were over, I saw the man in the hallway
and casually asked him, "Why didn't you cast any votes today?"

His gruff answer surprised me, "If I can't vote *against* something, I don't care to vote at all!"

When most people think of spiritual warfare and the confrontational temperament, they tend to associate the concepts with a negative attitude similar to that of the gruff old man. "They're always praying *against* something," or "They see devils behind every bush" are common judgements I hear regarding this school of prayer.

So is the glass half-full or half-empty? Do police officers fight crime or protect peace? Your ability to understand this temperament may well depend on whether you can see both sides of this coin. Although they are sometimes perceived as being too focused on the negative, the truth is, confrontationalists, if they are balanced and established in the Word of God, are actually as much for the kingdom of light as they are against the kingdom of darkness. They are God's foot soldiers, and they feel a calling to make sure nothing stands in the way of His sovereign working in the earth.

> "They're always praying against something," or "They see devils behind every bush" are common judgments I hear regarding this school of prayer.

This temperament is vital to the body of Christ for several reasons:

1. **It identifies and exposes evil.** Because Satan is very crafty, evil does not always appear as such on the surface. Just as the serpent lured Eve and Adam into sin with smooth talk and deceptive reasoning, Satan is still a master of disguises, often working through our own natural desires and emotions to create trouble. As most of us know from experience,

it is not always obvious when we are dealing with a person or situation that is leading us in the wrong direction. This temperament is very sensitive to the spiritual realm and can often discern the workings of the enemy more quickly than others.

2. **It upholds God's standards of holiness.** The holiness and purity of God resonates strongly in this temperament, causing it to expect nothing less from those who call themselves Christians. Just as Paul did, this perspective says that we are overcomers, fully equipped with the power of Jesus' name to live upright and blameless so that Satan has no opportunity to get his foot in the door.

3. **It protects the benefits that come with kingdom living.** Where God is in control, power, joy, eternal life and love abound. The Holy Spirit is able to move; the body of Christ is strong and unified, and peace drives out fear. This temperament fosters a winner's mentality, affirming the authority of every believer to have victory over all areas of their lives. It prays, "Thy will be done on earth just as it is in heaven—no violence, no hatred, no prejudice, no poverty!" Confrontationalists go to bat in the spiritual realm so that life for all of us in the natural realm can be filled with the hope of God's presence.

4. **It prepares the way for revival.** Ted Haggard's book, *Primary Purpose*, is one of the greatest written testimonies I know of concerning the power of confrontational prayer. In it, he tells the documented story of how, through spiritual warfare, the city of Colorado Springs was transformed from the witches' capital of America to the home base for hundreds of Christian ministries. He explains how evil forces were confronted and driven out through aggressive, authoritative prayer, in order that God's Spirit could begin to dwell in the city. As Ted and others who fought with him found out first hand, sometimes revival cannot happen until all the spiritual garbage is removed. To renovate a house and fill it

with nice, new carpet and furniture, you must first gut it. This style of prayer is essential to revival on any scale, big or small, because it paves the way for God to work.

Primary Purpose and Contemporary Expressions

The primary purpose of the temperament of confrontation is to establish the rule and reign of Jesus in individual lives and entire regions.

Although our western culture is highly resistant to many of the ideas that are foundational to this style of prayer, the amount of recognition it is receiving and the amount of literature being generated about it have exploded in this country in recent years. The man most people point to as the father of this movement in America is C. Peter Wagner, scholar, professor and author of many books on the topic. The whole area of spiritual warfare has become a powerful movement under the leadership of Dr. Wagner, and it has been thrust along by foreign missionaries from the United States who have seen the principles at work in other countries for years.

Because confrontational prayer is relatively new to us, much of what is going on today related to this temperament is education. Author Frank Peretti opened the eyes of many Christians with his best-seller, *This Present Darkness*, to a world they had never considered before. And now Peter Wagner and a host of other leaders are conducting spiritual warfare conferences throughout the year that are drawing thousands of people interested in finding out more about the supernatural realm.

Spiritual mapping is one prayer strategy that has sprouted out of the spiritual warfare movement. This plan of action diagrams communities, cities and regions according to the spiritual forces that are dominant in specific areas. Places with high concentrations of the symptoms of evil—crime, witchcraft, perversion, oppression, violence, hatred—are identified on the map and targeted as priority prayer points. Patterns of various strongholds are marked and dealt with as they become evident from the map. Maps such as these are used to create strategic prayer plans that will be effective in changing the spiritual climate of a region by driving out the darkness and making way for the kingdom of light to be established.

Another dynamic expression of confrontational praying is the story of Resistencia, Argentina, told by Ed Silvoso in his book, *That None Should Perish*. The plan of prayer-evangelism that was implemented in this city to convert thousands to Christianity was based strongly on a corporate model of the confrontational temperament of prayer. Silvoso summarizes the plan for reaching a city for Christ like this:

Step One: Establish God's perimeter in the city by identifying the remnant of people who are praying for revival.

Step Two: Secure God's perimeter in the city by identifying Satan's schemes and by tearing down strongholds.

Step Three: Expand God's perimeter in the city by slowly bringing others into the remnant through salvation, thereby building up the army of saints that will eventually attack the forces of darkness.

Step Four: Infiltrate Satan's perimeter by "parachuting behind enemy lines through a massive 'air assault' of specific and strategic intercessory prayer." In other words, create prayer cells to focus on praying for the unsaved people in the city.

Step Five: Attack and destroy Satan's perimeter by launching a campaign of direct spiritual warfare. Confront, bind-up and cast out evil spiritual powers that are ruling over the city, and proclaim the message of Jesus.

Step Six: Establish God's new perimeter where Satan's once existed by incorporating new converts into the body of

Christ and planting them firmly in local churches where they can grow and be discipled (294).

It is not hard to recognize the confrontational temperament at work! When utilized from strong biblical foundations, it is highly effective for achieving dramatic results in places where Satan has set up camp. Stories like the one in Argentina are not uncommon and are beginning to unfold in neighborhoods and cities in America. Crime rates are being reduced, unity among denominations is being strengthened, racial tensions are being dissolved and perverted businesses are being shut down. The people of God are gaining an understanding of what Paul meant when he said "our struggle is not against flesh and blood, but against . . . the spiritual forces of evil in the heavenly realms," and they are taking up the weapon of prayer.

Dear God,

Are there devils in the world? I think there is one in my class.

—John, age 9

Chapter 20

The Temperament of Perception

In the 1820's when railroads were spreading across this country as the up and coming form of transportation, not everyone had caught the vision of the tremendous possibilities they would open up. Just as with any significant shift of custom in society, proponents of railroads met with fierce opposition from people who could not see past the status quo to grasp the idea that there might be a better way. Consider this letter from Martin Van Buren, governor of New York at that time, to President Andrew Jackson:

> The canal system of this country is being threatened by the spread of a new form of transportation known as "railroads." The federal government must preserve the canals for the following reasons:
>
> 1. If the canal boats are supplanted by railroads, serious unemployment will result. Captains, cooks, drivers, hostlers, repairmen, and lock tenders will be left without means of livelihood, not

to mention the numerous farmers now employed in growing hay for the horses.

2. Boat builders would suffer and decline, whip and harness makers would be left destitute.

3. Canal boats are absolutely essential to the defense of the United States. In the event of unexpected trouble with England, the Erie Canal would be the only means by which we could ever move the supplies so vital to waging modern war.

As you know, Mr. President, railroad carriages are pulled at the enormous speed of fifteen miles per hour by engines which, in addition to endangering life and limb of passengers, roar and snort their way throughout the countryside, setting fire to crops, scaring livestock and frightening women and children. The Almighty certainly never intended that people should travel at such breakneck speed (Anderson 169-170).

Oh, how fearful we are of that which we do not understand! For Martin Van Buren it was the railroad; for many people in my generation, it was the personal computer. As you look back throughout history, two things become evident about change: it is never easy, and it is never really an option. If only we had the ability to see into the future, every generation would certainly have been surprised at what "evil" and "threatening" inventions became absolute necessities as progress pushed its way through heavily fortified lines of resistance.

View of God – A Bold Innovator

For those who pray in the perception temperament, God is a bold innovator who always has been and still is in the business of creating. He favors progress, creating new things and making all things new. There are no antiques in heaven—no such thing as depreciation—because everything gets newer every day.

The hallmark verse for this temperament is Revelation 21:5 which says, ". . . I am making everything new!"

He has given us a new covenant.
"This cup is the new covenant in my blood, which is poured out for you" (Luke 22:20).

He has given us a new love.
"A new command I give you: Love one another . . ." (John 13:34).

He has given us a new birth.
"Flesh gives birth to flesh, but the Spirit gives birth to spirit" (John 3:6).

He has given us a new nature.
"Therefore, if anyone is in Christ, he is a new creation; the old has gone, the new has come!" (2 Corinthians 5:17).

He has given us a new name.
"I will write on him the name of my God and the name of the city of my God, the new Jerusalem . . ." (Revelation 3:12).

He has given us a new song.
"And they sang a new song . . ." (Revelation 5:9).

He has given us a new home.
"In my Father's house are many rooms; if it were not so, I would not have told you. I am going there to prepare a place for you" (John 14:2).

From the perspective of this temperament, God is in no way limited to work within the current systems that we love and cherish. He is inventive and supremely creative, constantly giving birth to new works, new ideas and new ways of reaching lost and hurting people. He is full of surprises, not the least bit hesitant to violate our theology if necessary in order to accomplish His will in a new, more effective way. God is the originator of all things fresh and imaginative.

Prayer Profile

This is the temperament of dreams and visions. Those who pray in this school yearn to see and know what new things God is doing each day. In their prayer times, they often see images or pictures of events that happened long ago or have not yet happened. For example, God may reveal to a woman of this temperament a glimpse of someone's past in order to give her insight into how she can help meet a specific need. Or, He may show a man a vision about some future event for the purpose of giving clear direction or warning. On the other side of this coin, this group often has keen insight into the dreams or visions of others which need interpretation. Those who pray perceptively seem to be especially open to receiving this kind of revelation from God for the benefit of another person or group.

Since these people are acutely tuned in to God's frequency, they generally hear from God more often than most of us. They might perceive hidden agendas or unseen forces. They can often articulate God's heart in matters that have become encumbered with human opinions. They are intuitive, able to declare the mind and will of God, especially in the midst of trials or crises.

The language of this temperament tends to be futuristic or apocalyptic and is often laden with dates and predictions. While they may see images from the past, their focus is on the future and what God wants to accomplish. Journaling may be an important part of the perception pray-ers' prayer lives because they love to see things come to pass as they have been revealed. They may keep detailed notes and occasionally write out prayers in which God gave them a vision or interpretation.

While those who pray in this prayer style might have set times and places of prayer, they tend to be very spontaneous because they are always listening for the Spirit to speak. They are likely to have a vision not when they sit down for their morning devotional, but rather at the point of the need, be it in the dairy section of the grocery store or right after dessert is served at an intimate dinner party. They are like a blank screen for God's projector, capable of receiving a picture at any time, in any place.

Because they are often given the responsibility of heralding the message of new ideas or directions, they must be, at least to some degree, risk-takers, willing to go out on a limb to announce the coming of that which seems impossible, ludicrous or intimidating. They must not be afraid to communicate what they see, in spite of strong resistance. They are often ridiculed for being crazy or eccentric, and they are frequently misunderstood. Some people may accuse them of wanting attention. However, when visionaries truly hear from God, they will articulate their vision and then let it stand on its own merit.

> They are like a blank screen for God's projector, capable of receiving a picture at any time, in any place.

Finally, this group tends to be dramatic, excitable and demonstrative. Since what they envision is very real to them, they will sometimes "act out" the image in some manner to get their message across. They might make use of body language or symbolic movement when they pray, especially in front of other people. Like their love temperament counterparts, they may be somewhat emotional pray-ers.

Biblical Models

One of the best models in the Bible of this temperament is a man named Peter, one of the foremost disciples who emerged as their spokesman after Pentecost. Peter was apparently a good orator and a man of perception as he demonstrated in Acts 2:14-36 when he interpreted the Pentecost experience to the crowds who had gathered around the disciples in Jerusalem. God had done a new thing there in the Upper Room, and Peter explained to the Jews what they had witnessed, presenting the gospel so that they might believe. The Bible says that when Peter finished preaching, "about three thousand were added to their number that day" (Acts 2:41).

Peter was also bold enough to lay his own reputation on the line because he believed strongly in the new things Jesus had commissioned the disciples to do in His name. Although Jesus had performed many miracles while on earth, for his followers to do signs and wonders in His absence was a fairly innovative, risky endeavor. Yet in Acts 3, Peter prayed for a crippled beggar to be healed in the name of Jesus, marking the first recorded miracle of this kind following Christ's death and resurrection. When the man went running and leaping and praising God into the city, everyone who saw him was amazed. Once again, Peter had to explain to the people what had happened.

Later in the book of Acts, Peter had a vision that was so radically contradictory to the order of the day, it would have made the jump from canal boats to railroads look small. Until that time, the only people who had heard the gospel were the Jews, which included Peter and his friends. In fact, such a barrier existed between the Jews and the Gentiles that they were forbidden to speak to each other.

But one day, as Peter was on a rooftop praying and waiting for lunch to be served, he had a vision. He saw what looked like a sheet being lowered down from heaven by the four corners. On it were many animals, some of which were considered "clean" or edible and others which were considered "unclean." Although the Jews were forbidden to eat "unclean" animals, the Lord spoke to Peter saying, "Get up, Peter. Kill and eat" (Acts 10:13).

"Surely not, Lord!" replied Peter, unwilling to defy the Jewish laws. But the Lord reassured him that He had made the food clean. After this happened three times, the sheet disappeared. No sooner had the vision ended than three men came knocking on Peter's door. They had been sent by a well-respected Gentile named Cornelius, who himself had been instructed by God to seek Peter out and listen to his message. Peter immediately realized that the vision was not about what he could or could not eat; it was God's way of showing him that the barrier between Jew and Gentile was going to be removed. It was his license to go with the Gentiles to Cornelius's house and preach the gospel without fearing God's reproach. Because Peter received the vision, Cornelius and his whole household were saved that day, and a door was opened for the message of

> *As* is typical of those who pray in the perception temperament, Peter again found himself having to explain his behavior.

Jesus to reach an entire people group that had previously not heard.

Not surprisingly, most of the Jews misunderstood Peter's actions since they had not seen the vision. As is typical of those who pray in the perception temperament, Peter again found himself having to explain his behavior. It was not until they comprehended the chain of events that the people could rejoice with Peter over the exciting breakthrough.

Another man that strongly exhibited the characteristics of the perception temperament was Daniel. Trained as a young man to serve in the court of King Nebuchadnezzar, Daniel had an exceptional amount of wisdom. He received much notoriety and acclaim in the royal palace because he was able to interpret the Kings' detailed dreams with accuracy, even when all of the other astrologists, sorcerers and magicians could not. Three times the Kings under which Daniel served had dreams which revealed to them events that would take place in the future, and three times Daniel not only told the Kings what they had seen but also explained the full meaning to them (Daniel 2:24–45; 4:19–27; 5:18–28).

Daniel himself also received visions from God concerning the days to come and the kingdoms and empires that would rule in that region. Some of his visions had political significance, while others related to the futures of nations and people groups. Some were fairly simple to interpret, while others were extremely complex. Daniel, like Peter, was especially gifted at seeing into the future and then relating what he saw as God's messenger.

Benefits

It was not until just recently that I overcame my own fears about "new" things and got my first computer. Despite being convinced that they are tools of the enemy meant to rob us of personal sanity and peace, I resolved that if I was capable of operating heavy machinery and putting engines together, surely I could learn how to run a computer.

I was very proud of the first file I created. I was on an airplane, feeling a newfound camaraderie with all the other business people who had their laptops out on their tray tables. (I used to be impressed by this image until I realized that most of them were playing golf or solitaire.) I wrote a letter, gave it a name and then clicked the save button. That was easy. In fact, I was so impressed with myself that I wanted to look at the letter again, but I could not find it. I tried to "open file," but it was not there. Exasperated, I picked the computer up and shook it a little, binding the spirit of computer sarcasm, but to no avail. I was beginning to understand why that tiny blinking line is called the "cursor." My letter was lost, shot out of the printer port by mistake, I imagined, right into thin air.

As I have learned a little more about computers, I have come to have a great appreciation for the small rectangular boxes on my screen which are appropriately called "windows." Anytime I want to do something, I know I will find the key in one of those handy windows. For me, it is a little like "What's behind door number three?" because I never know exactly what I am going to find, but the excitement is addictive.

The perception temperament acts much like a window in the body of Christ. Full of surprises, it is a vital source for solutions and important information. It is often the portal through which God speaks to His people, and it offers us several valuable benefits:

> *The perception temperament acts much like a window in the body of Christ. Full of surprises, it is a vital source for solutions and important information.*

1. **It can warn of impending danger.** In Acts 11:28, a prophet named Agabus warned the people that a famine was coming upon their land, which gave them time to store up food and water for survival. This temperament can sound the alarm that some peril lies ahead, giving us time to prepare for the crisis.

2. **It can offer solutions to problems that seem to have no answer.** Because this temperament is given images from the creator and designer of the universe, it can often see a breakthrough in a situation that appears hopeless. The perception temperament may give direction or new ideas, supply a critical piece of information needed to move forward or it may simply act to confirm an important decision that has already been made.

3. **It is motivational and edifying.** Since this temperament focuses on the future, it tends to be a driving force, often coming into play to encourage a group or individual that is

moving in the direction of God's will. It can be the impetus that gets us off dead center and inspires us to act. As it reveals God's heart to us, it provokes and urges us to press on toward His calling.

4. **It can be interpretive.** As it was for Daniel, this temperament can be very intuitive to things of the Spirit and can often unravel mysteries and explain things we do not understand. In the midst of hardship, this temperament can bring hope by revealing a look at a brighter future. It might offer keen insights into events that seem unrelated but are in reality part of God's design for a person or group.

Primary Purpose and Contemporary Expressions

The primary purpose of the perception temperament is to provide specific information at a point of need, generally to confirm or give direction. It, like the confrontation temperament, has emerged in the last decade as a school of prayer that cannot be ignored, whether we fully understand it or not. Even though "prophetic ministries," as they are called, have stirred up some controversy over theological issues, many have proven themselves to be both reliable and biblical.

The prophetic movement itself is big in America today, giving rise to some modern day prophets who are hearing from God regarding political, national and spiritual issues. Because this gift is so easily abused, many people, even Christians, have a hard time swallowing the idea of new revelations and visions coming through just anyone. Nevertheless, God is still speaking today. I know this because on several occasions I have seen this temperament in action with humility and integrity. I have seen first hand how God can use dreams or specific revelations to encourage, heal, direct and confirm.

One such instance happened many years ago to a friend of mine named Mark Rutland. Now the president of Southeastern

College near Lakeland, Florida, Mark is one of the greatest preachers I have ever heard and truly a visionary man of God.

Back when Mark was still pastoring, he was often called on to do revivals because of his tremendous preaching ability. During one such revival outside of his home state, he opened the altar as he typically did for people to come and receive personal ministry and prayer. After praying for several different people, Mark noticed a lady kneeling at one end of the altar who was visibly distressed. He knelt in front of her and asked her what was wrong. She shook her head and shrugged, unable to articulate exactly what she was feeling. So Mark just began to pray for her in a general manner.

> *But* as he prayed, an image kept appearing in his mind. The image was so clear that he could not ignore it, although he had no idea what it meant.

But as he prayed, an image kept appearing in his mind. The image was so clear that he could not ignore it, although he had no idea what it meant. The picture he saw was of a little girl, dressed in a pink party dress trimmed in white lace, standing on a porch crying. When he finished praying, he described the vision to the woman and asked, "Does that mean anything to you?"

The woman was shaken and started to cry. After several minutes, she began to recount a story to Mark about her sixth birthday, when she had worn a pink party dress trimmed in white lace. Sitting around the table with her family, she had opened a birthday card which contained ten dollars, an exciting amount of money for a girl that age. Her face lit up as she held the bill, until her father reached across the table and snatched it from her hands. "What does a girl need with that kind of money?" he retorted, handing the ten dollars to her older brother, who stuffed it in his pocket with a grin.

As a small child, she was devastated—betrayed by her father and made to feel insignificant, even non-existent. She had harbored that shame and bitterness into her adult years, still feeling violated like a person of little worth.

Because Mark was available to receive the vision, he was able to minister the grace and healing touch of God to that young woman, helping her to leave at the altar that day a source of pain she had been carrying for years. The result of that single image, seared into Mark's mind, was profound, bringing closure to a painful memory of the past and giving new hope for the future.

Another expression of this temperament in action is one I just recently witnessed while guest preaching in a friend's church. This particular church is growing rapidly, on the cutting edge of what is happening spiritually in the twin cities of Bryan/ College Station, Texas, where I pastored for sixteen years. At the beginning of the service, the pastor invited a woman I have known for years to the microphone to share something that the Lord had spoken to her in her prayer time. A former member of my church, I knew her to be a woman of great integrity and humility. This is an excerpt of what she received:

> We are in a new season, a season of great need for the extra jar of oil (Matthew 25). This new oil we need will be supplied by the outpouring from the lampstand on High that is continually filled in heaven. It is ready to be poured out now! The Lord's fire on this earth will be spiritually ignited by the Hand of God. It is a consuming fire like that of the burning bush, and it will not be able to be quenched.
>
> Be the lamp for the Lord and be consumed as the wick of the lamp is saturated. We are to be saturated also with this new oil from the extra jar. We are to be the light; so also are we to be ready to supply oil and light to

cast out the darkness. Be ready! The match is in the hand of God and is ready to be struck and laid to the wick. Community Family Church is a wick the Lord sees getting prepared.

For a congregation stepping out into new territory, this word was encouraging, motivating and confirming. It stirred the hearts of the people to action and reassured them that they were on the right course. It especially lifted the spirits of the leaders of the church who were probably feeling some form of resistance to their innovative ministry ideas and creative programs.

As Christians, we need these "windows" around us to help us see things above and beyond our circumstances. While God is eager to speak to each of us personally, as I emphasized in Part Two, He does utilize this temperament in a unique way to reveal relevant information for the benefit of many.

Lord, every day I witness the power of electricity that flows into homes and businesses. Let your power flow through my life in visible ways, and help me learn how to use it.

—the prayer of an electrician

Chapter 21

The Temperament of Order

I was driving home from church one afternoon down an old country road, when I saw an old rancher, a member of my church, standing on the side of the road just at the edge of his property. As I got closer, I could see that he was looking down at a cow which was lying in the grass. I pulled my car over and got out.

"What's wrong?" I asked him.

"Anthrax goin' around, preacher. I'm afraid she's not gonna make it."

Now in those days, I was a zealot—young, green and too bold for my own good. So I said to him, "God can heal your cow. Can I pray for her?"

"Sure, okay, but I don't think it will do any good. She's on her last leg."

I took my coat off and loosened my tie. Squatting down in the grass, I took the cow's head and laid it in my lap. I prayed for her to be raised up and completely healed. I prayed against the anthrax, infection, disease and anything else I could think of

that might cause a cow to be sick. I thanked God for his faithfulness and for His attentiveness to our every need. "In Jesus' name,"
I finished, "be it done as I have said for this cow!" Then I looked
down into her big brown eyes. She looked back at me, let out an
agonizing final breath and died right there in my arms.

I did not even look up at the rancher; I did not want to see
the look on his face. Nor did he say a word. I simply got up,
brushed off my pants and went back to my car.

What do you do when prayer appears to fail—when you do
not get the answer you were hoping for? What keeps you from
giving up when you do not see immediate results? What motivates you to keep praying when the cow dies in your arms and
you feel humiliated and discouraged?

View of God

The temperament of order is made up of people who remain persistent in prayer because they see God as the rock of
salvation. They put their trust in and identify with the nature
of God that is solid, never changing, immovable and steady. Their
prayer life hinges on verses like these:

> The Lord is my rock, my fortress and my deliverer; my God
> is my rock, in whom I take refuge. He is my shield and the
> horn of my salvation, my stronghold. For who is God besides
> the Lord? And who is the Rock except our God? The Lord
> lives! Praise be to my Rock! Exalted be God my Savior!
> (Psalm 18:2, 31, 46).

> He alone is my rock and my salvation; he is my fortress, I will
> never be shaken (Psalm 62:2).

To fully understand the "rock" imagery, it helps to know
that the writer of the Psalms was probably not referring to little
pebbles but to the giant boulders that are scattered across the
countryside in Israel, some of which are bigger than a house.
To say that God is the "rock of our salvation" is to call Him
ever-present, firm, securely grounded, fixed. It is to say that He

is reliable at all times, now and forever more, because He will never falter or be moved. No matter what happens, we can believe on Him in prayer because He is unaffected by circumstances of life, unchanged by the storms and problems of this world.

These giant boulders also provide a high vantage point; likewise, God's vantage point is higher than ours. His perspective is eternal while ours is temporal. He is a refuge of safety, a fortress to run to when we need protection.

As **I looked over the detailed plan, I thought to myself, "The temperament of order, at its finest!"**

Prayer Profile

I once received a calendar in the mail that had been created to build a prayer force for a young boy who was sick. It was well done, neat and very helpful. Each day on the thirty-day guide contained a suggested scripture verse to be prayed for the boy pertaining to thirty specific needs of him and his family. As I looked over the detailed plan, I thought to myself, "The temperament of order, at its finest!"

Because of their view of God, order pray-ers have a propensity to look at prayer as a resource to be managed for the long haul. They want to put a system of prayer in place and set it into motion for a predetermined period of time. This type of prayer is what I call "perspirational" prayer as opposed to "inspirational" prayer because it is motivated more by sheer obedience than emotion. These people pray every day at the appointed time, regardless of feelings or circumstances. They pray in response to who God is, not in response to what the situation might look like. And since God is a rock, they often remain steadfast even when others have given up. When circumstances seem upbeat, this group might be described as "boring." But as soon as crisis hits, they are suddenly in demand, being perceived as "strong" or "resolute."

Those who pray in this temperament also tend to be lovers of structure. They generally work to organize prayer by placing it in a routine and supporting it with informational guides and helps. Their prayer resources may include maps, lists of names, topical scripture references, calendars or devotional guides. While they may keep detailed records of prayer requests and answers in some kind of journal, they probably do not write pages and pages of "mushy" stuff. Their entries would be brief and to the point and would be in keeping with a structured plan.

> *This group might be described as "boring." But as soon as crisis hits, they are suddenly in demand, being perceived as "strong or "resolute."*

As you might guess, these pray-ers tend to be more disciplined than some. They are seldom accused of being rash or impulsive. They may not readily pray in front of groups or on demand without preparation because spontaneity is not their strong suit. They prefer to commit to a specific prayer time and then carry out their commitment with discipline. They have what most of us would consider good prayer habits, making time to meet with God regularly and consistently. They are much more likely to gravitate toward ordered types of prayer, such as prayer rooms or prayer chains, than some other activities that involve more "freestyle" prayer.

Another hallmark of those who pray in the order temperament is that they typically embrace the concept of fasting. Not just limited to abstinence from food, fasting includes any self-denial of desires of the flesh such as television, caffeine, certain food groups or habits. It is the discipline of this activity that appeals to this group because it is an exercise in personal sacrifice and management. They fast to remove any distractions and sharpen their focus in prayer.

These organizers will take the lead in facilitating prayer in a group setting if they are allowed. Management is their strength, so they make great coordinators, even if the style of prayer they are coordinating is very different from their own. They might be excellent candidates for recruiting, planning, training and evaluating a variety of prayer initiatives because they can bring order from chaos. They have a natural propensity for making good use of raw materials.

Finally, the prayer language for this temperament emphasizes the steadfastness of God, the promises of God and the salvation of God. Much like the tradition temperament, those who pray in this school like to pray the promises of God, especially those that underscore His sovereignty, faithfulness and saving power. To them, salvation is the ultimate answer to prayer, which is always granted by God to those who earnestly seek Him. He is our Savior, the One who gives us eternal life in Jesus. To be rescued from an eternity of suffering is the greatest gift we can receive. The prayer language of order reflects hearts of gratitude and praise for the grace of unmerited salvation.

Biblical Models

Although we do not know a great deal about him, I believe James strongly exemplified this temperament of order. The letter he wrote in the New Testament is, more than anything, a call to Christians to live disciplined lives of faith, never giving up in the face of trials, always praying regardless of circumstances. Read what James writes to his fellow believers:

Consider it pure joy, my brothers, whenever you face trials of many kinds, because you know that the testing of your faith develops perseverance. Perseverance must finish its work

so that you may be mature and complete, not lacking any-
thing (James 1:2–4).

Blessed is the man who perseveres under trial, because when he
has stood the test, he will receive the crown of life that God
has promised to those who love him (James 1:12).

Be patient, then, brothers, until the Lord's coming. See how
the farmer waits for the land to yield its valuable crop and
how patient he is for the autumn and spring rains. You too,
be patient and stand firm, because the Lord's coming is near
(James 5:7–8).

Is any one of you in trouble? He should pray. Is anyone happy?
Let him sing songs of praise. Is any one of you sick? He
should call the elders of the church to pray over him . . . (James
5:13–14).

James was an advocate of faith in God, perseverance and
prayer at all times. Pray when you are happy; pray when you are
under stress; pray when you are sick. For James, prayer was the
visible manifestation of belief in an unchanging, saving God.
Almost everything he wrote was, in some manner, a challenge
to Christians to exhibit self-control through humility, good deeds,
obedience and respect. His theme was holiness through personal
management, and above all, unshakable faith.

Two other examples of this temperament, Simeon and Anna,
appear in the second chapter of Luke. Both lived in Jerusalem
and had one thing in common: they waited in prayer for Jesus to
be born and presented in the temple.

The Bible says of Simeon, "[He] was righteous and devout.
He was waiting for the consolation of Israel, and the Holy Spirit
was upon him. It had been revealed to him by the Holy Spirit
that he would not die before he had seen the Lord's Christ" (Luke
2:25–26). So Simeon waited in the temple and prayed; he prayed
and waited. He had faith to persevere because he knew Jesus, the
Savior, was on the way.

Scripture tells us of Anna, "She was very old. . . . She never left the temple but worshipped night and day, fasting and praying. Coming up to them [Mary, Joseph and baby Jesus at that very moment, she gave thanks to God and spoke about the child to all who were looking forward to the redemption of Jerusalem" (Luke 2:36–38). Clearly she, like Simeon, had hope that was not rooted in circumstances. While others came and went, these two remained steady until their prayers were answered.

Benefits

Years ago, a submarine sank off the east coast. When the rescue team divers reached it, they heard a faint tapping in Morse code coming from the inside of the metal structure, "Is there hope?"

1. **People today are looking for hope.** We want to know that there is hope for our children, hope for our dreams, hope for a brighter future, hope for justice. Out of the steadfast faith in an unshakable God, the temperament of order gives us the hope we seek. Always persevering, this temperament will not allow us to throw our hands up in despair at the first sign of trouble. Rather, it challenges us to push on, to keep praying in spite of this or that. It sets an appointment with prayer that is not subject to cancellation. Because God never changes, the temperament of order sees no reason to allow their relationship with God in prayer to be affected by the ebb and flow of life. With faith comes discipline, and with discipline comes eternal hope and optimism.

2. **The temperament of order puts wheels under visions.** It is the "nuts and bolts" school, excellent at planning and implementing strategies birthed through visions and revelations. It is always seeking a better way to pray, a better method for sustaining prayer over a period of time. It is detail minded and very pragmatic. Without this temperament, many of the creative ideas generated by other styles of prayer would fall by the wayside without ever having practical application.

3. **It fosters teamwork and builds relationships.** Because this temperament is prone to manage and organize, it serves as a catalyst to bring people together for a common purpose. It connects individuals to each other and to the group for maximum efficiency and productivity. It might birth prayer groups based on a shared interest or home cell groups for people that live close together. It encourages participation for every believer, regardless of age or level of spiritual maturity.

4. **It acts as a safety harness to keep us from being carried away by emotions—either good or bad.** Because of its steadiness, this temperament keeps our feet on the ground, reminding us of the need to pray even in the midst of prosperity, while scraping us up off the ground in the midst of trouble. It is far-sighted and tenacious, not operating according to the feeling of the moment. It recognizes that some things take time, and prays accordingly.

5. **Finally, this perspective offers new converts a place to operate in prayer.** Though not necessarily shallow, the temperament of order is where most people start their prayer journey. We do not generally enter into the Christian walk seeing grand visions or casting out demons. We enter at the point of simple obedience in response to salvation. It is here that we learn the importance of spending time in prayer and begin to explore what it means to communicate with God. Then, out of our early structured efforts develops a unique way of relating to our heavenly Father that becomes our prayer identity.

Primary Purpose and Contemporary Expressions

The primary purpose of this temperament is, as it is written in Hebrews 12:1–2, to help us "run with perseverance the race marked out for us" and "fix our eyes on Jesus, the author and perfecter of our faith. . . ." Its destiny is to be a lifeline of hope, abounding always in faith, setting our eyes upon the rock of salvation. It sustains prayer until the answer is received, never giving up or giving in.

This school of prayer has many expressions today, some of which represent a flourishing partnership with a very different temperament. One example of this kind of partnership is a prayer model called Houses of Prayer Everywhere, founded by a man named Al VanderGriend. Houses of Prayer Everywhere, or H.O.P.E., is a program working to establish small prayer groups in workplaces, homes, apartment units, businesses— virtually anywhere people

> *Its destiny is to be a lifeline of hope, abounding always in faith, setting our eyes upon the rock of salvation.*

gather. The purpose of the groups is to pray for unsaved family members, friends, neighbors or co-workers. It is a beautiful combination of the temperaments of love and order, resulting in a practical, well-organized prayer ministry of intercession. It brings people together to systematically stand in the gap for loved ones who do not know Jesus.

Another such partnership can be seen in the development of the World Prayer Center, the control nucleus for prayer rooms, worldwide spiritual warfare and intercession. This partnership involves several of the temperaments—primarily order, love, confrontation and mystery. The World Prayer Center will be the core of a global network of prayer, receiving and transmitting information regarding prayer requests and answers. It is a highly structured operation that will maximize the efficiency of prayer through the use of computers and modern technology.

There are many such partnerships, most of which have sprung up in the last decade as prayer has taken on a stronger identity in the areas of organization and management. The temperaments of order and immediacy pair up in a ministry called Prayerwalk USA!, which is organizing to prayerwalk every zip code in America by the year 2000. The prayer emphasis on the 10/40 window that I mentioned earlier in this book was a detailed plan of intercession for unreached people groups in that sector of the world. Another example is the way that Bill Bright of Campus Crusade for Christ has facilitated several nationwide fasting emphases for the spiritual revival of our country. As this temperament of order has come into its own with regard to prayer, the potential for organizing and implementing various prayer strategies on national and global scales is literally endless.

> *The temperaments of order and immediacy pair up in a ministry called Prayerwalk USA!, which is organizing to prayerwalk every zip code in America by the year 2000.*

A good example of the order temperament in its purest form is a ministry called Every Home for Christ, run by Dick Eastman. Dick is no newcomer to the order temperament; he is the author of a book entitled *The Hour That Changes the World* which contains one of the best, most applicable personal prayer models ever developed. The prayer model, which has helped push sales of this little book over the 500,000 mark, divides an hour into twelve, five-minute segments of prayer, each one having a different focus. The segments are: praise, waiting, confession, scripture praying, watching, intercession, petition, thanksgiving, singing, meditation, listening and praise. The model is simple yet yields multiple avenues for personal prayer. It can be applied as easily by a new Christian as it can by one more seasoned. It was one of the first prayer models to introduce the concept of these twelve prayer "stations" which have now become a standard part of prayer vocabulary.

The goal of Eastman's Every Home for Christ ministry is to distribute literature with the message of the gospel to every home in the world! The idea is to ensure that every person is reached with the good news of Jesus and has the opportunity to be saved. What a magnanimous application of this temperament that thrives on implementing systematic plans.

This prayer perspective is unique because it often acts as a carrier for the other six, making a way for prayer of all kinds to happen with consistency and integrity.

L ord, selling insurance reminds me of how important it is to have the assurance of eternal life. Help me to learn to talk to people about you so that they can be "spiritually" insured in you.

— the prayer of an insurance agent

Temperament	View of God	Defining Characteristic	Biblical Model	Primary Purpose
Tradition	Master Architect	Historical	Matthew	To see God's plan fulfilled in lives, cities and nations
Immediacy	Able Provider	Spontaneous	Mark	To reveal the ability and willingness of God to meet needs
Love	Righteous Judge	Relational	Luke	To reveal and implement the redemptive purposes of God
Mystery	Exalted King	Contemplative	John	To seek and safeguard the revelation of Jesus
Confrontation	Commander in Chief	Authoritative	Paul	To establish the rule and reign of Jesus in lives and regions
Perception	Bold Innovator	Visionary	Peter	To provide specific information at a point of need
Order	Rock of Salvation	Structured	James	To help fix our eyes on Jesus and always persevere in faith

Chapter 22

The Prismatic Movement

The temperaments were never meant to function in isolation. God did not create them to set up their own little prayer "camps" and compete. He created them to complete each other, working in harmony as the various instruments in a symphony. While each one has its own unique sound, they make the prettiest music when they play together, enhancing one another.

In order to show you how all of the temperaments might respond differently to the same real life situation, imagine with me for a few moments the following scenario. You are on an airplane (I promise, this is the last airplane illustration) cruising at 25,000 feet. On the flight with you are many other passengers, including the seven apostles that represent the seven temperaments: Matthew (tradition), Mark (immediacy), Luke (love), John (mystery), Paul (confrontation), Peter (perception) and James (order). Suddenly, you hear a loud "pop" which seems to jolt the plane off balance momentarily, causing drinks to spill and a few people to let out noticeable gasps. Within minutes, the captain's voice comes over the intercom, monotone and controlled yet somewhat urgent. He explains that the plane's engine has experienced a mechanical problem and that utilizing the backup system, he will try to land the plane at a nearby airport. "This is an emergency situation," he announces as slowly as he can. "Please remain calm and pray."

> **This an emergency situation," he announces as slowly as he can. "Please remain calm and pray."**

As the level of panic begins to boil, Matthew (tradition) is thinking, "Corporate repentance—we all need to repent! The judgement of God is on us for some reason . . . oh, what was it I saw in the paper just the other day . . . something about this airline and illegal hiring practices. Why didn't I read that article? Or maybe it's someone on the plane. . . ." He gets up and rushes to the front. "May I?" he asks the flight attendant as he reaches for the intercom microphone. "Who will be the first to confess? Let us pray and seek forgiveness—we must plead for mercy! If only we can reconcile the sin that has brought about this disaster, surely God will save us!"

While Matthew is doing his best to get to the root of the problem, Mark (immediacy) is going up and down the aisle, laying hands on people, praying over every seat. Bible in hand, he stops occasionally to comfort and minister to those who are especially distressed. "Just as you raised Lazarus from the dead, oh Lord, touch this engine and cause it to function properly," he prays out loud as he walks. "You are the God of miracles; the earth and everything in it responds to your command. In Jesus' name, bring us to safety." He sits down next to a woman who is

crying and puts his arm around her shoulder, speaking a quiet
prayer before moving on.

As you watch Mark making his way to the front of the plane
where he lays his hands on the door to the cockpit, you notice a
small group forming several rows back. Four people, including
Luke (love), are crammed into one row, holding hands and praying together. All their heads are bowed, and several are weeping. One is kneeling in the aisle. "Oh Jesus, we pray for the pilots
and the flight attendants on this aircraft—give them peace and
wisdom," you overhear one of them say. "Yes, Lord . . . peace
and wisdom," the others chime in agreement. "We stand in the
gap for all those on this plane who do not know you. Use this
situation not for destruction, but unto salvation!" They all affirm, "Amen." Over and over they speak the captain's name as
they continue to cry out to God, so engrossed in prayer that
they are seemingly oblivious to all the activity on the plane.

Meanwhile, John (mystery) has disappeared. He has retreated
to the solitude of the bathroom cubicle, where he is seeking a
revelation from God about the true meaning of life and death.
"Show us, Almighty God, what you will through this crisis. I
shall be happy to live or die, because either way, I will stand in
awe of your glory this day! You alone are exalted, high above
the earth. Reveal yourself to me, and demonstrate your greatness to all who are on this plane."

As the plane continues to descend rapidly, the pilot once
again addresses the passengers, "We are approximately one
hundred miles away from a small landing strip, but our communication with the air traffic control tower there seems to be
fading in and out. We are doing the best we can to bring this
aircraft to the ground safely, but we are losing altitude faster
than we would like to. Our chances for a safe landing remain
very questionable."

Above all the noise and commotion, one man's voice stands
out. Pacing up and down the aisle red-faced and perspiring,
Paul (confrontation) is piercing the walls of the plane with his

warlike prayers. Shaking his fists in the air, he binds the spirit
of fear and death. "I command you, Satan, to take your hands
off of this plane! You have no right to be in control here; in
the name of Jesus, I rebuke you!" he bellows. "Lord, as you
spoke to the wind and the waves to be still, speak now to this
mechanical problem to be corrected." He turns to face the other
side of the plane and continues, "I take authority over every
part in this engine and command through the power of God
that it function properly. Show your strength, oh Lord, by de-
feating the enemy and enforcing your perfect will in this situation!" Then he begins to sing, "Let God arise and His enemies
be scattered. . . ."

Peter (perception), who has been praying quietly to himself up to this point, is beginning to stir up excitement around
his seat. "I have received a word from the Lord! He has shown
me a vision that gives me hope!" Many people turn to listen as
Peter recounts what he has seen. "As I was praying, I saw in
my mind a bright light at the end of a long, dark tunnel. There
in the light, a celebration was taking place. I believe it is a sign
from God that we are not going to die! If we will trust in Him
and have faith, He will save us!" The response to Peter is var-
ied—some are looking at him like he is crazy, while others seem
to be comforted by his words. He moves out of his seat and
with a strange look of peace and tranquility mutters over and
over, "We are not going to die; He will save us!" As he reaches
another group of passengers who are panic-stricken and near
hysterics, he starts again, "I have received a word from the
Lord . . ."

The last apostle, James (order), though he has not been the
loudest or most noticeable person on the plane, has been quietly
organizing a prayer force throughout the whole ordeal. Remain-
ing relatively calm, James has identified most of the Christians
on the plane and has given each one of them a specific prayer
assignment. Some are praying for the pilots, others for the flight
attendants, some for the engine and still others for the passen-

gers. James has also managed to tear out some scripture verses from his Bible and give them to people as prayer prompts. He too, moves slowly up and down the aisle, encouraging those who are praying with comments like, "Don't lose heart. God is faithful. We must not give up the fight. Just keep praying—He will answer."

Moments later, the aircraft bounces on the small runway and screeches to a halt. The plane erupts with cheers as the passengers applaud the pilots. As they file off one by one, a celebration breaks out as Mark leads a praise dance around the plane. Matthew and Paul join in the parade, singing songs of victory to God and thanking Him for His mercy and forgiveness. Luke and James are visiting about the best way to start an intercessors' prayer group to cover all of the airlines with prayer, while Peter and John slip quietly away from the group, eager to record what they have seen and heard from the Lord.

Seven different responses to the same desperate situation— all of which were valid and helpful in some way for encouraging the whole group. Together, they saw to it that sin was confessed, comfort was conveyed, love was felt, Jesus was seen, hope was given, faith was built, and the devil came away from the ordeal with a tremendous headache! Each of the temperaments made a significant contribution to the prayer effort according to its own strengths and perspectives.

Jesus – The Sum Total of All

While various individuals throughout the Bible exemplify different temperaments, there is one man who embodied them all—Jesus. He was the supreme example of prayer perspectives, showing that He had full command over all styles of prayer during the course of His earthly ministry. He not only operated in them but He taught them. He was the very essence of everything that prayer was created to be. As he demonstrated the temperaments, He gave each of them credibility, and challenged us to move in and be moved by all of them.

Called our "high priest," Jesus operated in the traditional temperament as a mediator, helping relate God to man and man to God. He stood in between the two. John 17, which is called the "high priestly prayer of Jesus," is an example of the traditional prayer style because Jesus prayed from a heavenly perspective with regard to the Father's desire on earth. He acted as God's representative, praying, "I have given them the glory that you gave me, that they may be one as we are one: I in them and you in me. May they be brought to complete unity to let the world know that you sent me and have loved them even as you have loved me" (John 17:22–23). He also prayed in the Lord's Prayer, "your kingdom come, your will be done on earth as it is in heaven" (Matthew 6:10).

> *Again and again in the gospels, people came to Jesus hurting and desperate, and He touched them at the point of their pain.*

Jesus also prayed numerous times to provide for the needs of people. He lived out of an understanding that God wants to meet needs of every kind, and he prayed and ministered with a sense of immediacy. Again and again in the gospels, people came to Jesus hurting and desperate, and He touched them at the point of their pain. He healed lepers (Matthew 8:2), gave sight to the blind (Matthew 9:27-33) and restored the sick (Matthew 8:16). He performed miracles to feed the hungry (Mark 6:39–44); He gave intangibles such as peace (John 14:27) and life (John 10:10); He went about doing good (Acts 10:30). Jesus cared about people, and He seldom passed up an opportunity to act on the compassion of the Father.

The very reason Jesus was sent to earth defines the temperament of love—He laid down His life for us. The final sacrifice He made on the cross was the ultimate act of intercession through which He paid the supreme price for justice to be done on our behalf. All of the gospels paint an agonizing picture of Jesus in the Garden of Gethsemane when He was in the "press." The reason for His pain—He was in love with mankind and did not want us to be judged and condemned to an eternity in darkness. So He interceded, taking upon His own back our sin and standing in the gap to bridge the way for us to have eternal life. Hebrews 7:25 tells us that even now, Jesus lives to intercede on our behalf to the Father.

It is not hard to understand why Jesus classifies as a mystic. He often withdrew to lonely places to pray (Luke 5:16) and seek the face of God. In solitude, He found strength; in stillness, He received direction. Luke 9 gives an account of what we call the Transfiguration, a time when Jesus drew apart on a mountaintop to pray and was literally changed in appearance by the powerful presence of God. ". . . [H]is face changed, and his clothes became as bright as a flash of lightning" (Luke 9:29). Jesus knew that God was His source for everything, and so His first priority in life was to spend time one-on-one with the Father, seeking His face and basking in His closeness.

Jesus prayed occasionally as a confrontationalist, casting out demons (Mark 9:32) and opposing evil forces. In fact, the reason He was crucified was because He called to task the dead religious systems of the day. When He drove the money changers from the temple, He was praying for God, enforcing the rule and reign of holiness in that place of worship. He prayed and challenged anything that stood in the way of God's kingdom being established. He was Lord over His domain, commanding the dead to return to life and the wind and waves to be still. Jesus clearly knew that His enemy was Satan, but He also knew that He would have the ultimate victory.

Often Jesus prayed as a prophet, calling things into being that were not yet in existence. He was continually doing "new things" by perceiving the Father's will and then praying it into being. As we have already seen, He made all things new, and not everyone in that day was ready to accept His innovative ideas about religion and spiritual matters. His teachings were hard on systems that clung to the old for the sake of self-preservation and maintenance. The signs and wonders that followed His ministry were anything but typical. Because Jesus knew what the future held for Him, He walked in a depth of understanding that was beyond even His closest companions.

Finally, Jesus demonstrated the highest level of discipline and faith in His relationship to the Father. He exemplified well the temperament of order. Despite being one with God, He never took for granted the privilege of being able to communicate with Him. He never forsook spending time in prayer, especially early in the morning, regardless of circumstances around Him. When His popularity was at its highest and He was being sought out by crowds of people, He took time to get alone and pray. When His hours were numbered and He was facing the cross, He went to the garden to pray. On one occasion, He prayed and fasted for forty days (Luke 4). Prayer in Jesus' life had nothing to do with His emotions or His image. He prayed out of obedience, love and honor for His heavenly Father, and as a result, He was anchored in hope. He summed up this prayer perspective when he said, "So I say to you: Ask and it will be given to you; seek and you will find; knock and the door will be opened to you. For everyone who asks [and keeps on asking] receives; he who seeks [and keeps on seeking] finds; and to him who knocks [and keeps on knocking], the door will be opened" (Luke 11:9–10).

Spectrum of Color

I am not much of a physicist, but I have been told that the visible light spectrum, the wavelengths of light that our eyes are capable of detecting, contains seven colors. They are the colors of the rainbow: red, orange, yellow, green, blue, indigo and violet. While I find this hard to comprehend, I understand that what we see as white light is actually the sum of all seven colors of the spectrum. That is why, when a light beam shines through a prism which "bends" it ever so slightly, all of the colors spill out and make a little rainbow on the wall.

Similarly, Jesus, who shines radiant and white, is the expression of all seven temperaments together. He is the sum total of all prayer. When we pray, we are manifesting some aspect of Jesus' character that lives in us. As the light of His life is refracted through our humanity, we may shine red or yellow or violet but only because some part of Jesus is being reflected through us. The array of color in the body of Christ is as beautiful to God as a rainbow. But we must keep in mind that we shine the most like Jesus when we are connected to the other "colors" in the prayer spectrum.

> *When* we pray, we are manifesting some aspect of Jesus' character that lives in us.

The Glory of God

Just as oceans are both the source and the destination for all rivers, Jesus is the source and the destination of all prayer. It is inspired by Him, motivated by Him, carried by Him and answered through Him. All of the rivers of prayer, though they may tumble and weave their way through very different terrain, flow to one end—the glory and honor of God. Prayer is not a self-serving activity; rather, it pours out from us into something larger than ourselves. We pray to give reverence to God, and ultimately we become His glory. He shares it with us by displaying it through us.

The river of prayer is flowing. It started with Adam and Eve and has been flowing through time ever since, always the same yet dynamic and ever-changing. The purpose of understanding the temperaments is freedom—freedom to step into the river and embrace it as you see it. God did not create you to be like everyone else. He created you to participate in prayer in a special and unique way, and He gave you strengths and gifts that can benefit those around you, if you will only exercise them.

Myth #7
Prayer is a gift—some people have it, and some people don't.

Truth #7
As God's children, we all have the privilege of communicating with our heavenly Father.

Let the River Flow

Let me conclude this section with a few simple challenges:

1. **Let the river flow in you.** Do not strain and agonize trying to get it just right or be like someone else. Just relax, apply the brakes, get still, and allow the Creator of prayer to work in you. Trust in Him, not your own schemes and devices. Keep in mind that it is not up to you to produce anything; you must only participate.

2. **Be who you are, and encourage others to be who they are.** Promote teamwork, not competition, avoiding at all cost the quicksand of the comparison trap. As you observe the prayer lives of other people, you may not always understand the different perspectives. In fact, you may be quite certain

that some are a few eggs short of a dozen. But do not compare and do not judge. God created variety and He owes you no explanation. Pray with both confidence and humility, never underestimating the importance of your own gifts and strengths yet never setting yourself above others.

3. **Dare to step out of your comfort zone and discover what it is like to pray in other temperaments.** If you lean toward the temperament of order, try throwing caution to the wind and cut loose in a March for Jesus. If you are a stout confrontationalist, discipline yourself for a period of time to pray quietly in solitude. Ask God to show you something new about Jesus. If you identify strongly with the perception school of prayer, participate in a reconciliation and healing service in which sins of the past are being dealt with. Stretch yourself to experience and appreciate those prayer styles that seem the most foreign to you.

Dear God,

   Thank you for the baby brother, but what I prayed for was a puppy.

                                                —Joyce

(Hample and Marshall)

Epilogue

Just Like Noah

During the year that I worked on this book, I constantly harbored in the back of my mind the question, "How does it end?" Starting a project like this is always difficult, but sometimes it is just as hard to find a way to bring into focus the essence of all you have been trying to communicate. As I would think back to the very beginning of the book, trying to come up with some idea for a conclusion that would summarize the heart of this message, nothing seemed to strike the right chord in me—until I met Noah.

Thanksgiving Day, just weeks ago, as we were nearing completion of this project, I took off on my motorcycle to downtown Houston to watch the holiday parade. As I stood there waiting in the crowded street, a man shuffled through the people and stopped beside me. Neatly dressed and very handsome, He had a baby boy with him who I later learned was about one year old. Since neither of us had arrived terribly early, we did not have a very good view of the parade course from the ground. I offered to hold the baby in my lap up high on my bike so he could see better. "Sure," the man said. "This is Noah—Noah Christian." And he handed me the boy.

Now I have five grandchildren of my own, all of whom were, of course, exceptionally cute babies. But I must say, Noah Christian was one of the most beautiful little baby boys I had ever seen. Dark-complexioned and blue-eyed, his dimples overtook his round face when he smiled, which was often. He babbled and looked around, but he was much more interested in examining my glasses than he was the parade.

"Noah was conceived right here in downtown, just a few blocks over there under a bridge," his father, John, offered so unashamedly that it almost caught me off guard. I mean, how do you respond to that? My first thought was, "What in the world were they doing under a bridge?" Well, not really *what* were they doing—I supposed I knew the answer to that.

"Oh, really?" I managed to say, not sure that I really wanted to hear more.

"His parents still live there," the father continued, which cleared up a few questions but raised several more.

As we stood there in the street in the middle of downtown, bands and floats going by one by one, John, who turned out to be one of those rare people you meet that you will not soon forget, relayed the remarkable story of how Noah came to be a part of his family.

When John married his wife, Darleen, she had one teenage daughter, who is now eighteen and in her first year of college. Within five years, they had adopted three other girls: Nichelle, who is now ten; Hannah, who is five; and Zoe, who is just turning two. Although each of these precious children came to them in a unique and somewhat dramatic way, the circumstances surrounding Noah's adoption were almost unbelievable. What, for most of us, would have been a major life decision that merited months of consideration, calculating the risks and trying to foresee all the possible pitfalls, was for John and Darleen almost second nature.

Their oldest daughter, Shannon, was out one Wednesday evening with a group of her friends feeding the homeless in downtown—something they had been doing completely on their own for some time. But this Wednesday evening was special because Shannon came across Noah's biological parents. His father was a dark-skinned African American, and his mother was white, and obviously in the late stages of pregnancy. They lived under a bridge, begging and doing odd jobs for what little bit of money they could get. Concerned about the couple's baby and their growing need for food and blankets, Shannon told

> *They lived under a bridge, begging and doing odd jobs for what little bit of money they could get.*

her mom and dad about them, urging her mom to go talk to the woman to make sure she was getting proper medical care.

At the insistence of her teenager, Darleen went downtown to pay Becky and Jarvis a visit. They talked briefly, and Darleen left her phone number with Becky, offering to help in any way she could. Over the next few weeks, Darlene and Shannon visited the bridge several more times, so it was not too surprising when Darleen received a phone call from Becky in the hospital, "I'm going to have my baby. Will you come?"

As soon as the baby was born, Child Protective Services was on the scene, ready to take custody when he was released from the hospital. But the Johnsons (not their real name) intervened. They told Becky and Jarvis that they wanted to adopt the baby and give him a home as well as a chance to know his biological parents—something he would be forbidden to do in the custody of the state. Within twenty-four hours, they spoke to an attorney, and arrangements were made in a special court hearing for John and Darlene to take Noah as the newest member of their family.

As I watched John with this little boy, who was happy and obviously well cared for, I could not help but feel the irony of the situation, standing so near where little Noah might have been born. The difference between where he was conceived and where he was now living was enormous. They were two different worlds. His true heritage would not have given him much of a chance in life, but his adopted heritage will put the world at his fingertips.

> *The difference between where he was conceived and where he was now living was enormous.*

Although he will not understand for a long time, through a divine meeting under a highway in the inner city, Noah was granted the gift of hope.

But Noah was not the only one with a new outlook on life. On her college entrance exam, Shannon wrote about what she discovered under that bridge:

> Each year thousands of people in Houston fall victim to a terrible social malady known as homelessness. . . . [M]y baby brother had been destined to be one of the victims, shrouded beneath the blanket no one wants to uncover; but instead, he now peacefully sleeps cradled in loving arms, in a warm, peaceful and safe abode on Riverside Drive every night.

> As a result of the genuine concern and attention shown by strangers, Becky and Jarvis determined to seek the Lord and to make their lives better. Now that seven months have gone by, Jarvis holds down a steady job and has quit drinking. Becky and he have moved into their own apartment. Every once in a while they stop by to

see my baby brother Noah, who lives a happy and contented life as a member of my family.

Before I met this couple, I never realized what could be accomplished when you seek the Lord. Becky and Jarvis are now blessed to be where they are. They gave me a hope that I never had—a hope that I never knew existed. I am ready now for my future; I approach it with a new determination. Whenever I seem to lose confidence in myself, I recall the starving couple I once knew who lived under the bridge. I then have faith that all things are possible through Him.

I love this story of Noah, because it is my story also, and everyone else's who has been adopted into the kingdom of God and given a new life. Just like Noah, we are born destitute. But in Christ we have a new home, a new name, a new family and a new hope. Out of God's infinite mercy and love for us, He gives us life and expects nothing in return except our hearts. We become heirs to an inheritance which we did nothing to earn, and we are given all the privileges and benefits of the family name. Like Noah, we have very little to do with the whole process. It is our heavenly Father who reaches down and rescues us from our poverty.

When you pray, go to God with the confidence that is yours as part of the family! Do not hang on to the "bridge" mentality; He has brought you in off the streets and made you His precious son or daughter. You do not need to be afraid to tell Him what you need because it is His delight to provide for you and watch you grow. It was His great love for you that saved you, and He wants to have a relationship with you as a Father to a child.

Thank you God, for giving me a new life. I am your child, called by your name and regarded in heaven as one of the family. I can talk to you and you will listen and answer me because I am precious in your sight. I do not need to fear rejection; I am fully loved and accepted. I do not need to fear failure because to you, my prayers are as sweet as incense. I will not fear embarrassment; you created me and gave me a destiny unlike any one else in the world. I will enjoy the privilege of relating intimately with you in prayer because I know that I have nothing to lose and everything to gain! Amen.

Works Cited

Anderson, Leith. *A Church for the 21st Century*. Minneapolis: Bethany, 1992.

Braxton, Tony. "There's No Me Without You." *Secrets*. New York: LaFace Records, 1996.

Brooks, Garth. "Unanswered Prayers." *No Fences*. Nashville: Caged Panther Music, 1990.

Chambers, Oswald. *My Utmost for His Highest*. New York: Dodd, Mead & Co., 1935.

Dawson, John. *Healing America's Wounds*. Ventura: Regal, 1994.

Eastman, Dick. *The Hour That Changes the World*. Grand Rapids: Baker Book House, 1978.

Foster, Richard. *Prayers from the Heart*. San Francisco: Harper, 1994.

God's Little Devotional Book on Prayer. Tulsa: Honor Books, 1997.

Graham, Ruth Bell. "Worship and Worry." Comp. Alice Gray. *More Stories for the Heart*. Sisters: Multnomah, 1997.

Haggard, Ted. *Primary Purpose*. Orlando: Creation House, 1995.

Hample, Stuart and Eric Marshall, comps. *Children's Letters to God*. New York: Workman Publishing, 1991.

Hawthorne, Steve and Graham Kendrick. *Prayerwalking*. Orlando: Creation House, 1993.

Hochschild, Arlie Russell. *The Time Bind: When Work Becomes Home and Home Becomes Work*. New York: Metropolitan Books, 1997.

Hybels, Bill. *Too Busy Not to Pray*. Downers Grove: InterVarsity Press, 1988.

Keys to the Kingdom: Personal Prayers—Who I Am in Christ. Muncie: Prayer Point Press, 1998.

Lewis, C. S. *The Screwtape Letters.* Rev. ed. New York: Macmillan, 1982.

Lucado, Max. *The Great House of God.* Dallas: Word, 1997.

Mother Teresa. *No Greater Love.* Novato: New World Library, 1997.

Peretti, Frank E. *This Present Darkness.* Westchester: Crossway Books, 1986.

Silvoso, Ed. *That None Should Perish.* Ventura: Regal, 1994.

Strait, George. "Love Without End." *Ten Strait Hits.* Universal City: MCA Records, 1988.

Towns, Elmer L. *Biblical Meditation for Spiritual Breakthrough.* Ventura: Regal, 1998.

Yancey, Philip. *What's So Amazing About Grace?* Grand Rapids: Zondervan Publishing House, 1997.